*Constructing Democratic Governance:*
*Latin America and the Caribbean in the*
*1990s—Themes and Issues*

**Constructing Democratic Governance: Latin America and the Caribbean in the 1990s**
edited by Jorge I. Domínguez and Abraham F. Lowenthal

Available in separate paperback editions:

**Constructing Democratic Governance: Latin America and the Caribbean in the 1990s—Themes and Issues**
edited by Jorge I. Domínguez and Abraham F. Lowenthal

**Constructing Democratic Governance: South America in the 1990s**
edited by Jorge I. Domínguez and Abraham F. Lowenthal

**Constructing Democratic Governance: Mexico, Central America, and the Caribbean in the 1990s**
edited by Jorge I. Domínguez and Abraham F. Lowenthal

# Constructing Democratic Governance

## Latin America and the Caribbean in the 1990s—Themes and Issues

*edited by*
*Jorge I. Domínguez and*
*Abraham F. Lowenthal*

*The Johns Hopkins University Press*
Baltimore and London

The Johns Hopkins University Press
2715 North Charles Street
Baltimore, Maryland 21218-4319
The Johns Hopkins Press Ltd., London

The Library of Congress has cataloged the hardcover edition as follows:

Constructing democratic governance: Latin America and the Caribbean
 in the 1990s / edited by Jorge I. Domínguez and Abraham F. Lowenthal
     p.     cm.—(An Inter-American dialogue book)
   Includes bibliographical references and index.
   ISBN 0-8018-5385-0 (alk. paper)
     1. Latin America—Politics and government—1980– . 2. Democracy—
Latin America. 3. Caribbean Area—Politics and government—1945– .
4. Democracy—Caribbean Area. I. Domínguez, Jorge I., 1945– .
II. Lowenthal, Abraham F. III. Series.
JL966.C677    1996
321.8′098—dc20

96-12421
CIP

A catalog record for this book is available from the British Library.

ISBN 0-8018-5386-9 (pbk.)

# Contents

# Foreword

There is no more important challenge in the hemisphere today than building effective democratic governance. The understandable celebrations associated with the transition to constitutional, elected governments in Latin America over the past fifteen years have now yielded to growing concern that persistent obstacles stand in the way of constructing and consolidating genuine democracies. Free and competitive elections are no longer noteworthy events in the region. Yet progress is lagging behind in other key areas such as establishing civilian control over armed forces, fully protecting human rights, advancing the rule of law, strengthening the role of the legislature and the judiciary, fostering citizen participation, improving the performance of political parties, and redressing sharp social inequalities and ethnic divisions.

Analysts make many claims about the state of democracy in the hemisphere—and policymakers make decisions based on such assessments—but there have been few, if any, systematic attempts to understand and explain prevailing conditions in Latin America and the Caribbean. This volume is just such an effort. The editors commissioned twenty-one country studies and five chapters on crosscutting issues relevant to a number of the national cases. Abraham F. Lowenthal, the Inter-American Dialogue's founding executive director and currently a board member, and Jorge I. Domínguez, who is a member and associated fellow of the Dialogue, succeeded in attracting first-rate analysts from Latin America, the Caribbean, Canada, and the United States to prepare these studies.

The chapters went through several drafts. They benefited from the comments of the editors as well as from a major, two-day conference held in Washington, D.C., in September 1994 that brought together U.S. and Latin American senior government officials, representatives of multilateral institutions, congressional staff, policy analysts, and key leaders from many nongovernmental organizations. The conference prompted rich discussion on both the country and the thematic papers and helped bridge the worlds of policy and academia.

Many others deserve credit for their role in this project. Jeanne Kinney Giraldo, a doctoral student in political science at Harvard University, provided detailed, critical commentary on all the chapters. We would also like to extend our appreciation to Javier Corrales and Robert Hemmer for their fine translations and to the Dialogue interns who contributed to this project: Robert Bettman, Corrine Castagnet, Sarah Connelly, Cindy Garret, Alex Gross, Robyn Prinz, James Rogan, Eduardo

Romo, and John White. Special thanks are in order for Nicola Lowther, who skillfully performed the countless editing and other tasks that finishing such a volume entails, and to Jenny Pilling, for her unfailing patience and dedication in coordinating the project.

The Inter-American Dialogue's research and publications are designed to improve the quality of public debate and decision on key issues in western hemisphere affairs. The Dialogue is both a forum for sustained exchange among leaders and an independent, nonpartisan center for policy analysis on U.S.–Latin American economic and political relations. The Dialogue's one hundred members—from the United States, Canada, Latin America, and the Caribbean—include prominent political, business, labor, academic, media, military, and religious leaders. At periodic plenary sessions, members analyze key hemispheric issues and formulate recommendations for policy and action. The Dialogue presents its findings in comprehensive reports circulated throughout the Americas. Its research agenda focuses on four broad themes: democratic governance, inter-American cooperation, economic integration, and social equity.

The Inter-American Dialogue wishes to express its gratitude to the National Endowment for Democracy and the A. W. Mellon Foundation for their support for commissioning the papers, the September 1994 international conference in Washington, and the publication of this volume. Mead Data Central–Lexis/Nexus Research Information Services gave us crucial research assistance. We are also pleased to acknowledge the broader support that the Dialogue has obtained from the Ford, A. W. Mellon, and William and Flora Hewlett foundations and the Carnegie Corporation of New York.

Michael Shifter  
*Program Director, Democratic Governance*  
*Inter-American Dialogue*

Peter Hakim  
*President*  
*Inter-American Dialogue*

# Contributors

**Alan Angell** is a fellow of Saint Antony's College and a former director of the Latin American Centre, University of Oxford. He has written extensively on Chilean politics and more recently has been working on the politics of social sector reform.

**Jorge G. Castañeda** is professor of political science and international affairs at Mexico's National Autonomous University (UNAM). He was previously senior associate of the Carnegie Endowment for International Peace in Washington, D.C., and a visiting professor at Princeton University and the University of California, Berkeley.

**Jorge I. Domínguez** is Frank G. Thomson Professor of Government at Harvard University. Previously he was visiting senior fellow at the Inter-American Dialogue, of which he is a founding member. A past president of the Latin American Studies Association and member of the Council on Foreign Relations, he is a member of the editorial boards of *Mexican Studies, Cuban Studies, Political Science Quarterly*, and the *Journal of Inter-American Studies and World Affairs*. Dr. Domínguez is a leading authority on Cuban and Latin American politics and is widely published on these topics. With James McCann, he recently co-authored *Democratizing Mexico: Public Opinions and Electoral Choice.*

**Edward L. Gibson** is assistant professor of political science at Northwestern University. He previously taught at the University of Michigan, was an academy scholar at Harvard University's Academy for International and Area Studies, and served as assistant director of the Industry Council for Development from 1981 to 1985. He is the author of *Class and Conservative Parties: Argentina in Comparative Perspective* (1996). He holds a Ph.D. in political science from Columbia University.

**Jeanne Kinney Giraldo** is a Ph.D. candidate and has been a teaching fellow in the department of government at Harvard University. Her papers include "Democracy and Development in Chile: Alejandro Foxley and the Concertación's Economic Policy," which she presented to the Latin American Studies Association in March 1994.

**Frances Hagopian** is associate professor of political science at Tufts University. She has taught at the Massachusetts Institute of Technology and Harvard University. Professor Hagopian's research has focused on Brazilian politics and democratization in Latin America. She is the author of *Traditional Politics and Regime Change in Brazil* (1996) and several articles on democratization in Brazil and South America which have appeared in such journals as *World Politics* and *Comparative Political Studies.*

**Abraham F. Lowenthal** is president of the Pacific Council on International Policy and director of the Center for International Studies at the University of Southern California. From 1982 to 1992 he was the Inter-American Dialogue's founding executive director. He was previously the founding director of the Latin American Program at the Woodrow Wilson International Center for Scholars and director of studies at the Council on Foreign Relations. He is widely published.

**Deborah J. Yashar** is assistant professor of government and of social sciences at Harvard University and a faculty associate of Harvard's Center for International Affairs. Dr. Yashar is the author of *Demanding Democracy: Reform and Reaction in Costa Rica and Guatemala* (forthcoming) and of a number of articles on democracy, representation, and protest in Latin America. She holds a Ph.D. from the University of California, Berkeley.

# Acronyms and Abbreviations

## General

CEPAL • Economic Commission for Latin America

EC • European Community

ECLA • Economic Commission for Latin America

ELG • export-led growth

FBIS • Foreign Broadcast Information Service

FDIC • Federal Deposit Insurance Corporation

GATT • General Agreement on Tariffs and Trade

GDP • gross domestic product

GNP • gross national product

ISI • import-substituting industrialization

LDCs • lesser developed countries

MDCs • more developed countries

MERCOSUL/R • Southern Cone Common Market

NAFTA • North American Free Trade Agreement

NGOs • nongovernmental organizations

OPEC • Organization of Petroleum Exporting Countries

PSOE • Socialist Workers Party of Spain

SOFRES • French Polling Association

VAT • Value Added Tax

## International Organizations

IDB • Inter-American Development Bank

IMF • International Monetary Fund

NACLA • North American Congress on Latin America

OAS • Organization of American States

UN • United Nations

UNDP • United Nations Development Program

USAID • United States Agency for International Development

## Anglophone Caribbean

CARICOM • Caribbean Common Market

JCF • Jamaican Constabulary Force

OECS • Organization of Eastern Caribbean States

PNP • People's National Party (Jamaica)

## Argentina

CGT • General Confederation of Labor

FG • Left-of-center political organization

FREPASO • Center-Left coalition

MID • Movement for Integration and Development

MODIN • Movement for National Dignity and Independence

PJ • Peronists

UCEDE • Union of the Democratic Center

UCR • Radical Civic Union

## Bolivia

ADN • Democratic and Nationalist Action

AP • Patriotic Accord

CBN • Bolivian National Brewery

COB • Bolivian Worker Central

COMSUR • Mineral Company of the South

CONDEPA • Conscience of the Fatherland

COPAP • Political Council of the Patriotic Accord

ENAF • National Smelting Company

ENDE • National Electricity Company

ENFE • National Railroad Enterprises

ENTEL • National Telecom Enterprises

FELCN • Special Counternarcotics Force

LAB • National Airways

MBL • Free Bolivia Movement

MIR • Revolutionary Movement of the Left

MNR • National Revolutionary Movement

MRTK • Tupac Katari Revolutionary Movement

NPE • New Economic Policy

RTP • Popular Radio and Television

UCS • Solidarity Civic Union

YPFB • National Hydrocarbons Enterprises of Bolivia

## Brazil

ARENA • National Renovating Alliance

"Diretas-Já" • Direct Elections Now campaign

IBOPE • Brazilian Institute of Public Opinion

IDESP • Institute of Social Economic and Political Research

MDB • Brazilian Democratic Movement

OAB • Brazilian Bar Association

PCB • Brazilian Communist Party

PDS • Democratic Social Party

PDT • Democratic Labor Party

PFL • Liberal Front Party

PMDB • Brazilian Democratic Movement Party

PMDB+PFL • Democratic Alliance

PRN • Party of National Renovation

PSDB • Brazilian Social Democratic Party

PT • Workers' Party

PTB • Brazilian Workers Party

## Chile

CD • Concertation for Demoncracy

CODELCO • National Copper Corporation

MIDA • Communist Party

PPD • Party for Democracy

RN • National Renovation

UCC • Center-Center Union

UDI • Independent Democratic Union

## Colombia

AD M-19 • Democratic Alliance M-19

ANAPO • National Popular Alliance

ANDI • National Association of Industrialists

ANIF • National Association of Financial Institutions

CAMACOL • Colombian Chamber of Construction

CGT • General Confederation of Labor

CRIC • Regional Indigenous Council of the Cauca

CSTC • Syndical Confederation of Workers of Colombia

CTC • Confederation of Colombian Workers

ELN • National Liberation Army

ELP • Popular Liberation Army

EPL • Popular Army of National Liberation

FARC • Armed Forces of the Colombian Revolution

FEDECAFE • National Federation of Coffee Growers

FEDEMETAL • Colombian Federation of Metallurgical Industries

FEDESARROLLO • Foundation for Higher Education and Development

FENALCO • National Federation of Merchants

M-19 • Nineteenth of April Movement; *see also* AD M-19

MSN • National Salvation Movement

NFD • New Democratic Force

PEPES • Persecuted by Pablo Escobar

SAC • Colombian Agricultural Society

UP • Patriotic Union

UTC • Union of Colombian Workers

## Costa Rica

CBI • Caribbean Basin Initiative

OIJ • Judicial Police

PLN • National Liberation Party

PUSC • Social Christian Unity Party

TSE • Supreme Electoral Tribunal

## Cuba

CCD • Cuban Committee for Democracy

CODEHU • Human Rights Organizations Coordinating Committee

PCC • Cuban Communist Party

## Dominican Republic

PLD • Dominican Liberation Party

PRD • Dominican Revolutionary Party

PRI • Independent Revolutionary Party

PRSC • Social Christian Reformist Party

PUCMM • Pontifical Catholic University"Madre y Maestra"

## Ecuador

CONAIE • National Confederation of Indigenous Nationalities of Ecuador

FUT • United Federation of Workers

PSC • Social Christian Party

PUR • United Republican Party

## El Salvador

ABECAFE • Salvadoran Association of Coffee Cultivators and Exporters

ASCAFE • Salvadoran Coffee Association

ANSP • National Academy of Public Security

ARENA • Nationalist Republican Alliance

CD • Democratic Convergence

COPAZ • Commission for the Consolidation of Peace

FAES • Armed Forces of El Salvador

FMLN • Farabundo Martí National Liberation Front

FPL • Popular Liberation Forces

ILO • International Labor Organization

IUDOP • University Institute for Public Opinion

MAC • Christian Authentic Movement

MNR • National Revolutionary Movement

MSN • National Solidarity Movement

MU • Unity Movement

PCN • Party of National Conciliation

PDC • Christian Democratic Party

PN • National Police

PNC • National Civilian Police

ONUSAL • United Nations Mission in El Salvador

SIRES • Application for identification an card

TSE • Supreme Electoral Board

## Guatemala

CACIF • Chambers of Commerce Industry and Finance

CERJ • Council of Ethnic Communities "We Are All Equal"

CONAVIGUA • National Steering Group of Guatemalan Widows

FDG • Guatemalan Republican Front

GAM • Mutual Help Group

INC • National Instance for Consensus

MLN • Movement of National Liberation

PID • Institutional Democratic Party

UCN • National Center Union

URNG • Guatemalan National Revolutionary Unity

## Haiti

CEP • Provisional Electoral Commission

FNCD • National Front for Democratic Convergence

KID • Convention for Democratic Initiatives

KONAKOM • National Committee of the Congress of Democratic Movements

MOP • Organizing Movement of the Nation

OPL • Popular Organization Lavalas

PLB • Barye Workers Party

VSN • Volunteers for National Security

## Honduras

BANFAA • Armed Forces Bank

CCIC • Chamber of Commerce and Industry of Cortes

DNI • National Investigative Directorate

FPM • Morazanista Patriotic Front

HONDUTEL • Telecommunications monopoly

IPM • Military Pensions Institute

PDC • Christian Democratic Party

PINU • Innovation and Unity Party

PL • Liberal Party

PN • National Party

## Mexico

AC • Civic Alliance

EZLN • Zapatista National Liberation Army

FDN • National Democratic Front

IFE • Federal Electoral Institute

ISI • Import-substituting industrialization

IVA • Value Added Tax

PAN • National Action Party

PARM • Authentic Party of the Mexican Revolution

PPC • Popular Christian Party

PPS • Popular Socialist Party

PRD • Democratic Revolutionary Party

PRI • Institutional Revolutionary Party

PRONASOL • National Solidarity Program

## Nicaragua

AMNLAE • Nicaraguan Women's Association Luisa Amanda Espinosa

ATC • Farmworkers Association

COSEP • Superior Council of Private Enterprise

CST • Sandinista Workers Federation

EPS • Sandinista Popular Army

ESAF • Enhanced Structural Adjustment Facility

FISE • Emergency Social Investment Fund

FNT • National Workers' Front

FSLN • Sandinista Front for National Liberation

IEN • Institute of Nicaraguan Studies

MRS • Sandinista Renewal Movement

PALI • Authentic Liberal Party

PLC • Liberal Constitutionalist Party

PLI • Independent Liberal Party

PLIUN • Liberal Party for National Unity

PLN • National Liberal Party

UNAG • National Union of Farmers and Ranchers

UNO • National Opposition Union

## Panama

ARI • Inter-Oceanic Regional Authority

FP • Public Force (national police)

MOLIRENA • National Liberal Republican Movement

PDF • Panamanian Defense Forces

PRD • Democratic Revolutionary Party

## Paraguay

ANR • Colorado Party

EN • National Encounter

PLRA • Liberal Radical Authentic Party

## Peru

APRA • American Popular Revolutionary Alliance

CCD • Democratic Constitutional Congress

FREDEMO • Democratic Front

IFI • International financial institutions

IU • United Left

PPC • Popular Christian Party

SIN • National Intelligence Service

## Uruguay

FA • Broad Front

PIT–CNT • Interunion Workers Council–Workers National Caucus

## Venezuela

AD • Social Democratic Party

Causa R • Cause R (a new unionist party)

CN • A personal vehicle for Rafael Caldera

CONINDUSTRIA • Council of Industrial Producers

CONSECOMERCIO • Council of Commercial Enterprises

COPEI • Christian Democratic Party

CTV • Venezuelan Workers Confederation

FEDECAMARAS • Federation of Chambers of Commerce and Production

MAS • A democratic party of the Left

MEP • People's Electoral Movement

RECADI • Foreign Exchange Agency

UNO • Odríist National Union

URD • A personal vehicle for Jóvito Villalba

*I*

# Introduction: Constructing Democratic Governance

## Abraham F. Lowenthal and Jorge I. Domínguez

Democratic political norms and procedures are increasingly common throughout Latin America and the Caribbean. But effective democratic governance—the daily practice of constitutional rule under law with stable political institutions that mediate among power contenders, restrain the dominant, and protect the weak—is far from consolidated; in many countries it is not even gaining strength. In fact, effective democratic governance has yet to be constructed in most countries of the region.

That mixed message is the main finding of this project on the state of democracy in the Americas in the mid-1990s. We aim neither to celebrate democracy's recent progress in the hemisphere nor to lament its continuing shortfalls. Rather we seek to analyze the sources of Latin America's current democratizing tendency as well as the remaining obstacles to democratic governance, to understand what has been achieved and how, and to illuminate what remains to be done.

In commissioning essays for what we hope will be a benchmark survey for the mid-1990s, we turned primarily to specialists on the politics of individual countries of Latin America and the Caribbean, often na-

This introduction draws on points made in various chapters of *Constructing Democratic Governance*. It also draws on a vast literature about democratic transitions, consolidation, and construction. We have been influenced by many other authors of whom we would cite the following, in alphabetical order, as particularly helpful: Giorgio Alberti, Nancy Bermeo, Catherine Conaghan, Robert Dahl, Larry Diamond, Jonathan Fox, Manuel Antonio Garretón, Jonathan Hartlyn, Samuel P. Huntington, Terry Karl, Juan Linz, Scott Mainwaring, Guillermo O'Donnell, Robert Putnam, Adam Przeworski, Karen Remmer, Aníbal Romero, Philippe Schmitter, Ben Ross Schneider, Alfred Stepan, J. Samuel Valenzuela, and Laurence Whitehead. We are especially grateful to Michael Shifter for his comments on this and several other chapters in this collection.

We would like to express our special appreciation to those at Harvard's Center for International Affairs and David Rockefeller Center of Latin American Studies and at the Center for International Studies of the University of Southern California who help us try to keep up, in both cases, with too many projects. We are also very grateful to all those mentioned in the Foreword by Peter Hakim and Michael Shifter.

tionals of these countries. In order to facilitate comparability, we asked the authors of country chapters to address a common set of issues. Among the topics we posed were the nature of the electoral process; the condition of parties and other political institutions; executive-legislative, civil-military, and church-state relations; the rule of law and the state of the judiciary; the roles of civic, professional, business, and labor organizations and of the media; the treatment of minorities and women; the impact of socioeconomic inequities; and the challenge (when relevant) of incorporating into politics those who until recently had employed violence to secure their objectives. We also asked contributors to highlight special issues salient in particular countries, such as the impact of ethnic movements, the narcotics trade, or gross corruption. No one chapter in this collection addresses all these questions in detail, but most of them take up many of the topics, with the result that the collection as a whole provides a nuanced set of appraisals.

To capture some of the important insights to be gained from cross-national analysis, we invited essays on central issues faced in several countries: the challenge for constructing democracy of incorporating the formerly extraconstitutional Left and the equally thorny task of taming the extraconstitutional Right; the difficulties of building effective democratic governance in fundamentally unjust societies; the issues posed by the growing and more active indigenous movements; and the tension between traditional power structures and the modern political forms they still sometimes dominate. Because our project permitted the exchange of drafts over many months, authors of these crosscutting chapters were able to draw on evidence from the country studies, and many of the authors of country studies, in turn, were able to incorporate insights from the topical essays into their final drafts; we believe these "conversations" among contributors have considerably enriched our efforts.

The positive side of our mixed message should not be underestimated or taken for granted. It is noteworthy that politics throughout Latin America and the Caribbean has moved unevenly but steadily toward electoral democracy. U.S. president George Bush surely overstated matters in 1992 when he proclaimed the western hemisphere, apart from Cuba, as the "first completely democratic hemisphere in human history," and Clinton administration officials engaged in similar hyperbole at the December 1994 Miami summit of democratically elected heads of governments. But, such flights of politically motivated rhetoric aside, it is undeniable that one Latin American nation after another has moved from authoritarian rule toward democratic politics.

In 1975 only two countries in all of South America had elected presidents, while Central America was still governed by praetorian dictators in every nation but Costa Rica. Since that time, governments of force have almost everywhere given way to regimes chosen in national elections, most of them reasonably free and fair, and the elected authorities have almost without exception served out their constitutionally stipulated terms. Whenever an internal attempt has been made to overthrow an elected government during the past decade, the attempted coup has been put down immediately or soon thereafter reversed. In the more ambiguous case of Peru, where an elected government itself closed down democratic institutions to rule by decree, internal and external pressures combined to produce a gradual restoration of democratic legitimacy; a similar *autogolpe* (auto-coup) in Guatemala was reversed even more quickly.

Acting through the regional organization the Organization of American States, Latin American governments have reduced strict doctrinal adherence to the norm of nonintervention in order to make a meaningful regional commitment to collective action in defense of democracy. The internationally endorsed multilateral effort to restore President Jean-Bertrand Aristide to office in Haiti was a stunning display of the new regional consensus. If Cuba's personal autocracy still persists in the mid-1990s, it is ever more conspicuous as an anachronistic exception. And even Cuba has undertaken some political reforms in a democratic direction, albeit modest ones.

The core democratic idea—that, to be legitimate, government authority must derive from periodic free, fair, broadly participatory, and genuinely contested elections—has gained broad acceptance throughout the Americas. Both elites and masses from many different perspectives and ideological backgrounds have come to support the fundamental democratic notion of popular sovereignty as well as the understanding that, for democratic elections to be legitimate, there must be freedom of opinion and of association and a free press to which all competitors have access. People from across the political spectrum—military officers and former guerrillas, peasants and industrial workers, intellectuals and industrialists—agree on the desirability and feasibility of democratic governance.

It was not always thus. Just thirty years ago, even twenty-five years ago, vanguards on the Left and guardians on the Right openly proclaimed their disdain for democratic institutions, and each current had considerable support. It was often argued that cultural and religious traditions predisposed Latin Americans toward authoritarian rule and that democracy was a foreign transplant, bound to be rejected by the body politic.

Throughout the chapters of this collection, there is ample evidence that Latin Americans today want democratic governance and are trying to build it. Perhaps the most dramatic illustration of this transformation came in Chile and Nicaragua, where entrenched rulers let power be taken from them as a result of internationally observed elections they certainly could have prevented. But less dramatic examples abound. The presidency has been turned over from incumbents to oppositions in numerous countries. Where that has not yet occurred, it has become imaginable. Elected civilian presidents have survived military coup attempts in half a dozen nations during the past few years. And military coups have become unlikely in several other countries where it was still a ready option, frequently invoked, just a generation ago. Even in Central America, where military officers have for so long dominated politics, the growth of civilian institutions is clearly taking place.

All this is true and important. Latin America's broad and forceful transition toward democratic governance is a paradigm shift of historic dimensions. Whatever the shortfalls of performance or the detours and reversals along the way, these chapters emphasize the significance of Latin America's turn toward democracy. That this turn has occurred and been sustained during a period of major economic stress and structural change is all the more impressive.

But what is equally evident in these chapters and just as significant is that holding fair elections and avoiding successful coups are not by themselves sufficient to produce effective and enduring democratic governance. Effective democratic governance requires not only that the governing authorities be freely and fairly elected but that the public share the expectation that the rulers will remain subject to periodic popular review and that they can be replaced through equally fair elections. It also implies that executive authority is otherwise constrained and held accountable by law, by an independent and autonomous judiciary, and by additional countervailing powers.

Effective democratic governance involves clear and consistent subordination of the military and the police to civilian political institutions, especially parties, that are autonomous, stable, and powerful enough to express and aggregate social interests and also to constrain self-aggrandizing power grabs by the executive. It implies the organizations and procedures of civil society, of intermediary institutions engaging in the interests and values of diverse individuals and groups. Yet for democratic governance to work well, government officials must also have enough authority and legitimacy to take and implement decisions that are intended to privilege public and national interests over those of sectors, classes, regions, or private actors. The tension between effective authority and accountability is built into democratic governance and provides a constant challenge, even in those societies where democracy has been most fully achieved.

These chapters suggest that it is premature and indeed misleading to talk about "consolidating" democratic governance in Latin America and the Caribbean. Electoral procedures are being institutionalized in a number of countries, to be sure, but all too often these coexist with pervasive clientelism, imbedded injustice, massive corruption, flagrant impunity, and reserved domains beyond the authority of government or the rule of law. Throughout much of the region, the frustrations in advancing effective democratic governance have at times shaken Latin Americans' confidence in and commitment to democracy itself.

In most nations, effective democratic governance is still incipient, inchoate, fragile, highly uneven, incomplete, and often contradicted. Democratic governance in Latin America needs to be nurtured, constructed, and reinforced, bit by bit and country by country. In their assessment of Latin America's progress toward democracy, these essays underline that a great deal remains to be accomplished.

How hard it is to build effective and enduring democratic governance is highlighted by considering the United States, the hemisphere's most established democracy. Effective democratic governance in the United States has been deteriorating in recent years with the marked decline in public respect for parties and virtually all other political institutions; the deep rejection of professional politicians and incumbents; the decline of interconnectedness among citizens in the communities where they live; growing struggle over identity, culture, and values that cannot be resolved by compromises over "more or less"; consistently high levels of violent crime; the privatization of security and the use of deadly force; and an erosion of confidence in law, courts, and access to equal justice. Any inclination to think that democracy in the western hemisphere is close to being consolidated must be challenged throughout the Americas, North and South.

This is not the place for extended comments on what can be done to strengthen the prospects of constructing democratic governance.[1] But one strong implication of these essays is that we should rethink the sharply dichotomous categorization of "democracies" and "non-democracies." The tendency to think about democracy in "on-off" terms focuses too much international policy attention on holding and monitoring elections and on preventing or reversing coups. Elections and attempted coups are clearly defined moments of decision, and the steady reinforcement of international norms in favor of free elections and against coups has certainly been important in making democratic governance possible.

But effective democratic governance depends fundamentally on the quotidian building, exercise, and maintenance of democratic political

1. We have dealt with this issue in an Inter-American Dialogue Policy Brief, *The Challenges of Democratic Governance in Latin America and the Caribbean: Sounding the Alarm,* and the Dialogue has recently published an entire volume on international efforts to promote Latin American democracy: Tom Farer, ed., *Beyond Sovereignty: Collectively Defending Democracy in the Americas* (Baltimore: Johns Hopkins University Press, 1996).

practice. The most urgent and important task today is to help make democracy in the Americas work day to day: to maintain order peacefully with the consent of the governed, to represent the interests of all citizens fairly and effectively, and to extend the rule of law to all corners and all issues in the hemisphere. These are the challenges all true democrats must confront.

*II*

# 1

# Incorporating the Left into Democratic Politics

## Alan Angell

Historically the Left . . . has always presumed the existence of an objective, a program, an organized force capable of carrying out that program, and a theory that explained the logic of the system. The program may have been improvised, the objective unreal, and the organized force nothing of the kind, but this was how the Left thought about change, at least how it legitimized its activities. All this is now open to question.[1]

This quotation from José Aricó well captures the ideological dilemma that faces the Left in Latin America since the collapse of international communism in the late 1980s. The Latin American Left always sought legitimation in an appeal to a broader context than the purely national one. This was partly the heritage of a Left that was firmly rooted in Marxism as its ideological model and Leninism as its political practice. It is difficult, for example, to explain the important political role of communist parties in Latin America, in spite of their limited popularity, and even more limited success as promoters of revolution, unless this international and ideological dimension is taken into account. Communist parties in Latin America were seen as the direct representatives of an international movement of world revolution, giving them an importance beyond their specific electoral appeal or political power. It is true, of course, that the impact of the Cuban Revolution on the Latin American Left was shattering, not least on those orthodox communist parties that claimed a monopoly of the truth. But in a sense what happened was that the center of the Latin American Left was transferred from Moscow to Havana, and Marxism became combined with a kind of revolutionary voluntarism rather than with strict Leninism. The Latin American Left still had its international reference point and its revolutionary orthodoxy.

The collapse of international communism profoundly changed the Latin American Left. The significance of what happened after the revolutions of 1989 in Eastern Europe was as important for the Latin American Left as the Bolshevik revolution of 1917. No longer could the Left claim a special significance as part of an international movement. No longer could the Left appeal to a particular ideology as containing the inevitable laws of historical development. With the collapse of international communism, the Left lost the mobilizing vision of a socialist society to be achieved by revolution. In the words of Jorge Castañeda, the idea of revolution became not simply unimaginable but even undesirable.[2]

The Left in Latin America now found itself facing a newly defined political context that was national rather than international. This might be seen as an advantage. The Left would no longer have to justify or excuse the undemocratic practices of the Communist bloc.[3] It no longer had to defend regimes that offended liberal democratic beliefs. The Left no longer had to face the same degree of hostility from the United States. It could begin to free itself from the charge that the Left in power will automatically degenerate into authoritarianism.

But no movement changes completely overnight in response to external events. The Left in Latin America did not suddenly become social democratic. Old practices persisted, not least that of an elitist Leninism still practicing a style of party government that was far from democratic and participatory. The far Left saw in the collapse of communism not the result of an excess of Marxist practice but, on the contrary, a lack of it. There are still practitioners of revolutionary violence. There are still adherents of a state-centered doctrine of economic planning.

These groups might be seen as remnants of the past fighting a rearguard action against the social democratic modernizers. This interpretation would be more plausible if the modernizers had a clear ideological program and widespread support. But the prevailing ideological climate in Latin America is not favorable to the Left, in whatever form. In the first place, the prevailing economic doctrine of the free market runs counter to the idea of central state planning, which has dominated the thinking of the Left since its inception. If the idea of state planning is discredited, then the Left has somehow to make its long-term objectives compatible with a free market system. But in practice the Left has little credible alternative to offer to the casualties of the economic adjustment packages that had in many cases stabilized national economies, though at great social cost. Second, the Left still faces the electoral dilemma that had haunted its history: how can it move outside its core of organized labor and leftist intellectuals to reach social sectors previously indifferent to its message, but necessary for any prospect of electoral success? Third, given the dismal record of the Left in power—for whatever reasons, the economic performance of Allende's Chile, Castro's Cuba, or Sandinista Nicaragua was not inspiring—how can the Left establish credibility as competent administrators?

The perplexity of the Left in facing this conjuncture is well expressed in this statement by José Pasos, deputy chief of the FSLN's (Sandinista Front for National Liberation) international department, after the Sandinista defeat in 1990.

We have to become a modern party. There are some principles that don't change: political pluralism, non-alignment, mixed economy. Our anti-imperialism stays the same, but it is not the anti-imperialism of Marx or Lenin. For us, it means non-interference in our internal affairs and it's the United States that interferes. We continue to believe in socialism as the goal. But it's definitely not the socialism that has come up in the East, nor the socialism of Cuba, nor perestroika. Perhaps the most acceptable for us would be Swedish socialism, but it's very expensive. What kind of socialism a poor country can have is a discussion that we're now going to begin. (*Guardian* [London], April 30, 1990, interview)

The previous models of socialism widely prevalent in Latin America have lost their appeal, and there is little consensus on a new model. There is a problem of defining the aims of the Left in the new order.

There is also a problem of defining the means by which the Left can effectively gain power. How can the Left mobilize the poor effectively? What strategy of alliances should it pursue to win power in a way that still leaves intact some identifiable socialist project? How can the Left relate to the social movements of Latin America without arousing suspicion of political manipulation by the Left?

There is, in addition, the issue of the appropriate form of organization for mobilizing support for the Left. There are serious questions about whether this can be done simply by continuing with the same kind of party organization and structure as in the past, not least because of the need to respond to changes in social structure which have weakened the traditional base of the Left, namely, the dramatic reduction in the power and influence of the trade union movement in countries as diverse as Bolivia and Argentina, for example.

## The Shadow of the Past

The present crisis has to be seen in the context of the historical development of the Left in Latin America. What were the weaknesses of the Left, and which of those weaknesses survive to the present? What were the strengths of the Left, and which of those strengths survive?

The Left historically has been characterized by deep and bitter divisions and has rarely, if ever, been united. In most countries one should talk not of the Left, but of the Lefts. The most public manifestations of disunity were differences, often bitter and violent ones about ideology and strategy, about who could legitimately be included as being "on the Left."[4] There is less fundamental disagreement today about ideologies: battles between orthodox communists, Trotskyists, and Maoists are increasingly irrelevant. There is more agreement today on the need for unity and consensus on the Left, for building wider coalitions, and for working with other parties. In some countries, notably Chile, this tactic has been pursued with some success by one part of the Left, namely, the socialist parties, but was opposed with catastrophic effects on its own following by the other part, the communist movement. In most countries, however, the unity of the Left is, if not so far away as it was in the days of heated ideological debate, still an objective to be achieved rather than something attained.

However, the disunity of the Left has never been a function of purely doctrinal issues. The Left in most countries is best seen as a combination of a variety of parties, social movements, and ideologies, and these three elements do not necessarily overlap nor agree. The ideology of the Left, of Marxism, has always been much more influential than the organized parties of the Left, and often the adherents of the doctrine were among the strongest critics of the leftist parties.[5] The real influence of Marxism in Latin America was felt not so much through the parties of the Left, but at the level of ideology and as a stimulus to political mobilization and action, not least in the trade union movement and among students and intellectuals, including, from the 1960s, radical Catholics.

The problem that faces the current Left is precisely how to regain that sense of ideological commitment, and how it can do so to rival the enhanced ideological commitment and appeal of the Right with its doctrine of the free market.[6] One of the major strengths of the Left was precisely its firm belief in the validity of its ideas. In order to recover that strength, the Left needs to develop ideas appropriate to the era of post-Marxism—and that is a challenge that faces the Left worldwide, not just in Latin America. The Left can no longer behave as if the logic of historical development is on its side.

To talk of redefining ideologies, of devising policies, and of making tactical alliances implies a Left structured around political parties and associated organizations such as trade unions. Yet this pattern of political organization applies to relatively few countries, notably to Chile and Uruguay, and (to a lesser extent since 1989) to Venezuela. But in other countries, the Left is relatively diffuse, similar to the Mexican Left which encompasses a large number of parties, political groups, labor unions, organized popular movements, and mass publications that continually fluctuate in both form and composition. Such dispersion can be a source of strength, if there is a broadly unifying party or movement (such as the PT [Workers' Party] in Brazil and, more questionably, the PRD [Democratic Revolutionary Party] in Mexico). But if this unifying factor does not exist, then such dispersion can be a source of weakness (as in Peru or Bolivia).

Historically, the Left sought its base in the union movement which, in its turn, sought to act as representative of the urban, if not the rural, poor. But the recent period has seen the decline of unions in general, and those that remain powerful are in the public sector and do not always enjoy broad social support for their demands. There has also occurred the growth of community-based organizations, often suspicious of manipulation by political parties, including those of the Left. These grass-roots movements express powerful demands for citizenship rights; they draw some inspiration from radical Catholicism; and they incorporate groups that had not been politically active in the past, especially women and the unemployed. Their demands are rarely political in the first instance, but when the political environment is unresponsive or even hostile, then a general demand for democracy is inevitably linked to their specific aims. Popular movements tend to be of protest and opposition. They flourished when military dictatorships limited political participation. They created a powerful opposition consciousness, with a strongly corporatist element: they believe in the state and not in the market.

These so-called new social movements are not always hostile to parties. In Brazil the role of the Left, especially the PT, in the neighborhood organizations is important. The PT helped these organizations transcend their immediate material perspectives, fostered coordination on a broader scale, and raised general political issues. But in other countries these social movements can, and often do, express an explicit rejection of, or disillusionment with, political parties. In Peru, areas where the Left and APRA (American Popular Revolutionary Alliance) had been traditionally strong voted in 1990 for the politically unknown Fujimori as president and for his untried party, Cambio 90. Fujimori received 40 percent of his total Lima vote from the twelve poorest districts, far exceeding the vote for the left-wing coalition, the Izquierda Unida (United Left).[7]

The electoral challenge to the Left from these movements is formidable for these populist figures are often capable of winning considerable support from the urban or rural poor. In societies where class structures are less firm, and certainly less institutionally expressed through class-based organizations, the Left faces a strong challenge. What can it offer to the urban poor that is more attractive than the promises of an effective populist politician? One partial answer at least is that of efficient local government, and this is an area where the Left is trying to establish a distinctive profile to contrast with the clientelism and corruption that are held to be characteristic of local government generally in Latin America.[8]

The problem that the Left has faced in mobilizing the poor of the shantytowns is part of a broader problem that has faced and still faces the Left in Latin America, that is, the electoral and popular challenge of the populist parties. The political space traditionally occupied in Europe by social democracy was occupied in Latin America by nationalist populist parties. These parties were never constrained by ideological orthodoxy and in the past drew heavily upon the ideas and practices of the Left. A crucial and continuous political problem for the Left was, and in many ways still is, the nature of its relationship with such parties of greater ideological flexibility, greater political appeal, and broader social support.[9] The Colombian Left has never been able to establish a continuing electoral presence outside an alliance with the Liberal party, in part a consequence of the Colombian electoral system which penalizes small independent parties. One of the reasons why sectors of the Colombian Left have preferred violent tactics has been the overwhelming political weight of the two traditional parties.

However, populism in Latin America has recently emphasized its hostility to political parties as such. This has been manifested not only at the national level by leaders such as Fujimori in Peru or Caldera in Venezuela, but also at the local level where a number of mayors of major cities have been elected on antiparty tickets. This presents real problems for the Left. Not only does it have to combat the appeal of genuinely popular leaders, but it also has to combat a widespread indifference to, or even rejection of, the political party as such.

One of the most enduring divisions of the Left in Latin America has been over the justification of the use of violence to achieve political objectives, a tactic that was given an enormous boost by the Cuban Revolution. The election of Allende in Chile was an equally dramatic moment for the Left and seemed to legitimate the peaceful road to socialism. This was the first experiment in trying to create a socialist society through peaceful, constitutional means and posed a question of universal relevance for the Left: could there be a peaceful transition to socialism in a pluralistic and democratic society? This was no imposition from above of a rigid revolutionary dogma, but a pluralist and democratic government attempting to win popular support for the most part by argument and persuasion.

With the coup of 1973, however, other questions were posed: what could the Latin American Left learn from the mistakes of the Chilean Left? How could the Left anywhere hope to attain power in the face of opposition from the national and international Right? The effect of the failure of the Unidad Popular (Popular Unity) government was to polarize the Left in Latin America. The more radical groups, such as the Sandinistas in Nicaragua and pro-Cuban groups elsewhere, resolved to intensify armed conflict. Their argument was that the coup showed that a peaceful road to socialism was simply an illusion. The far Left argued that in face of the opposition of the Right, the military, and the United States, armed revolution was the only hope of achieving power.

If one response of the Left to the coup was to advocate the need for violence, another response was diametrically opposite—arguing that the Left should now moderate its policies and actions so that the conditions that gave rise to coups would not occur. The revisionists argued that the Left should stop visualizing power exclusively in terms of force, as something to be physically possessed. The Left should stop concentrating on property relations to the exclusion of other factors: a simple transference of ownership to the state would not solve anything and could indeed create more problems than it resolved. The military could not be defeated by force. A radical government had to achieve such widespread legitimacy that the conditions that gave rise to military intervention—social disorder, political conflict outside the parliamentary and electoral arenas—did not occur. That meant concessions to the Right and a determined effort to win the support of the middle classes and to achieve a working relationship with the business sectors. Political alliances were seen as necessary, and democracy was seen as a value in its own right.

In a way the modern debate on the Left in Latin America began with the Chilean coup and is not yet concluded. Some parties of the Left, not least the Chilean Socialist party, can be placed firmly in the camp of the revisionists. But other movements of the Left, notably guerrilla groups in Colombia and Peru, still pursue the armed struggle. Yet others, such as the Sandinistas in Nicaragua or the former guerrilla groups in El Salvador, are making an uneasy transition from armed movement to political party.

This debate was conducted largely clandestinely or in exile for much of the 1970s and 1980s as the Left was a passive witness to forces that it could barely influence. Military authoritarian governments brutally attacked the Left. Parties and unions were suppressed, and many leaders were killed or exiled. Intellectual debate was stifled. The period of authoritarianism saw changes in society and the economy that were unfavorable to the Left: the growth of informal as opposed to formal employment, the emergence of free market economics as the dominant mode, the reduction in the size of the state. These trends continued into the period of transitions to democracy. And, if this state of organizational weakness and ideological uncertainty was not enough, then to the misfortunes of the Left was added the collapse of international communism.

## The Latin American Left in the 1990s

It should be clear from the analysis so far that, in common with many other parts of the world, the Left in Latin America in the 1990s faced multiple challenges, and faced them from a position of organizational weakness, ideological uncertainty, and minority electoral support. Yet the Left in some countries had strengths that it could draw upon. The Left had opposed, often with great courage, the authoritarian governments of the 1970s and 1980s and could claim a greater democratic credibility than the movements of the Right. The Left in some countries, notably Brazil, organized the new movements in the unions and neighborhoods and acted as the representative of the poor. In others, the Left had a tradition of organization and had created a subculture of socialism that resisted the drift to the Right. There are also the seeds of future growth of the Left in the twin failures of many of the restored democracies of Latin America: the failure to create adequate safety nets to deal with the social costs of the economic adjustment programs and the failure to halt the corruption of the governing elites. The Left owes its origins to protest above all, and given the social condition of the poor in Latin America, there is still a great deal to protest about.

How far can we identify general trends? How far can we say that the Left in Latin America unambiguously accepts democracy? How far is the Left a serious political force in Latin America? The answers to these questions are not easy, and to some extent national diversity is greater now, in the postcommunist era, than in the past. If there are no completely uniform trends, it is still possible to make some distinctions that are broader than the national level.

There is a strong social democratic Left in a number of countries. In these countries—Chile, Venezuela, Uruguay, Brazil, Mexico are the leading examples—there are parties firmly committed to the democratic system, and with significant electoral support. They each have a popular leader, though not policies for dealing with economic and social issues which are substantially different from the predominant free market ones.

In other countries, notably those of Central America and Colombia, there is a Left emerging from the guerrilla experience, forced by a mixture of necessity and rethinking to accept the rules of competitive party politics. The commitment of these movements is much more conditional, and they contain within them groups that prefer the armed method of seizing power.

Yet there still exists an active tradition of leftist insurgency. This is most sharply present in Peru with the Maoist-inspired Sendero Luminoso movement. It is true that this movement has suffered a sharp reversal of its power with the arrest of its leader, Abimael Guzman. But it is equally characteristic of such movements that they can appear suddenly and with little advance warning, as happened with the Zapatista movement in Chiapas in Mexico.

Other countries are characterized by the eclipse of the Left and its electoral and political insignificance. Peronism in Argentina has turned its back upon its leftist past and has created a vacuum on the Left. In Bolivia, a once powerful leftist movement based on the unions, above all the mining unions, has collapsed as the unions have been decimated.

The political influence of the Left in any country will be at maximum when four factors coincide and reinforce each other: a united party, widely based social support, ideas that are seen as relevant and credible, and a popular leader. These factors rarely coincide in this neat fashion, but some Latin American countries combine them, notably those where political parties are reasonably well structured and where, arguably, there is a social democratic tradition of some weight. In these countries it can be argued that the commitment of the Left to electoral politics is not just a matter of expediency but of principle. Indeed, perhaps it is given that if the violent road is ruled out for a variety of reasons, then the only alternative open to the Left is through the maximization of electoral gains. It could also be argued for these countries that the incorporation of the Left into democratic and constitutional politics is less problematic and less conditional than is that of the Right.

### The Social Democratic Left

One response to the decline of orthodox communism, and the increasing unattractiveness of the Cuban model—and in contrast to the violence associated with the guerrilla movements of countries such as Peru, Colombia, and El Salvador—was a renewal of interest in socialism of an essentially parliamentary and electoral form. The reaction to years of military dictatorship, and the suppression of basic freedoms of the Left, was a much more positive evaluation of the benefits of formal democracy. The growth of social democratic movements in Europe, notably the Spanish socialist party of Felipe González, provided a source of inspiration. The work of the Socialist International in Latin America provided international links, further encouragement, and some financial assistance. Closer analysis of the social structure of Latin America led the more moderate Left to realize the importance of appealing to the middle classes and to the growing popular organizations that were not trade unions, nor expressions of class struggle, and that owed more to church-inspired institutions than to the Marxist Left.

These parties in the 1990s advocated a number of policies very different from those of previous decades. Instead of the centralized state, they advocated decentralization and participation of the community in local decision making. Instead of a Leninist model of internal party government, they emphasized inner party democracy and positive discrimination for women. Instead of concentrating power in the executive, they emphasized the need for checks and balances and turned their attention to issues such as an independent judiciary and an independent central bank. They sought to establish their credentials by efficient administration of the local governments they controlled. They emphasized that, against the corruption that had emerged so much into the open with the return to democracy, they would be, by contrast, honest and accountable if elected. What is happening in practice falls short of the rhetoric, but there are countries where the Left is trying to present itself, with some success, as a modern, capable, and incorrupt political force.

The countries where the social democratic model of the Left prevails have a number of features in common. They are all countries with relatively strong institutional frameworks, and with reasonably developed party systems. These systems have allowed the Left to develop as an institutional force and to learn the rules of political competition and party behavior. They are all countries with relatively modern economic and social structures, providing a social base for the Left to develop electoral and political support. Though all countries have seen periods of repression—indeed of intense repression in some cases—it has not been continuous, nor has it been the norm. And, in all of them, the ideas of socialism and Marxism have been vigorous and widespread.

The Chilean Socialist party, though always containing a variety of ideological factions, had moved to the left during the 1960s, partly under the influence of the Cuban Revolution. During the Popular Unity government, it was more radical than the Communist party and supported worker and peasant takeovers of factories and farms. It was savagely repressed after the 1973 coup, and most of the leadership of the party was forced into exile, where the party divided into a moderate wing and a Marxist-Leninist wing. This difference partly reflected the experience of exile. Those exiled in France, Italy, or the Scandinavian countries were influenced by the changes taking place in European social democracy, and they came eventually to dominate the whole party. The party was forced to a profound reconsideration of the meaning of democracy.[10]

The Chilean socialists embraced a political alliance with the Christian Democrats in opposition to Pinochet in the plebiscite in 1988. After the elections of 1989 they entered the government coalition. They shed the dogmas of the past and embraced the market and modernization of the economy with even greater enthusiasm than the Christian Democrats. Both entrepreneurs and the military found the newly fashioned socialists more congenial politically than the Christian Democrats. The socialists are divided into two parties, but this enhances rather than diminishes their appeal. The Socialist party appeals to the traditional subculture of socialism in Chile, based on the trade union and the local party. The Party for Democracy (PPD), founded to fight the 1988 plebiscite, appeals to the less ideological sector of the electorate, to a wide spectrum of middle-class urban groups, and gains support through the leadership of the socialist politician most credible as a future president, Ricardo Lagos. In the 1993 elections the socialists combined gained just under 24 percent of the vote. What the Chilean socialists have done, and done very effectively, has been to establish themselves as efficient administrators, as a party of government and not just of opposition.

The Venezuelan Movimiento al Socialismo (MAS, Movement to Socialism) was formed in 1971 by dissident members of the Communist party, and many of them had participated in the 1960s guerrilla movement. Though the party has rarely gained more than 5 percent of the vote, its importance in the political system has been greater than that

figure would suggest, for the ideas it has disseminated have been influential, and it helped to consolidate democracy in Venezuela by lending
its support to the system established in 1958. The MAS was influenced
by the experience of the Italian Communist party and by the Eu-
rocommunist movement. It emphasized that there must be individual
and national roads to socialism and rejected the idea that there was one
correct model. It was critical of the Leninist style of party organization
and argued for a participatory party structure. It criticized the Communist party for underestimating the role and importance of the middle
classes in the Venezuelan political system. Although many of the
members of the MAS came from the Communist party and the far Left,
the party committed itself to democracy, both for the country and in its
own internal structure. The MAS emphasized the need for honesty and
accountability in public life, and sought to present itself as the true
representative of the values that the major parties—AD (Acción Democrática [Democratic Action]) and COPEI (Comité de Organización Política Electoral Independiente [Committee for Independent Electoral
Politics])—had once embodied but had compromised in the struggle for
political power.

In the 1988 elections, running in alliance with another left-wing
party, the MAS won 10.2 percent of the vote, and in the first direct
elections for state governors held in 1989, it took the industrial state of
Aragua and came second to AD in several others. But the MAS suffered
from its lack of a popular and union base, and its decision to support
Caldera in the 1993 presidential election was seen by many as succumbing to the temptation to gain power at the cost of principle. It has
been challenged on the left by Causa R, a trade union–based party from
the provinces. Causa R takes as its model the Brazilian PT. It has established a powerful presence in the union movement, achieved popularity as an efficient and honest government of the state of Bolívar, and
has an attractive leader in the trade unionist and governor of the state
of Bolívar, Andrés Velásquez. Causa R gained 20.5 percent of the vote in
the 1993 congressional elections compared with 28.2 percent for AD,
28.6 percent for COPEI, 12.8 percent for the MAS, and 11.8 percent for
the coalition supporting Caldera.[11]

The Venezuelan Left has not established credibility as a party of central government as in Chile. But it has done so at the local level. It
emphasizes honest government in contrast to the rampant corruption
of the major parties: it emphasizes participation in contrast to the elit-
ism of the major parties. This appeal has prospered as the economy in
Venezuela went into decline, as accusations of corruption multiplied,
and as Causa R was able to break the stranglehold of AD in the trade
union movement.

The Left in Uruguay was unusual in the way that it seemed less affected in its ideas and strategy by the long years of military dictatorship

than the Left in Brazil or Chile. However, more than the other countries of the Southern Cone, the restoration of democracy in Uruguay was precisely that, a restoration of the previous system. In fact, the Left changed rather more than the two dominant parties in Uruguay, Colorado and Nacional. The Left made a strong showing in the 1971 elections when, organized as the Frente Amplio (FA, Broad Front), it won 18 percent of the vote. In the first elections following military rule in 1984, it won 21.3 percent of the vote and in 1989, 21.2 percent. But there were changes in the composition and politics of the FA.

In 1973 the main parties in the FA were the communist, the socialist, and the MLN (National Liberation Movement)-Tupamaros. By 1984 the vote going to the radical Left, the MLN, fell as a proportion of the total Left vote from 23 percent to 6.7 percent; to the Communists from 32.9 percent to 28.2 percent; while the major gainers were a new moderate Christian Democratic–inspired party, the Movimiento por el Gobierno del Pueblo (Movement for the People's Government), which won 39.3 percent of the FA's vote compared to the 10.3 percent that had gone to moderate parties in 1971. The FA was clearly less extreme than in 1971, and its commitment to electoral politics was firm. It lost the support of the most moderate group in 1989, which formed the Nuevo Espacio (New Space) party that took 9 percent of the popular vote, but its share of the vote remained constant. Moreover, the FA won a plurality in Montevideo, with 37 percent of the vote, and elected the mayor there.

The FA, as its name implies, is a broad coalition held together by the peculiarities of the Uruguayan electoral system, which encourages broad coalitions of many parties. It gained support partly because it was the only credible alternative to the traditional two-party dominance at a time when those parties were increasingly unpopular for their handling of the economy. The FA consolidated its hold on the Left by its opposition to the law that grants amnesty to military officers for human rights abuses. The FA benefited from the Uruguayan union system which, in contrast to most countries of Latin America, has a history of autonomous development unincorporated into the state machine and not colonized by one of the two major parties.[12] But the FA is weak outside Montevideo, where it gained only 9 percent of the vote, and unionized workers who vote heavily for it constitute only 19 percent of the adult population of Montevideo and are insignificant elsewhere. The exit from the FA of the moderate parties reduced its overall chance of electoral gains.[13] To some extent the FA's survival was testimony to the overall immobility of the Uruguayan political system rather than to the development of a new and innovative leftist movement.

Like Venezuela, the Left in Uruguay benefited from disenchantment with the two dominant parties, established a reputation for efficient local government, has a popular leader in the former mayor of Montevideo, Tavaré Vásquez, has significant support in the union movement, and also mobilized support around the human rights issue. In the 1994 elections the FA won 30 percent of the national vote, but what was impressive was that it made significant gains in the interior of the country as well as in Montevideo. It elected a new mayor of Montevideo, in part a vote of confidence in the record of the previous FA administration. Its overall national support is now more or less equal to those of the traditional parties, though like those two parties it also has divisions and factions. The FA's experience demonstrates the benefit the Left can derive from efficient local administration.

The most important development on the Left in Latin America came with the formation of the Brazilian Partido dos Trabalhadores (PT, Workers' Party). The PT grew out of the new unionism that developed in the massive metallurgical industries of the São Paulo region. By 1978, after a year of labor militancy, the new union leaders, especially Luis Inacio da Silva (Lula), came to believe that workplace militancy was inadequate to achieve their broader aims. In Lula's words:

> In my view the Brazilian left has made mistakes throughout its history precisely because it was unable to comprehend what was going on inside the workers' heads and upon that basis elaborate an original doctrine. . . . I do not deny that the PCB [Brazilian Communist Party] has been an influential force for many years. What I do deny is the justness of telling the workers that they have to be Communists. The only just course of action is to give the workers the opportunity to be whatever suits them best. We do not wish to impose doctrines. We want to develop a just doctrine which emanates from the organization of our workers and which at the same time is a result of our own organization.[14]

The PT has become the largest explicitly socialist party in Latin America. Its electoral support increased from 3 percent of the total vote in 1982 to 7 percent in 1986. In the 1988 elections for mayor, PT candidates took control of thirty-six cities, notably São Paulo, where the candidate was a woman migrant from the impoverished northeast, Luiza Erundina. The PT's vote overall in Brazil's one hundred largest cities was 28.8 percent of the total. Though the party had its roots in the urban union movement, it has also grown in the rural areas where it has the support of the radical Church and the local base communities. In the first round of the 1989 presidential elections, Lula, the PT candidate, won 16.08 percent of the vote, narrowly winning the second place over Brizola (PDT, Democratic Labor Party) with 15.74 percent. In the second round, Lula (37.86%) was defeated by Fernando Collor de Mello (42.75%), despite the party's having moderated its radical political platform in order to appeal to the Center—a tactic that almost worked. In the 1993 presidential elections, the PT was again the major challenger, and indeed for months was the frontrunner in the opinion polls. In the end it lost to the social democratic candidate, Fernando Henrique Cardoso, but increased its first ballot vote to 27 percent and gained a larger representation in Congress.

The PT also sought to adopt a new model of internal organization that would, unlike that of the PCB, respect the autonomy of the union movement. The party was not to lead the workers but to express their demands in the political sphere. The organization of the party emphasized participatory democracy. The core organization of the party would be the *núcleo de base*, composed of affiliated members from either a neighborhood, professional group or workplace, or social movement, and engaged in permanent political, rather than occasional electoral, activity. The party was meant to dissolve the differences that normally exist between social movement and party. If, in practice, many nuclei do function largely as electoral bodies, the level of participation of the estimated 600,000 members of the PT is still extraordinarily high by Brazilian party standards.

Such a participatory structure was very appropriate for the oppositional politics made necessary by the imposition of military rule. It is less clear that such a structure is functional for a competitive democracy. Many of the members and leaders of the party came from Catholic radicalism rather than Marxism, and they were more concerned to maintain the autonomy of union and popular organizations than they were to create a disciplined political party. There were many conflicts inside the PT, not least between the PT members of Congress and the party leaders outside Congress. The three Brazilian Trotskyist parties all worked within the PT, even though the largest of them, the Convergência Socialista (Socialist Convergence), conceives of the PT as a front to be radicalized under the direction of a revolutionary vanguard, combating in the PT the influence of the church and the parliamentary group.[15] Such a variety of political positions did not lead to party discipline, but the defeat of the Trotskyists in the 1991 Congress led to a more unified party.

The PT is undoubtedly novel, not just among the parties of Brazil but even among the socialist parties of Latin America. It is firmly rooted in the working class and controls some 60 percent of unions in the public sector, and only slightly fewer in the private sector. In Congress the PT is the party with the largest proportion of deputies linked to organized labor and social movements. It has tried to develop new policies and practices, for example, 30 percent of seats in the Central Committee of the party are to be held by women. But there are problems that it faces for further development.

The PT is an ideological party in a party system that is very unideological. It faces the challenge of other parties on the Left, notably the old radical populist party of Brizola, and the social democratic PSDB (Brazilian Social Democratic Party). It reaches out to the organized poor in town and countryside, but most poor Brazilians are neither members of unions nor of social organizations, and in 1989 these sectors voted more heavily for the right-wing Collor de Mello than for Lula. Like all parties of the Left, the PT has difficulties in proposing policy alternatives for dealing with the economic crisis which do not look either like the unsuccessful formulas of the past or simple imitations of the orthodox neoliberal policies. While the PT's attachment to a radical ideology helps to develop committed party members, that very commitment limits its ability to compete in the fluid and populist world of Brazilian party politics.

For all the differences between political systems, there are parallels in Chile, Venezuela, Uruguay, Brazil, and elsewhere in Latin America in the emergence of a socialism that stresses participation and democracy, rejects the past orthodoxy of one correct model, and is firmly based on national structures rather than international doctrines.

As usual in Latin America, it is difficult to fit Mexico into any comparative category, but with the 1988 presidential election, a new party of the Left did emerge to shake the political dominance of the PRI (Institutional Revolutionary Party). The political coalition put together to support the presidential candidature of Cárdenas was a heterogeneous coalition of dissident members of the PRI, the independent parties of the Left, and the satellite leftist parties that had traditionally revolved around the PRI (such as the PPS, Popular Socialist Party). In the 1988 elections it was the satellite Left that saw its vote sharply increase while that of the independent Left fell. Although normally these parties gained only a small vote—4.7 percent in 1979 and 2.96 percent in 1982—their vote rose to 21.04 percent in 1988 when they were supporting the candidature of Cárdenas in the FDN (National Democratic Front) coalition.

The attraction of this coalition was based on the popularity of its leader, Cuauhtémoc Cárdenas, the son of the reformist president, on its revolutionary nationalism, and on its being an effective vehicle for anti-PRI protest. The coalition emphasized political democracy and the autonomy of mass organizations, but its message was vague enough to create uncertainty as to whether it was simply the Left of the PRI or a genuinely new socialist departure. The coalition was a fragile combination of very disparate elements from the anti-Communist PARM (Authentic Party of the Mexican Revolution) to the Stalinist but opportunist PPS. It faced bitter opposition from the PRI because it competed directly for those groups and voters that have been the backbone of the PRI. It is also similar to the PRI in its rather undemocratic internal practices, and it suffers from continuous internal dissent and disagreement.

In March 1990 the renamed PRD (Partido Revolucionario Democrático [Democratic Revolutionary Party]) agreed to incorporate popular movements into the party, but the relationship between the party and the movements is by no means clear and is unlikely to parallel the close organic relationship between the social movements and the PT in Brazil. What is novel about the rise of *neocardenismo* for the Mexican Left is that it involves a repudiation of attempts to establish a clear separation between the socialist agenda and the ideology of the Mexican Revolution. The eternal dilemma for the Left in Mexico, and this applies to the PRD as well, is how to free the mass organizations such as the unions from control by the state, without looking as if they are just seeking to replace PRI control with their own.

Unlike the Brazilian PT, however, the Mexican PRD did badly in its second presidential campaign, coming a poor third in the contest. The history of the Left in Latin America is a constant story of advance and reversal, and in the case of Mexico reversals are usually greater than the advances. The PRD faced problems of lack of internal unity and, above all, lack of an alternative economic strategy.[16] Moreover, in an age when electioneering is increasingly dominated by television, the PRD's leader did not prove to be an effective media performer.

What explains the relative strength of the Left in the countries we have examined? In all cases, there was a tradition of leftist political activity on which to build. There was and is a trade union and popular movement influenced by socialism. In all these countries there is a competitive electoral system that does not discriminate blatantly against the Left (even in Mexico, the system did not disguise the support for Cárdenas in 1988, though it probably did diminish it). In all cases there is a relatively free and vigorous press that allows the Left to make its case. In all the countries (except Chile) there is opposition to the existing government for neglecting the suffering of the poor and for abuse of power. Popular feeling on these issues has translated into support for the Left. And, in the case of all the countries examined, the Left has shown, in central or local government, that it is capable of exercising power with restraint and efficiency. These conditions are not present in most of the other countries of Latin America.

### The Insurgent Left

Very different from any other country in Latin America is Peru, with its Maoist-inspired Sendero Luminoso guerrilla movement. Sendero professes admiration for the ideas of Mao at the height of the cultural revolution, when some of the Sendero leadership had been present in China. It also drew on the *indigenista* ideas of Mariátegui. Its largely mestizo leadership is hostile to any grass-roots organization other than the party. It recreated the authoritarian structures of Andean society, replacing the rule of the landlords with that of the party. It is organized in a highly secretive cell structure, which is difficult to penetrate. It is extremely ruthless and violent and uses terror to impose its rule.

Sendero made a substantial shift in strategy in 1988, declaring that the cities were "necessary" rather than "secondary." Sendero gained some support in the urban shantytowns of Lima and in some industrial unions. The capacity of Sendero to wreak havoc on the fragile political system in Peru was not in doubt; but what is in doubt is whether the movement could do more than that. The capture of its leader, Guzmán, in 1993 is undoubtedly a setback for the movement, but such a powerfully organized clandestine movement is hardly likely to disappear unless the conditions that gave rise to it are addressed.

The growth of Sendero created problems for the mosaic of other parties—orthodox communist, Trotskyist, pro-Chinese, Castroite—that make up the Left in Peru. The story of the Left in Peru is a never-ending process of temporary and fragile unification followed by division. The Left did well in the 1978 elections for the Constituent Assembly, with 29.4 percent of the vote. But the withdrawal of the Trotskyists weakened the coalition, and there were five separate leftist slates competing in the 1980 elections with a combined vote of only 14.4 percent. Most groups on the Left combined to form the Izquierda Unida (IU, United Left) in 1980, and the Left vote rose to 29 percent in the Council elections of 1983, with the leader of the IU, Alfonso Barrantes, taking control of Lima with 36.5 percent of the vote.

Yet the Left was far from united. As mayor of Lima, Barrantes faced a spate of land invasions organized by the far Left within his coalition. This lack of unity led to a fall in the leftist vote to 21 percent in 1985, though it was still the second electoral force. But the divisions intensified, reflecting on the part of important elements of the IU coalition an ambiguous attitude toward democracy (shared, it should be said, by some groups on the Right and even by the APRA government). The issue of political violence remained a dividing line between those who wished to collaborate in the democratic process, for all its faults, and those who wished to bring it down and replace it with a different order. Barrantes was criticized by those who argued that the major focus of activity should be the streets and factories and not the Congress. The first national congress of the IU in January 1989 led to a decisive split as Barrantes took with him moderate delegates to form a rival coalition, the Izquierda Socialista (Socialist Left). The leftist vote in the council elections in 1989 collapsed to 11.5 percent; and the two leftist candidates contesting the presidential election in 1990 gained only 11 percent of the vote between them.[17] In the 1995 elections the Left was virtually eclipsed, as indeed were all the traditional political parties.

Any explanation of the peculiarities of the Left in Peru has to be rooted in the sharp economic decline in that country, arguably the worst in all of Latin America. More than 50 percent of Peruvians in Lima live in poverty, 10 percent in extreme poverty. Conditions are even worse in the countryside. Added to that is ethnic antagonism, a series of governments that since 1968 have made extravagant promises of reform exceeded only by the extravagance of their failures, persistent inflation developing into hyperinflation, and a left subculture in which the dominant ideology became Maoism. This combination of features is peculiar to Peru and accounts for the failure of Sendero to set off would-be imitators in other Latin American countries.

The political fortunes of any party in Peru—whether of the Right, the Center, or the Left—look bleak at present. It is not so much that the democratic Left is rejected in Peru, but that all forces of democracy are weak while the initiative lies with an authoritarian president who rejects parties as such.

### The Left Lays Down Its Arms, Conditionally

The experience of the Left in the countries of Central America and Colombia has been rather different from that of the rest of Latin America. The Left in Central America really gained power only through force and still feels it needs arms to defend itself against possible future attacks from the Right. It is not entirely clear that it can evolve into some kind of social democracy. Its history has been marked by more prolonged and sustained repression than has occurred in other countries in Latin America.

The loss of the elections in 1990 faced the Sandinistas with the task of creating a political party in opposition. The Sandinistas were at core a vanguard party, and one that had held neither a congress nor conducted internal elections during its entire existence. While it had avoided many of the normal Leninist traits, it retained a strong *dirigiste* impetus, not least because its original guerrilla origins had been reinforced by the need to fight a war against the Contras. Defending a successful revolution against attack calls for characteristics very different from those of a party competing for power in competitive elections in a formally democratic system. As yet elements of both party and vanguard military force coexist uneasily in a political system that itself is far from seeing the end of violence used to advance political positions.

The same kinds of dilemmas face the insurgent movements in El Salvador. How do you move from guerrilla force to political party when you do not entirely trust the other forces to abandon the use of violence? How far will movements such as the FMLN (Farabundo Martí National Liberation Front) accept electoral results if they are unfavorable to them? How far will the ex-guerrilla movements resist the provocations of the Right? How far can movements like the FMLN, whose discipline has been enforced by military necessity, accept the kinds of internal disagreements that affect all political parties? The FMLN achieved a fairly remarkable set of agreements in the peace accords in

1992, demonstrating a high degree of political skill. But constructing a viable leftist party while simultaneously creating a viable democratic system and rebuilding a war-devastated economy are enormously formidable tasks.

There has been a notable change in the language of the leaders of the guerrillas. In the words of one of the leading Salvadoran guerrilla leaders, Joaquín Villalobos, "We Salvadorean revolutionaries at first were ideologically rigid, by necessity, in order to survive and develop. But later new conditions were created which offered the opportunity to develop our own thinking. The FMLN is proposing an open pluralist project, which will be pragmatically inserted in our domestic and geopolitical reality. What is fundamental is not its ideological definition but whether it resolves El Salvador's problems or not."[18] The question then remains, what if it does not solve El Salvador's problems? Although the FMLN did well in the 1994 elections, its candidate for the presidency, Rubén Zamora, gained only 24 percent of the vote in the first ballot and 32 percent in the second; and the FMLN has only twenty-one out of eighty-four congressional seats. It faces a formidable challenge not only to overcome the ascendancy of the Right, both politically and ideologically, but also to overcome its own internal divisions.

The Colombian Left has faced dilemmas similar to those of the Left in Central America. On what conditions do you lay down arms and at what cost? Like Peru, Colombia has its peculiarities that render comparisons difficult. Political violence has not been used only by the Left. On the contrary, the major parties, the Liberals and the Conservatives, have a much longer and more sustained tradition of political insurrection. The Left has, in a way, only conformed to one powerful tradition in a country where a weak state has been unable to control political insurgency.

The Colombian Communist party had a small guerrilla arm, the Fuerzas Armadas de la Revolución Colombiana (FARC, Armed Forces of the Colombian Revolution), though rather more as a result of conformity to political practice in the republic than an indication of a desire to seize state power. The FARC controlled some isolated rural municipalities, thus allowing the Communist party to claim that it was pursuing a revolutionary strategy while in practice finding that electoral politics was a more congenial occupation.[19] The participation of the FARC in the peace process in Colombia has been rather ambiguous because the dispersed organization of the group makes it difficult to impose any central direction. Guerrilla leaders may decide that the time has come to lay down arms, but they cannot guarantee that their commands will be followed locally.

The success of Castro set off many would-be imitators in Colombia. The Ejército Popular de Liberación Nacional (EPL, Popular Army of National Liberation) was a small Maoist group. The Ejército de Liberación Nacional (ELN, Army of National Liberation) was a Castroite group founded in Cuba in 1963–64 and advocated the *foco* approach of Che Guevara, but had more success and gained a considerable fortune by its attacks on internationally owned oil installations. If the motives for the violence of the traditional parties have been sometimes obscure, so it is for the guerrilla groups as well. In part, guerrilla violence has become a business in which the language may be that of a rather stale Marxism or Maoism, but the reality looks more like that of the Mafia.

The most important of the recent guerrilla groups to emerge in Colombia was the M-19, formed in 1970 in protest at alleged electoral fraud that prevented the former dictator, General Rojas Pinilla, from taking power. Such antecedents hardly qualify the M-19 to be counted as a leftist movement, and its program amounted to little more than a combination of vague nationalism and spectacular armed actions. The M-19 accepted participation in the peace process and gained considerable public support as a result, securing strong representation in the Constituent Assembly called to frame the Constitution of 1991. But as the M-19 showed itself to be little different in practice from the other parties, it lost its identity and suffered increasing electoral reversals. As Chernick and Jimenez write, the M-19's

> deep seated vanguardist and exclusionary sensibilities presented serious obstacles to the development of a strategy combining electoral coalitions with popular nonviolent mobilization in order to implement the historic leftist program of dismantling elite economic and political power. In the absence of a political party with an organizational base of support and participation, the ground swell of enthusiasm for the M-19 leading up to the constitutional assembly could thus prove as ephemeral as the vote for ANAPO [National Popular Alliance] in the presidential elections of April 19, 1970.[20]

Subsequent elections have borne out this prediction.

While a relatively weak Colombian state was unable to repress the guerrillas, they did not amount to a serious threat to the status quo—much less than the traditional parties did when they, too, entered the armed struggle to compete for power. The guerrillas undoubtedly gained some local support in certain areas, such as the banana zone of Uraba with its harsh labor regime, and Arauca where the newly found oil wealth brought few benefits to the poor. But support for the guerrillas remained local, their aims confused, their rivalry endemic, and their power infinitely inferior to the real threat to Colombian democracy that developed with the illegal drugs trade in the 1980s.

The conditions for the development of a successful social democratic Left in these countries looks more doubtful than for the countries examined in the first part of this section. The social base for the development of the Left is weaker in these societies that are more rural and less industrial. The Left has suffered almost continuous repression and has responded by developing insurgency as its main tactic. Even in Colombia with a much stronger electoral tradition, many of the leftist guerrillas who went into politics were assassinated by their former enemies, by the drug cartels, and by paramilitary groups. The Colombian FARC set up the Unión Patriótica (Patriotic Union) in 1985 to contest elections. In the next few years some fifteen hundred members of the party were assassinated. It is hardly surprising that the FARC mistrusts the democratic process. In such circumstances, to expect a Left to develop along the lines of the Chilean Left looks most unrealistic. The Left does not determine its own fate. In the case of Central America, if democracy really results from the present phase of pacification, then the Left may be transformed into a conventional party or parties—but that depends upon an equally massive transformation of the other political forces.[21]

### The Left in Retreat

It is less easy to group developments on the Left in other countries into neat categories. In a number of countries, parties that were once on the Left have virtually abandoned any resemblance to their former allegiances. Such would be the case, for example, of the Peronist movement in Argentina, the MIR (Revolutionary Movement of the Left) in Bolivia, or the formerly leftist parties in Ecuador. In these countries it can be argued that a series of factors has reduced the Left to a marginal role at best. Hyperinflationary experiences, combined with structural adjustment programs, erode the organizational basis of the Left, namely, the union movement, and popular preoccupation with solving the problem of inflation takes precedence over any concern with social justice. Indeed, in the case of Bolivia the ability to combine a successful anti-inflationary program with a relatively successful safety net program for the poor has strengthened the government and reduced the influence of the Left even further.[22]

It would be premature to assume that the Left has no future in countries such as Argentina or Bolivia. Indeed, one of the big surprises of the elections in Argentina for a constituent assembly in 1994 was the 12 percent of the national vote, and the 37 percent of the Buenos Aires vote, that went to a new leftist coalition, the Frente Grande (FG, Broad Front). This, however, was more of a protest vote against the Menem government by disaffected Radical party voters than the birth of a new Left in Argentina. Although the newly named leftist coalition, FREPASO (Frente Solidario País [National Solidarity Front]), gained almost 30 percent of the vote in May 1995, this once again represented the collapse of the Radicals. FREPASO is a very fragile alliance with no real coherent program or organization.

The Left in Argentina and Bolivia, among other countries, has suffered with the decline of the union movement. Successful control over hyperinflation has brought benefits to the government in power, not least from the poor who suffer most from the process. The Left in these countries looks like a remnant from the past, without ideas or policies to confront the future. Protest movements in these countries are equally likely to be apolitical, or rightist-linked, as they are to be an expression of support for the Left. The Left has been discredited by its past excesses, from Monontero violence in Argentina to militant syndicalist protest in Bolivia.

## Conclusion

What role can the Left play in the consolidation of democracy in Latin America? Does it, in fact, have a significant role to play? In some parts of the world, ethnic strife or religious fundamentalism have pushed the Left off the political stage. Some parties of the European Left have moved so far from their original positions that it strains credibility to call them parties of the Left any more: the Spanish PSOE (Partido Socialista Obrero de España [Socialist Workers' Party of Spain]) is a case in point.

This has not been the fate of the Left in Latin America. It is true that the Left in the 1990s has no distinctive policies to offer that are politically attractive and represent a true alternative to those of the neoliberal Right. The agenda for debate on the Left looks rather unoriginal (though this is far from saying that it is unimportant). Questions of inner party democracy go back to the very formation of mass political parties. Methods of strengthening popular participation through decentralizing government functions is hardly a novelty. Many of the issues on the Left in the developed world, especially concern for the environment and gender discrimination, hardly feature yet in any real sense on the Latin American Left.

But the strength of the Left in Latin America drew traditionally more upon the unacceptable nature of life for the majority of the people than upon the viability of policy options. The Left has drawn upon a powerful tradition of protest. The factors that brought the Left into being in the first place have hardly disappeared. The economic recession of the 1980s accentuated inequality and worsened poverty in Latin America. Political power is still disproportionately controlled by forces of the Right. The poor and dispossessed have little recourse to justice within existing legal and institutional systems. Corruption has eroded the legitimacy of government in Brazil and Venezuela.

In this sense the Left has a dual task: to seek a way of aggregating social demands into effective political ones, and to do so in a way that consolidates the fragile democratic systems on the continent. Indeed, it could be argued that unless the Left is able to channel potentially explosive demands into reasonable political options, then the democratic systems will be further undermined.[23] In other words, the evolution of the Left will inevitably affect the nature of the transition to democracy, especially in regard to two central challenges: consolidating democratic rule and complying with popular demands for socioeconomic development and distributive justice. The Left's response will influence not only the prospects for the survival of democracy, but also the type of democracy that emerges by shaping the character and content of socioeconomic and political structures. That response so far has been uneven, though in view of the international upheavals, and the national repression that have affected the Left in almost all countries, a limited response so far is hardly a cause for surprise. But there does seem to be a shift toward commitment to democracy as a value in itself, toward creating a stable and inclusive political order even in war-torn Central America, and toward establishing the Left's reputation as honest and efficient administrators.

The Left may be short of ideas at present, but that too may be inevitable as the Left struggles to adapt itself to a new political framework and a new institutional order. No doubt the temptation to revert to an authoritarian Leninist past will be too great to resist for some sectors, and there is the terrible example of Peru where the major force on the Left embodies all the worst features of dogmatic, violent revolution. No doubt in some countries the Left will continue to be politically irrelevant. In most countries, however, the Left is not now predominantly insurrectionary, nor irrelevant, but on the contrary attempting to contribute positively to building a new political and social order that, while not reverting to the central state model of the past, seeks to redress the social costs associated with the new model of economic development.

# 2

# Conservative Party Politics in Latin America: Patterns of Electoral Mobilization in the 1980s and 1990s

**Edward L. Gibson**

In the 1980s a new and unexpected phenomenon swept much of Latin America: conservative electoral activism. This was a development that few could have predicted from past historical experience, especially in countries that had recently emerged from authoritarian rule. The expectation of most observers had been conservative electoral estrangement rather than activism. The literature on democratization thus tended to address the likely political action of the Right as a potential problem of democratization, particularly where powerful socioeconomic and political actors, incapable of effectively organizing themselves for the electoral struggle, might exercise the many options for "exit" available to them in nondemocratic realms. As such, the Right was seen as a force to be "pacified" or "neutralized" while democratic agendas became consolidated. This view was nicely captured in a quote from one of the most influential scholarly texts on democratization in the early 1980s:

> Put in a nutshell, parties of the Right-Center and Right must be "helped" to do well, and parties of the Left-Center and Left should not win by an overwhelming majority. . . . The problem is especially acute for those partisan forces representing the interests of propertied classes, privileged professionals, and entrenched institutions. . . . Unless their party or parties can muster enough votes to stay in the game, they are likely to desert the electoral process in favor of antidemocratic conspiracy and destabilization.[1]

The worst fears of these political observers were not borne out by events. In fact, the view of conservatism as an estranged or at best passive player in electoral politics was contradicted by events. In the 1980s the Right did well in the electoral game without much "help." It won power outright through the electoral process in Brazil, Uruguay, Ecuador, and El Salvador. It also had a major impact on the political process, shaping the terms of the political debate as well as the policymaking process, in Peru, Mexico, Chile, and Argentina. Further-more, toward the end of the crisis-ridden 1980s, conservative leaders and their core constituencies emerged as major coalition partners of governments embarked upon free market reforms, even in countries where they had lost the elections to populist or nonconservative gov-ernments. Democracy in the 1980s, therefore, revealed surprising ca-pacities for conservative electoral mobilization. However, what is striking about this experience is that, just as this mobilization was ef-fective, it also appears to have been institutionally ephemeral in a number of important cases. New coalitions between the state, conser-vative political leaders, and business groups have now emerged on the scene. In the process, the conservative party institutions that gained visibility in the 1980s have receded from view in the seemingly more governable democratic politics of the 1990s.

The experience of the previous decade of democratic politics thus raises a number of key questions: what conditions facilitate the emer-gence of conservative parties in the region?[2] To what extent has the conservative electoral mobilization of the 1980s led to the institution-alization of participation by socioeconomic elites in democratic politics? What might all this indicate about the future relationship between the political action of social elites and democratic governance?

## Democracy and the Right: From "Lost Decade" Mobilizations to Governing Coalitions

In rough terms, the political evolution of the Latin American Right since the start of the democratization wave of the 1970s and 1980s can be divided into two phases. The first of these can be labeled the "lost decade" mobilizations, which saw the rise of new mass-based move-ments advocating free market economic reform.[3] This catapulted new parties onto the political stage and made the Right an important player in electoral politics. Party politics thus became a central arena for both advancing the agendas of conservative movements and expanding its leadership and constituent base. The second phase of the political evo-lution of Latin American conservatism might be labeled the "govern-ing coalition" phase. While still in its infancy, a number of trends seem already to have emerged from this phase. The first of these is the forg-ing of new governing coalitions between the state and socioeconomic elites that have provided vital social support for the market reform pro-cess and have stabilized the civilian governments carrying out these reforms. These reforms have been followed by new sociopolitical ar-rangements highly favorable to socioeconomic elites. If, as Ruth and David Collier suggest, state-labor relations served as a "coalitional fulcrum" during previous crucial phases of Latin American political de-velopment, then it can be argued that, in this period of regime restructuring, the coalitional fulcrum has shifted from state-labor relations to state-business relations.[4]

In terms of the political evolution of conservatism, the effect of this phase has been ironic. It has resulted in highly favorable political and economic conditions for the core socioeconomic constituencies of conservatism. It has also resulted in the withering or outright collapse of conservative party organizations that had played such a prominent role during the "lost decade" mobilization in the 1980s.

These developments also render the relationship between governability and conservative political action somewhat ambiguous. In the short to medium term, they have provided important political stability to governments embarked upon wrenching economic reforms. Today economic elites support democratic governments and are pivotal coalitional partners. Democracy is thus more stable because it counts on the vital support of the propertied and socially powerful. In the long run, however, the withering of conservative parties and electoral movements raises questions about the future institutional capacity of elites to influence politics through democratic channels. Much of this depends on whether these coalitions will result in longer-term electoral alliances, or whether they prove to be another instance of the ephemeral marriages of convenience between populists and plutocrats that have long marked the region's checkered political history.

## Democratic Stability and Conservative Parties in Latin America: The Historical Argument

Stable democracy in Latin America, as everywhere else, has historically been linked to the existence of strong national party systems. Strong national party systems have historically been linked to viable conservative parties. Logically, this should not be surprising. The importance of conservative parties to democratic stability lies in the pivotal social position of their constituencies and in the fact that they will be inevitable and important participants in the struggle for power. The organizational forms of their political participation will have major consequences for the relevance of different political institutions. If the organizational forms of upper-class power are weakly linked to political parties, regimes—or the major decision-making arenas of regimes—will be structured accordingly. Democracy in Latin America has endured where elites have possessed the institutional means to control it and where the challenges of mass politics could be regularly addressed through elite-controlled democratic institutions.

The argument here is not that conservative parties have made democracy "better" or more representative, only more stable. This proposition is supported by evidence from a growing number of comparative-historical studies of social conflict and political development in Latin Amer-

*Table 1* Conservative Parties and Democratic Rule in South and
Central America: From the Advent of Mass Politics to 1990

| | Competitive National Conservative Party(ies) Prior to Mass Politics? | Years of Democracy (restricted or full) | Years of Nondemocratic Rule | Ratio Years Democratic/ Years Nondemocratic |
|---|---|---|---|---|
| Chile | Yes | 45 | 24 | 1.9 |
| Colombia | Yes | 45 | 9 | 5.0 |
| Costa Rica | Yes | 48 | 2 | 24.0 |
| Uruguay | Yes | 67 | 20 | 3.4 |
| Average | | | | 8.6 |
| Argentina | No | 40 | 38 | 1.1 |
| Brazil | No | 24 | 36 | 0.7 |
| Ecuador | No | 25 | 40 | 0.6 |
| Peru | No | 30 | 30 | 1.0 |
| Venezuela[a] | No | 35 | 20 | 1.8 |
| Bolivia | No | 20 | 40 | 0.5 |
| Mexico | No | 8 | 62 | 0.1 |
| El Salvador | No | 6 | 53 | 0.1 |
| Honduras | No | 24 | 18 | 1.3 |
| Nicaragua | No | 0 | 54 | 0 |
| Guatemala | No | 14 | 45 | 0.3 |
| Panama | No | 15 | 35 | 0.4 |
| Average | | | | 0.7 |

*Source:* Edward Gibson, *Class and Conservative Parties: Argentina in Comparative Perspective* (Baltimore: Johns Hopkins University Press, 1996).

[a]The Christian Democratic Party (COPEI) plays a crucial role as the founding conservative party in interparty agreements for democratic regime inaugurated in 1958. Thereafter, upper-class representation is gained in the two major parties, Acción Democrática and COPEI.

ica.[5] It is also supported by the data presented in Table 1, which compares two groups of countries with different historical legacies of conservative party organization. The first group is characterized by strong historical legacies of conservative party organization. National oligarchic competitive party systems were established in the nineteenth century, when political competition was restricted to the socially privileged. As a result, conservative party structures were in place to deal with the challenge of mass politics when the expansion of popular participation took place. In the second group of countries such legacies of oligarchic competitive parties were largely absent, and national conservative party organization during the advent of mass politics tended to be weak or fragmented. Taking the initiation of mass politics as the historical point of departure, we can see that the durability of democratic regimes during the twentieth century was affected by this "genetic legacy" of conservative party organization. Those countries where national conservative parties were in place during the expansion of participation tended to experience significantly longer periods of democratic rule than those countries where conservative party organization was weak.

The data in Table 1 indicate the importance of historical legacies of conservative party organization to the continuity of democratic institutions. Countries that had viable, competitive national conservative parties in place at the start of democratic politics exhibited far greater democratic stability during the twentieth century than countries that did not. The average ratio of years under democratic rule to years under authoritarian rule for the four countries with strong legacies of conservative party organization was almost 9 to 1. For countries with weaker legacies of national conservative party organization at the start of mass democracy, the average ratio was 0.7 to 1.[6]

The point to be stressed here is that, regardless of the multiple arenas available for the organization of elite interests, one of the massive facts of democratic development in Latin America has been its positive association with stable upper-class participation in party politics. For countries with legacies of authoritarianism and weak conservative party organization, the development of new conservative parties is thus a central issue in the study of democratization.

## Latin American Conservatism and the Lost Decade Mobilizations

The question asked by much of the Latin American Left in the early 1980s as it faced transitions to democracy might well have been asked by Latin American conservatism: "why participate?"[7] In fact, democracy posed even thornier dilemmas for conservatives as they pondered their options during the return to democracy. In contrast to the Left, neither the leaders nor the core constituencies of conservatism had traditionally needed the protection of democratic institutions to prosper as political or economic actors. Their control over economic influence, and the privileged access they enjoyed to the institutions of state power, raised doubts about their need for democratic institutions as well as the advantages of devoting resources to the tasks of electoral mobilization.

Two factors played a role in changing the calculus of participation for conservative leaders. The first of these was the negative experience of authoritarian rule. The second was exclusion from state power during the early periods of democratic government.

The authoritarian experience that preceded the recent transitions to democracy in many countries raised doubts about the "certainty" of benefits from authoritarian rule for the leaders and constituencies of Latin American conservatism. One of the distinguishing features of this authoritarian period was that it produced important strains in the system of quid pro quos that governed conservative-authoritarian alliances in the past. Conservative political leaders had accepted control of the state by authoritarian powers in exchange for privileged access to its most important policymaking institutions, usually economic policymaking institutions. Similarly, business leaders abstained from autonomous political action in exchange for the benefits that discretionary state power under authoritarian rule could provide: the repression of competing claims from labor and a privileged position for business in channels of access to the state.

This is what snapped in the 1970s and 1980s. Conservative leaders and the upper classes learned a common lesson during this period: discretionary state power under authoritarian rule can be a double-edged sword. While an effective check against popular challenges, it had also proven to be a growing threat to the interests of political and economic elites. Argentina provides a telling case. The military had proved an uncontrollable partner, driven by its own agendas and internal conflicts. The effective implementation of policy under these conditions was problematic, to say the least. Business elites also often found channels to state policymakers closed. Ultimately, the military led the country to a reckless war against Argentina's historic trading partner and cultural referent. The subsequent collapse of the armed forces as a political actor also meant that it would not be available as a source of pressure against nonconservative governments.

Additional incentives for party building were provided by the fact that, during the government of the Radical president, Raúl Alfonsín, access to state power was completely closed off to conservative leaders. There would be no room in the top institutions of economic policymaking for the technocratic elite that had filled the leadership functions of the Argentine conservative movement. If influence was to be exercised over governmental decisions, it would have to be from without, through the mobilization of opinion and the construction of electoral coalitions.

This pattern of disenchantment with authoritarian rule and exclusion from state power also spurred conservative party building in other countries in the region. In Peru the leftist turn of the armed forces during the 1968–75 period of rule by General Velasco Alvarado introduced a major rupture in the conservative civil-military relationship. The country's first elected president after the transition, Fernando Belaúnde Terry, had himself been overthrown by the armed forces in 1968 and had based his comeback campaign in the founding elections of 1980 on a platform of opposition to the military regime.[8] The exclusion of conservatives from the 1985–90 APRA (American Popular Revolutionary Alliance) government of President Alan García, and the markedly populist cast of its economic policies, gave impetus to new strategies of conservative organization. During the late 1980s, party politics became a major arena for conservative political action in the country's chaotic democratic regime. This was bolstered by the mobilization of business behind party politics in the late 1980s, as business elites turned to the electoral arena in opposition to a government that exhibited growing hostility to business interests.

For Mexican conservatives, embracing the agenda of the Partido Acción Nacional (PAN, National Action Party) for political democratization was vital to challenging the ruling party's monopoly over political decision making. It also became important to business elites made wary by government-sponsored antibusiness campaigns and an increasingly systematic use of discretionary state power against business interests during the 1970s and early 1980s. Electoral politics thus became a vehicle for political leaders and business elites alike for challenging the actions of an increasingly antagonistic state.

In all these cases, therefore, the impetus for conservative party building lay in a break in state-elite relations. Support for democracy was spurred by the new uncertainties associated with authoritarian rule and the hopes for more favorable contexts for state-elite relations under democratic governments.[9] Exclusion from state power by democratic governments after the transition from authoritarianism made party politics a much-needed vehicle for reasserting influence over state decision making.

In many countries these developments sparked the rise of new leadership within conservative movements. They opened the way for the emergence of a more diverse conservative political class that saw in the manifold ideological and organizational tasks of party politics a route to influence and political advancement. In Argentina a new conservative party, the Unión del Centro Democrático (UCEDE, Union of the Democratic Center), was founded in 1982 by liberal ex-technocrats closely linked to previous authoritarian governments. Within a few years the internal pluralization of the party sparked challenges to established leaders and set internal struggles in motion that transformed the UCEDE's power structure and its appeals to the electorate. The new leaders that flocked to conservative party politics gave it a new ideological content. They introduced new agendas and discourses that permitted the party to appeal to a broader cross-section of supporters. Their interest in gaining access to tightly controlled leadership structures also made them advocates for internal democratization, and increased the importance of *political* liberalism as an ideological banner for rallying their followers. In addition, and most important for the electoral Right's growth, they sought to challenge established leaders by building new bases of support outside their parties' traditional electorate through strategies of electoral popularization.

The combination of ideas, organization, and political practice that came to be known as *la nueva derecha* was thus an outgrowth of internal struggle. The transformation of Latin American conservatism was not generally carried out by its established leaders. It was the synthesis of a clash between old and new, between traditional leaders and newly politicized activists contesting them for primacy.

In Mexico the PAN's protagonism in the democratization process attracted new activists and business elites into the party. Catholic *solidarista* currents that had dominated the PAN were displaced by *neo-panista* currents that gave the party's ideological orientation a far more liberal content.[10] They also expanded the party's prodemocracy platforms with new antistatist appeals and agendas of liberal economic reform.

The Peruvian electoral Right's transformation in the late 1980s was marked by struggle between the liberal activists and intellectuals that rallied behind Vargas Llosa's Movimiento Libertad and the veteran party leaders of the long-established Acción Popular and the Partido Popular Cristiano (PPC, Popular Christian Party). Libertad's activists were generally new to party politics. They brought new agendas of anti-statism and "popular liberalism" that clashed with the "social-Christian" doctrines of the PPC and with the paternalistic orientations of Belaúnde's Acción Popular. The new activists eventually came to shape Peruvian conservatism's appeals to the electorate in the late 1980s, but before reaching that stage they had to impose their agenda on a resistant conservative movement.

### Business and the Lost Decade Mobilizations

Throughout the early 1980s, as *la nueva derecha*'s appeals gained ground in the electorate, a major question loomed over their prospects for growth: would they succeed in mobilizing the support of business for their free market, antistate, coalitions? Historical evidence gave them few reasons for optimism: generally, stable business-party ties have been weak in the region. Latin American business has remained an aloof ally in the electoral struggles of conservative parties. At election time conservative parties may do well among the upper social strata; as individuals, business executives may vote for such parties and contribute financial support to their campaigns. But the organizational expressions of Latin American business, such as trade associations, large companies, or even prominent business elites, have rarely identified themselves with electoral politics. The political action of Latin American business has been focused directly on the state either through firm-state contacts or corporatist institutions.

The most important reason for this lies in the historical evolution of Latin American business, particularly the region's industrial sectors. Business development has taken place largely under the protection and tutelage of the state. State dependence has strongly conditioned business patterns of collective action and has made business elites wary of identification with partisan political action. In Argentina this wariness persisted throughout the 1980s, in spite of efforts by conservative parties to enlist business support. Despite the severity of the economic crisis, the Radical government of Raúl Alfonsín carefully maintained working relations with the business community. Continued business access to policymaking institutions hindered conservative efforts to mobilize active business support for its antistate agendas of economic reform.

In other countries, however, this pattern was broken. Three democratizing countries—Peru, Mexico, and El Salvador—experienced significant business electoral mobilization during the 1980s. In each of these cases the cause of that mobilization was a break in relations between business and the state. In addition, this mobilization helped to make conservative parties national electoral contenders. It catapulted Peru's new Frente Democrático (FREDEMO, Democratic Front) coalition and Mexico's PAN to the fore of national politics. It also led to the capture of national power by El Salvador's Alianza Republicana Nacionalista (ARENA, Nationalist Republican Alliance).

Long-standing ties between the state and the business community deteriorated progressively in each of these countries in the years preceding the late 1980s business mobilization. In Peru, relations between APRA president Alan García and the business community, initially cordial when García came to power in 1985, became marked by open hostility. The government intensified its populist policies, and business groups became increasingly reluctant participants in the government's plans for industrial development.[11]

In Mexico the business community had historically acted as a "stealth actor" in the nation's politics. It abstained from open political activity in exchange for informal but regular access to policymaking elites within the state, and to the rent-seeking opportunities that such access could provide. This arrangement came under strain during the 1970–76 administration of President Luis Echeverría, whose populist orientation and antibusiness rhetoric marked a change from the previously collaborative stance of earlier governments toward business. These business-state tensions continued into the 1976–82 government of President López Portillo. By the late 1970s and early 1980s, business took to increasingly open forms of political mobilization through interest associations and support for the growing party of opposition, the Partido Acción Nacional.[12]

In El Salvador, previously close ties between the state and business were broken by the reformist turn of the state after 1982 and the advent of the reformist Christian Democratic government of Napoleón Duarte in 1984. In an effort to consolidate popular support, and to counter the growing support of leftist opposition, the Christian Democratic government initiated socioeconomic reforms that, while imperfectly implemented, put business and agricultural elites on the defensive. Under siege by a powerful leftist movement demanding radical change, and excluded from a government committed to social reform, economic elites embarked upon major organizational and ideological mobilization. Business leaders also began to flow toward a party linked to agrarian elites and controlled by paramilitary groups, the Alianza Republicana Nacionalista.

The spark that crystallized the business-conservative party alliance in all these countries was the attempted nationalization of the banking system by the reformist governments, which took place in Mexico and El Salvador in the early 1980s and in Peru in 1987. Activated business elites found willing allies in the once-distant pro-free market politicians that were transforming the conservative party landscape. The party leadership's antistate agendas, once in tension with the business community, now became an effective ideological vehicle for challenging the dangers of discretionary state power. They also provided the ideological glue for linking business concerns to a more diverse set of democratization and economic growth issues capable of generating multiclass support.

The electoral mobilization of business galvanized conservative party politics. The open support of the Peruvian business community for the electoral challenge mounted by Mario Vargas Llosa's Movimiento Libertad endowed the movement with resources and credibility that allowed it to assert its hegemony over other parties in the conservative movement and emerge as a major contender in the 1989 presidential elections.[13] In Mexico, the defection to the PAN by important national business interests after the 1982 nationalizations solidified *neo-panista* control over the party and gave major credibility to the party's pro-democracy and pro-free market challenge against the governing party. During the 1980s the PAN became a serious electoral contender in a number of regional elections and, for the first time in its history, presented a credible national challenge to the governing PRI (Institutional Revolutionary Party) in the 1989 electoral campaign.[14] In El Salvador the mobilization of business behind ARENA produced an important leadership change in the party, as Alfredo Cristiani, a figure linked to agricultural and business interests, displaced the party's paramilitary leader, Roberto D'Abuisson. After a series of ARENA advances in congressional elections during the 1980s, the party captured the presidency in the elections of 1989.[15]

Just as business-state ties can break, however, they can also be mended. As Soledad Loaeza wrote regarding the later years of de la Madrid's presidency in Mexico, "all that the de la Madrid government [1983–89] needed to do was to restore harmony between the state and business for the latter to abandon its support for party opposition."[16] Under the presidency of Carlos Salinas de Gortari, the state overtures toward business intensified, resulting in an open alliance between the government and business groups behind the Salinas administration's program of economic reform. These developments produced a hemorrhage of business support from the PAN, particularly by the larger business and industrial interests that had mobilized behind it after the attempted bank nationalizations of 1982. Similarly, amid the general deflation of conservative party activity in Peru that followed the rise to power and the embrace of free market economic reform by Alberto Fujimori, there has been a renewal of state-business ties and a dissolution of the business party links that had characterized the post-1987 period. Only in El Salvador, where ARENA continues to control the national government, have the links forged between the conservative party and business during the 1980s endured.

A comparative look at the Latin American experience in the 1980s thus suggests that the potential for the electoral mobilization of business is negatively associated with the strength of the state-business relationship. Furthermore, where conservative parties are poorly institutionalized, the electoral fortunes of such parties are particularly sensitive to fluctuations in this relationship. Where significant ruptures in state-business ties take place, business can become a powerful force for the expansion of conservative party influence in electoral arenas. However, the withdrawal of business support can impose major constraints on the institutionalization of these parties and can prevent the maintenance of viable strategies of opposition. This vulnerability to the fickleness of business support constitutes one of the most important impediments to the development of conservative parties in the region.

## Governing Coalitions and the Deinstitutionalization of Conservative Party Politics

The new conservative parties that emerged from the lost decade mobilizations were essentially forgers of protest coalitions. Their coalition-building process reached a climax in the presidential elections that swept the region in the late 1980s. But now we must take a step further and ask, what has happened after those elections? To what extent have these coalitions, born out of protest, been forged into stable conservative electoral coalitions?

The institutionalization of these parties depends a great deal on what party leaders do *between* elections. This is especially important for those parties that failed to win presidential elections and cannot now benefit from the fruits of power. If these parties are to become consolidated, a considerable degree of leadership specialization and continuity will be required. Coalitions must be stabilized, organizations built, financial resources mobilized, and ideological appeals reforged. These are the tasks of political leaders. In Latin America, however, the incentives for sustained strategies of party opposition tend to be weak.

There are many reasons for this. The hyper-presidentialist nature of most Latin American regimes, and the often attendant marginalization of the legislative branch, remove an important potential arena that could provide incentives for sustained strategies of party building and political opposition between elections.

Since the last elections, however, another development has posed a threat to conservative party continuity: in countries where conservative parties lost, governments adopted their agendas of liberal reform and in many cases brought conservatives back into the state to help implement those programs. In Peru much of President Fujimori's economic team was taken from the conservative FREDEMO coalition he had just defeated. In Mexico the PAN "cogoverns" with the PRI by rubber-stamping its economic reform initiatives in the National Assembly and controlling regional power bases. It has, however, lost the national initiative it once possessed as the country's most important electoral advocate of free market reform and democratization.

One of the most dramatic instances of this was Argentina, where the Peronist government's economic policymaking institutions became a veritable revolving door of conservative party appointees. What impact did this development have on the UCEDE? The Peronist government's economic reform program, with which conservatives had cast their political fortunes, has been an important success.

Ironically, conservatives did not share in any resulting electoral benefits. In fact, the period of economic reform has been marked by a massive decline in the electoral fortunes of the country's most important conservative party, the UCEDE. Between 1989 and 1991, the UCEDE lost more than 60 percent of its electoral support. In the 1993 elections the UCEDE did not even register a chemical trace in the national elections, and in its home base of Buenos Aires only received 8.7 percent of the vote, the lowest percentage in its short history.

The reason for this is quite simple, beyond the identity crisis caused by the appropriation of a party's agenda by a government in power. As governments controlled by other parties open their doors to conservatives, this produces a drain of leaders from the activities of party organization, who join the government in technocratic roles. The parties become demobilized.

What the postreform period seems to indicate is that, in the tentative institutional context of democratizing regimes, just as leaders can choose to become involved in party politics as a means of gaining influence over the political process, so too can they choose to abstain from party politics once new opportunities to gain access to state decision making are opened to them.

The primary victim of this process is the institutionalization of conservative party politics. As long as conservative parties remain merely part of a varied arsenal for pressure against the state, rather than as institutions permanently organized for the capture of power through elections, it is difficult to foresee their consolidation as shapers of the political process in Latin American democratic politics.

## Conclusion: The Possible Futures of Conservative Political Organization

After almost two decades of democratization in Latin America, the institutional forms of upper-class representation are still very much in question. The early fears of upper-class subversion of democratic government have by and large receded, as new and more favorable arrangements in the economic and political realm have emerged from the turbulent experiences of the 1980s and early 1990s. The propertied and the socially powerful today support democratic governments. However, their connection to democratic institutions continues to be tenuous.

As a possible scenario for the future of conservative political organization, the consolidation of existing conservative parties as influential and regular players in democratic politics should by no means be ruled out. El Salvador's ARENA has shown signs of moving in this direction. Its hold on power since 1989, reaffirmed by its comfortable victory in the presidential and local elections of 1994, has given it the opportunity to evolve beyond its pre-electoral status as an elite-based opposition movement.[17] In Mexico the PAN has, after fits and starts, established itself as a major challenger to the PRI's hegemony in key regions of the country. If it is able to forge ties with national business, and build to a critical mass from incremental regional gains, it may challenge the PRI's hold on national power. However, in most of the countries discussed here, the possibilities for such an institutionalization scenario seem more remote. Thus three other scenarios might be advanced as plausible futures for conservative political organization.

The first scenario is merely a return to the time-tried pattern of state-centered pressure politics (relying on economic power, military power, or both). In this case, the current state-conservative coalitions will serve only as temporary marriages of convenience, leaving no lasting institutional legacies in the party realm, other than the erosion of the party institutions built in the 1980s.

However, things have changed in much of Latin America, and there are reasons to hope that the current disarticulation of conservative party politics does not merely represent a return to old historical patterns. The combined experiences of disastrous military rule and lost decade mobilizations have left their mark on the structure of politics and the incentives guiding conservative political action. Burned bridges with erstwhile military allies, as well as the surprising effectiveness of the electoral routes chosen in the 1980s, may have rendered old conservative ways unfeasible or unattractive to political leaders and much of the business community. Conservatives jumped into the arenas of electoral politics and mass persuasion in the 1980s, and there may be powerful factors preventing easy exit. Thus, while the deinstitutionalization of conservative parties seems to be a widespread phenomenon, it might well be part of a transition to "something else" in the electoral realm rather than a return to past patterns of electoral marginalization.

Thus a second and more hopeful scenario for the consolidation of Latin American democracies might be termed the "conservatization of populism." It would be a sequel of sorts to the ideological and programmatic "conservatization" of populist parties that shaped policymaking in the aftermath of the lost decade mobilizations. Where this leads to successful economic policies and favorable electoral dividends, it may help to bring about deeper changes at the institutional and coalitional levels. The "populist conservatization" scenario would involve (and in several cases has already involved) the absorption of conservatives into the leadership ranks of populist parties. More fundamentally, however, it would be driven by a shift in the social bases of these parties.

Changes in the region's political economy, particularly the lessening of business-state dependence as developmentalism yields to new economic models, would lead to new patterns of upper-class political representation. In this scenario, the formerly "populist" parties could become the electoral carriers of conservatism—the modern guarantors of market stability with a ready-made popular base. Historic state-business ties would yield to more stable party-business ties. The ideological and pragmatic convergences that have brought populist leaders together with business groups today would thus lead to longer-lasting institutional unions.

In this scenario, the social base of populist parties would become increasingly transformed by the addition of upper- and upper-middle-class voters. At the interest group level, the support of business groups for populist parties would become solidified and increasingly open, making business a pivotal base of financial and political support and displacing the parties' more traditional labor and middle sector constituencies. In effect, this development would constitute a core constituency shift for populist parties, rendering them effective advocates of upper-class political agendas while maintaining mass support for these agendas.

Trends in this direction are already visible in Argentina, where the Peronist party has succeeded in mobilizing important electoral support from upper-income voters and has deepened its ties with the large business community. This budding core constituency shift appears now to be prompting a leadership union, as important conservative party leaders have joined the Peronist party ranks. The PRI in Mexico has also shown signs of moving in this direction. In Chile the reformist Christian Democratic Party's promarket and probusiness stand in the last few years has eroded support in both the electorate and the business communities for the country's traditional conservative parties. The election to the presidency of Christian Democrat Eduardo Frei, an economic conservative with close ties to the business community, leaves open the possibility for such a shift in the social bases of support for the party. The ideological and coalitional shifts experienced by the Bolivian Movimiento Nacional Revolucionario (MNR, National Revolutionary Movement) in the last decade may provide another instance of populist conservatization.[18]

However, the realization of a populist conservatization scenario is fraught with obstacles. Any such transition would be marked by considerable conflict. Old guard elements on both the populist and the conservative side stand ready to undermine the union at every turn. Victory by radical populist leaders in internal elections could split the alliances apart. In addition, loyalties to old party labels and standards can prove surprisingly resilient. In these situations, economic success might not be a strong enough glue to keep the pragmatic alliance from unraveling before the power of entrenched ideological and institutional legacies.

A third scenario would thus fall between the two mentioned above: a new "rapid deployment" model of conservative party politics. The 1980s gave important lessons to conservatives. In a very short period of time they proved able to change the terms of the political debate and gain support for their agendas through the electoral process. They did so without the help of their erstwhile uniformed allies and, in many cases, without prior party structures. Given the structural power of their core constituencies, control of vital mass media outlets, contacts with influential intellectual circles, international ties, and the now tested financial power of a mobilized business community, conservatives have found themselves to be quite adept at mobilizing national electoral movements quickly and when crisis conditions warrant them.

That they have proven equally willing to abandon party building when possibilities for state-centered strategies emerge does not preclude a return to electoral mobilization if conditions change. In a future post-Fujimori crisis, a new conservative coalition might well emerge from the ashes of the short-lived FREDEMO and Movimiento Libertad, with familiar leaders wearing new and unfamiliar party labels. Rapid deployment for presidential elections might also be an effective strategy for conservatives that are institutionally weak nationally but have strong regional parties that safeguard their interests between presidential elections.[19] Knitting together the familiar constellation of regional conservative party networks and business interests behind new candidates and institutional facades, Brazil's regionally fragmented conservatives may, again and again, thwart the long and hard-fought bid of the Workers' Party for national power.

As a model of conservative political action, "rapid deployment" might blend the old and the new of conservative party politics in Latin America. It remains true to its historic institutional fluidity in much of the region, yet it also incorporates the significant changes in political practice that came with the lost decade mobilizations. Its impact on democratic development in the region, however, is hard to foretell. On the one hand, it would represent an advancement over previous military coup models of conservative political action. On the other, it is just as much a crisis-driven form of political action, one that does little to solidify the institutional bases of democratic politics.

It can be said that conservatives "discovered" party politics in many countries during the 1980s. It might be too much, however, to expect that the stable institutionalization models of party development imported from other regions or countries should result from this. Rather than the long-term development of conservative parties, we might see electoral mobilization emerge as a new and potent weapon in a varied arsenal of elite-based political resources, one whose relevance will rise and fall in response to changing opportunities that present themselves to conservative leaders and their core constituencies.

# 3

# Democracy and Inequality in Latin America: A Tension of the Times

Jorge G. Castañeda

Democratization in Latin America has been the object of a great deal of study, introspection, and doubt over the years. Every wave of democratic institution building has been accompanied by analysis and speculation about its origins, duration, and inevitability; every rush of dictatorships has generated endless reflection about its motivations, contingent nature, or fatal rooting in the political culture, history, or social configuration of the hemisphere. When, in the 1950s, it seemed that a recently created middle class had finally laid the ground for the emergence of democratic rule, great emphasis was placed on this social determinism as an explanatory factor. In the 1960s the Alliance for Progress and the Venezuelan and Colombian paradigms were rapidly explained by economic and social change, as well as by international considerations. Together with the ideological justification of two-party systems, they were quickly prescribed as the best antidote to the spread of the Cuban Revolution. More recently and with much more sophistication, the transitions from authoritarian rule that began in the early 1980s and came to fruition mostly in the course of that decade were analyzed and theorized with much detail and substance. Many authors attributed the new wave of democracy to the application this time around of the well-learned lessons of the past. The transitions would be successful and lasting on this occasion, it was hoped, because the factors that contributed to democracy's ephemeral nature in previous eras were neutralized by maturing leaders, a fortified civil society, and more responsible international partners.

Whatever the nuances—and they were not unimportant—one of the central points stressed by the transition theorists as well as by the politicians in charge of or involved in the transitions themselves was that the just-born democracies not be "overloaded" by political, but mainly economic and social, demands. The concern of nearly all observers and participants was that emerging, fragile, and "thin-skinned," so to speak, political systems not be suddenly and immediately submitted to overwhelming demands of an economic and social nature that would strain them to the breaking point. These demands, if presented and insisted upon, it was thought, would lead to a breakdown of the infant democracies and entail, however unwittingly, serious prejudice to the very sectors of society that would be most favored by the satisfaction of the demands that short-circuited the system. Whether this involved retribution for past human rights abuses, a rapid repayment of the social debt, or a more general redistributive economic policy, it was believed—not unreasonably—that by insisting upon these demands and not allowing the new regimes a breathing spell, something like a honeymoon, they simply would not last.

Largely because in nations like Chile, Argentina, Brazil, and to a lesser extent Uruguay many of these conditions for successful transitions were met, the new democracies did endure, or, more specifically, the transitions from authoritarian rule were consummated. And despite sporadic or localized setbacks—Peru after April 1992, Venezuela during that same year, perhaps Chile as long as Augusto Pinochet remained in place—Latin America was by and large considered, quite rightly, to have begun to consolidate its democratic regimes and credentials. One after another, elected presidents were succeeded by other elected administrations, human rights were to a large extent respected, a free press flourished, basic freedoms were safeguarded, and most of the trappings of representative democracy were preserved. But three preoccupations rapidly surfaced both in the literature and in real life, all pointing to the same dilemma.

## Problems with Democratic Consolidation

First, many naysayers and pessimists wondered whether the virtuous identity established between the consolidation of democratic regimes and the implementation of economic reforms along radical free market lines (that came to be known in Latin America as the neoliberal program) would not be sundered by a populist backlash. Would not demagogues or those nostalgic for bygone times take advantage of the short-term discontent provided by unpopular economic policies and of the democratic openings guaranteed by the liberalization dynamic to jeopardize the entire process by pressuring for redistributive policies or running on populist programs? What, they asked, could be done to retain the economic reforms on the one hand and democracy on the other, given that some were using the latter to fight the former? Many doubted that the current reforms and marvels of free market Latin America would last, given the region's penchant for doing the wrong things and its proverbial incapacity to stay the right course, tough as it may seem at first glance.

Second, others—more knowledgeable, sophisticated, and less enchanted by the market for the market's sake—expressed doubts about the depth of the democratization process in the light of what appeared to constitute the indispensable conditions of its success. It seemed that the only way for the nascent democratic regimes to last was if they guaranteed the permanence of the economic and social policies that had been carried out by the dictatorships that had preceded them. The example of Pinochet's Chile was often waved by these skeptics: the necessary (and indeed, sufficient) condition for a return to more or less democratic rule in Chile lay in the absolute maintenance of the free market, free trade policies pursued during more than fifteen years by the military regime. Democracy was fine, as long as it did not make too much of a difference insofar as economic and social matters were concerned. But how long could this sort of arrangement last, given the pent-up social demands accumulated during and the economic biases built up by the long period of authoritarian domination?

Third, and perhaps most crucially, many observers of the current democratic interlude in Latin America asked a harder question. Was the region's ancestral, abysmal inequality no longer the apparently insurmountable obstacle to democratic rule that it had been in the past? Inequality has been a permanent fixture of Latin American reality since independence. Alexander von Humboldt had made the point as early as 1802: "Mexico is the country of inequality. Perhaps nowhere in the world is there a more horrendous distribution of wealth, civilization, cultivation of land and population." The bishop of Michoacán, Fray Antonio de San Miguel, had written at the same time: "On the one hand, we see the effects of envy and discord, of skill, theft, and the penchant for hurting the rich in their interests; on the other, we see the arrogance, the hardness, and the wish always to abuse the weakness of the Indians. I do not doubt that these ills are born everywhere from great inequalities. But in America they are even more horrendous because there is no intermediate point; one is rich or miserable, noble or infamous in law and in deed."[1] Was this inequality not the cause of the absence of democratic rule, had the situation improved, or was the interminable inequality of Latin America no longer the obstacle to democracy it always had been?

After some soul-searching and much hand-wringing, a certain consensus began to emerge among students of the region's politics in relation to the type of question that needed to be asked, even if broad disagreements remained over the answer that the question called for. How compatible, it was asked, could democracy and widespread inequality and injustice be? Could representative democracy coexist with poverty of one sort or another affecting between half and two-thirds of the population? Could democratic rule survive in conditions of growing and acute inequality? And if not, wherein could the right answer to an ultimately perverse question be found?

This drawn-out preamble is justified by the need to emphasize that the current debate in Latin America about the nature of the region's new democracies and the possible tensions between the latter and the type of economic and social structures presently in place is not totally new. Nor is it limited to present-day discussions regarding the compatibility, or lack of it, between free market programs and democratization processes. Indeed, what is perhaps most interesting about the contemporary worries over the precarious nature of the region's institutions and advances is that they reproduce previous debates and doubts. And they reflect an underlying commonality: somewhere in the abstract thinking about and the everyday politics of Latin America there is a tension between the region's social configuration and its political aspirations. That tension is at the center of the discussion addressed here.

Before proceeding with that discussion, and having noted that it is not an entirely new one, it is nonetheless important to warn that a significant dose of today's tensions between these two trends is novel. The problem is no longer exactly what it was in the 1950s, when the identity of an emerging middle class and the possibility of two-party alternation was posited by numerous students of the region. The tension is greater than ever before because, on the one hand, the numbers are worse, yet on the other, the aspirations for and the roots of democracy are deeper.

There is a great deal of current debate in Latin America and in the multilateral agencies that deal with the region over exactly what occurred in the hemisphere during the 1980s in relation to inequality. There are undeniable problems of lack of reliable data, noncomparable series, baselines, and underreporting. In some countries the data is sufficient and illustrative, such as in Mexico and Brazil, and it is distressing. If in 1960 in Brazil the poorest 50 percent of the population received 17.7 percent of national income, in 1970 its share dropped to 15 percent, by 1980 to 14.2 percent, and in 1990 to 10.4 percent. In Mexico a similar process took place: in 1984 the poorest 50 percent of the population received 20.7 percent of national income; by 1989 the proportion had fallen to 18.7 percent, and by 1992 to 18.4 percent. Conversely, the richest 10 percent saw its share rise from 32.7 percent in 1984 to 37.9 percent in 1989 and 38.1 percent in 1992. According to the World Bank, of the twelve countries of Latin America for which comparative figures exist, in eight "the income distribution—measured by the Gini coefficient—deteriorated in the 1980s."[2] According to a review of other studies and sources of information regarding income distribution in Latin America before and after the "lost decade," "while most groups during the adjustment process saw their share in total income falling . . . the top ten percent—the richest to begin with—improved their relative position (with the exception of Colombia)."[3]

If data were available in relation to distribution of wealth and no longer simply of income, the early 1990s would almost surely show the same process of concentration as with income, or even worse. This is particularly true in countries with significant formerly state-owned sectors of the economy that were largely privatized in the first years of this decade. Regardless of the merits and motivations of these privatizations, given that they virtually all were carried out by sales to existing private sector conglomerates and without any of the share dispersion that at least nominally took place in Britain, for example, there is little doubt that they further concentrated assets in nations where small numbers already controlled huge chunks of the national patrimony. Suffice it to say that the thirteen Mexican billionaires on the *Forbes* list of the world's richest individuals own upwards of 10 percent of the nation's annual gross domestic product.

But there is not only more inequality; it is of a different nature. There is a new inequality, and a new poverty, in the hemisphere produced by the conjunction of the rush to the cities and the disappearance of economic growth at the rates most of Latin America became accustomed to between 1940 and 1980. The large majority of the poor and excluded are now in the cities, even if a greater proportion of the total number of each nation's rural inhabitants is poor. The new urban poor labor in the informal economy, on the streets and corners of the sprawling metropolises of a now overwhelmingly urban hemisphere. They live in the shantytowns overlooking the hills and in the increasingly segregated "poor" neighborhoods of cities removed from the ocean. They are, more recently, the laid-off or part-time employees of shut-down plants or streamlined bureaucracies that perhaps did not need them and that left them indigent in the streets.

But these urban poor are no longer the first generation to have left the countryside. In many cases, they are the sons and daughters of the originators of the rural exodus of previous decades; they have gone at least to grade school, they read and write and watch television, and are directly exposed to the trappings and opulence of middle-class and wealthy urban life. They do not live in another world; they live in the metaphorical cellars and tenements of the same high rise the penthouse occupants dwell in.

Yet, at the same time that the deterioration in income distribution was occurring, the democratization processes of Latin America were coming to fruition. Democracy did come to Brazil during this period, if by it we understand at least the prevalence of basic freedoms, alternation in power by different parties, competition for power exclusively through electoral means, the rule of law, and so on. It did not come to Mexico, although the demands for it were rapidly building. In both cases the pressure being built by the deterioration in the distribution of income, as good an indicator of inequality as any other, was rapidly growing. Thus while rights and choices were being granted to broader sectors of the population, the inequality that breeds growing demands and tensions was also increasing. Little wonder that the democratic transition was being resisted by Mexican officials, or that the fiscal crisis of the Brazilian federal government and of virtually every state government reached astronomical dimensions.

The fact that the democratic institutions of Latin America *are* more firmly rooted than in the past is another innovation. The national security dictatorships of the 1970s and early 1980s, the dirty wars and torture chambers, did leave a chilling lesson that was mostly well learned. It is better to build strong institutions that protect democracy than to do without them. Civil society is stronger, the middle class is larger, respect for human rights more widespread. Third, the international context is different. It is far from certain that the United States has, after the cold war, truly become a force for democracy in Latin America. But it has probably ceased to be a force against democracy, no longer combating it when it threatens its economic or, more important, geopolitical interests, as it did from the 1950s to the 1970s in much of the region. Finally, the ramshackle Latin American welfare states of the past are being dismantled today and are often being replaced by radical free market policies that, in addition to cutting inflation, tend to aggravate existing inequalities, at least in the short run. Thus the entire inequality/democracy debate, while not just born in Latin America, and though unquestionably part of the region's political and ideological tradition, is cast in a new light today.

Simply stated, the dilemma is that the kind of representative democracy that Latin America has sporadically enjoyed, and that it seems to be consolidating today, is not compatible with the region's social structures, and particularly with the enormous gaps between rich and poor, black, brown, and white, town and country, industrial powerhouses and rural backwaters. Whatever stance one may want to adopt regarding the causality and sequence between the emergence of some sort of broad middle class constituting a majority of the population and the viability of representative democracy, a certain simultaneity must prevail for the latter to endure. Because in Latin America today there is more inequality than before, and because Latin America was already more unequal than any other part of the world, the fragile democracy whose birth or resurrection it has witnessed in the past decade is likely to be short-lived.

Before proceeding any further, it is crucial to distinguish between the analytical statement that in principle and in the region today there is a tension between poverty and/or inequality on the one hand and democracy on the other, and the political call for the postponement of democracy until the continent's economic and social lags are surmounted. One statement is strictly analytical in nature and has no prescriptive value in itself other than to imply, as we shall see, that without progress in the attempt to reduce inequalities, there is a risk for democratic rule. The other statement—that democracy should wait until poverty is eradicated, as has been so often argued, tacitly or explicitly, by authoritarian regimes in Latin America of all ideological inclinations, but mainly by those on the Right—is politically motivated. It can mean that democracy should be suspended until inequality is reduced, or it can imply that given inequality and poverty, certain shortcomings in the organization and functioning of democratic rule in Latin America are more or less inevitable. But there is no causal or substantive link between the two types of statements. One can both detect the tension between inequality and democracy *and* be a firm supporter of democracy; or one can be a committed opponent of democratic rule in Latin America, for whatever reasons, and at the same time not believe there is any incompatibility between inequality and democracy. In fact, the political statement subsumes and implies the analytical judgment, but not the other way around.

The reasons for the presumed incompatibility mentioned above are clear. Democracy means giving free rein to the expression of pent-up demands of downtrodden or even marginalized sectors of society, and then finding and implementing solutions or giving satisfaction to at least part of those demands soon, if not immediately. The demands cannot be forestalled: they are too pressing. And satisfaction cannot be indefinitely postponed because those who do so proceed at their own peril given that they can be removed from office just by losing the next election. The gradualism and various virtuous cycles that made democracy and capitalism compatible in Europe and North America since late last century do not operate in Latin America today, at least from this perspective.

There is every reason to believe that the problem thus stated does exist, and in order for democracy and existing inequalities to cohabit in Latin America, it is the second term that must be addressed in order for the first one to survive. "Something special," that is, changes beyond what inertia and "natural" mechanisms will provide, must take place in order for the tension between both terms not to become unmanageable. But it is worth stressing that this incompatibility is not impervious to time and circumstance; it is so abstract a statement that its verification in practice can be a drawn-out matter. The dilemma must be formulated as a general principle or premise that will materialize only if a certain number of circumstances coincide. Conversely, if certain conditions of a different nature are all present, the consequences of the incompatibility can be avoided, though generally only for a set period of time.

Recent empirical work carried out by economists—and even by the World Bank—shows that there is a clear link between democracy, inequality, and economic growth. The traditional Kaldorian or Kuznetsian approach, whereby it was believed that inequality fostered growth because the rich saved more than the poor, and consequently high rates of investment demanded a greater concentration of wealth and income among the rich, has fallen into disfavor. A different and contrary correlation is currently posited, and some empirical evidence seems to indicate that it is more accurate. According to this view, most recently researched, among others, by Alberto Alesina and Roberto Perotti for the National Bureau of Economic Research, high inequality correlates with political instability, which then generates low investment rates. Working with data from seventy countries for the period between 1960 and 1985, these authors have found that "income inequality increases socio-political instability which in turn decreases investment," which obviously leads to lower growth.[4] They add that more acute inequalities also make for stronger pressures in favor of fiscal redistribution, which can act as a deterrent to investment.

## Prospects for the Construction of Democracy

In Latin America the recurrent cycle of democracy, overwhelming social and economic demands, public spending, inflation, devaluation, and middle-class and power elite disenchantment followed by a tragic outcome is well known. The reasons for this cycle, regardless of whether on occasion they are identified with a simplistic assessment of mere economic policy mistakes, are quite evident. The inequities in Latin American society, the information available to broad sectors of the population about how matters could be different, and the obvious injustice prevailing throughout the region are all such that most lasting democratic experiences give way to elections that bring to office governments or leaders that try to satisfy these aspirations. But given the scarcity of resources and the overall economic obstacles existing throughout the region, it is impossible to satisfy virtually any demand in a significant manner without engaging in some sort of redistributive exercise. This implies alienating or ostracizing the powerful sectors of society from which the resources to be redistributed must be obtained.

In most Latin American nations this signifies turning these sectors against the democratic process that brought up the redistributive issue in the first place. Given this dynamic, which has actually appeared in Latin America on multiple occasions, some have reached the conclusion—self-serving or sincere—that until the gaps between rich and poor are reduced, and thus the intensity of the poor's demands is defused, democracy will simply not work. It is not so much a question of the *desirability* of having inequalities and democracy coexist, but of the *impossibility* of that coexistence. Thus the political statement previously made explicit encloses the substantive premise: the reason democracy should be suspended until inequality is reduced is that otherwise it simply will not work.

This dilemma is specific to the region and to the contemporary era. It is, in a sense, a strictly historical problem and largely located in Latin America, the "middle class" of world societies as Alain Touraine has often said. It is a historical problem because of the compressed nature of modern evolution in Latin America, and it is a localized problem because of the specific traits of Latin America.

First, it is a localized problem. In the world's industrialized nations, although inequalities do subsist and are probably widening, they are sufficiently narrow to be manageable. A large enough majority of the population is equal unto itself, and democratic institutions are sufficiently old and well rooted that the undeniable contradiction that does persist between the basic premise of equality in principle before the law and the market, and the inequality that in fact prevails in much of modern society (between poor and rich, black and white, foreign and national, men and women, adults and children, and so on) remains within the bounds of what democracy will countenance. In the wealthy nations, the tension between democracy and inequality is just that: a tension that can be adequately managed or has been from the end of the last century until now.

Latin America has always been the most unequal of the world's poorer regions. Even in 1978, for example, just as the period of the continent's sustained economic expansion came to a close, the share of total income received by the poorest fifth of the population was lower than for any other area: 2.9 percent compared to 5 percent for southern Europe, 6.2 percent for East Asia, 5.3 percent for the Middle East and North Africa, and 6.2 percent for sub-Saharan Africa.[5] If, in many Latin American countries, the richest 10 percent of the population obtains today between 40 and 50 percent of national income, in East Asia the average is in the mid-30 percent range.

In the utterly destitute nations of the world—Africa and most of Asia—either inequality is far less dramatic than in Latin America, though poverty may be much more acute, or, more commonly, democratic governance is a relatively new phenomenon whose vicissitudes are understandable, given youth and the awesome challenges of economic development. Most of the nations of Asia and Africa did not exist as independent entities as recently as forty years ago. The others either have democratic governance and a high standard of living—Japan, for example—or low levels of inequality, even though they have not enjoyed democratic rule—China, Korea—or have levels of inequality below those of Latin America and something like electoral democracy at work—India, of course. It is useful to recall that India, despite its abject poverty, has a ratio of income shares of the richest 20 percent of the population and poorest 20 percent far lower (better), at around 10 percent, than countries such as Mexico (15–17%), Colombia and Venezuela (20%), or Brazil and Ecuador (25% and 45% respectively).[6] One reason for this difference might be the Indian political system and the redistribution that the lasting existence of even as skewed a system of representative democracy as India's entails.

Only in Latin America are the degree of inequality, the size and existence of a middle class, the level of economic development, and the sufficiently consummated process of nation building all far enough along to explain the number of attempts to establish democratic rule over the past century and a half. And only in Latin America have those attempts proved so frequently unfruitful that the issue is truly a burning one. In a nutshell, only in Latin America is there both enough democracy for it to be at risk and so much inequality for it to be a problem.

But the tension we are dealing with is also a historical phenomenon. It did not occur elsewhere in other times, although conceivably it could have. In principle, the immensely poor and unjust societies of nineteenth-century Western Europe or the United States could have been forced simultaneously to live with emerging democratic rule and social forms of organization and economic development that excluded vast sectors of the population from the benefits of the market, employment, mass consumption, and so forth. What difference is there truly between Dickens' England and the suburbs of São Paulo?

The answer lies in the different historical rhythms involved. Democratic rule expanded only at a slow pace, and sector by sector of the population, in most of Western Europe until after World War I. The franchise itself was extended by segments of society; in England it was only granted to all males late in the century. For practical purposes, democracy and incorporation into the modern market economy went hand in hand, and while early attempts did emerge to push democratic rule further ahead than the economic and social situation of the "dangerous masses" warranted (the Chartist movement, the revolutions of 1848 on the continent, even the Paris Commune of 1871), the little they temporarily achieved was swiftly rolled back. A certain contemporaneity prevailed: no idea or reform was truly "ahead of its time."

But in Latin America, of course, matters were quite different from the very caricatured outset. Just after independence, nations that virtually did not exist adopted sophisticated, enlightened liberal constitutions inspired by French philosophers and American founding fathers. And this diachronic feature continued through the first hundred, then hundred and fifty years of independence, although often certain formulas were employed to alleviate the pressures it generated. Thus elections were scheduled now and then, and, in some countries at some moments in time, power was actually contended for at the ballot box; in fact, extraordinarily few people voted.

As late as 1960 in Brazil, for example, there were only 16 million registered voters, of which barely 11.7 million actually voted in federal elections.[7] This was in a country of 80 million inhabitants at the time. In the 1940s the situation was of course much worse, not only in Brazil but throughout Latin America: where elections were held, only few voted. Still, the franchise was extended to everyone, and as democratic regimes consolidated in the early 1980s they awoke to a paradox illustrated, again, by the Brazilian example. In the 1989 presidential elections in that country, there were 75 million registered voters, a large majority of which went to the polls. But only 7.5 million Brazilians paid taxes; that is, schematically, only a tenth of the electorate was actually incorporated into one of the basic aspects of citizenship and modernity. Throughout Latin America the same paradox surfaced: on the one hand, the hemisphere had adopted, nearly across the board and from a historical perspective virtually overnight, the political structures for governance and transferring power of the industrial democracies, but the social structure of those nations was anything but present in Latin America.

The gradual extension of involvement in the market economy, the construction of a social safety net, and the granting of the franchise could not all occur in Latin America little by little or more or less simultaneously. No one can be easily denied the right to vote in the late twentieth century either because they cannot read or write, or because they do not own property, or because they are black, or because they are women. In a sense, the right to vote is either denied to everybody by authoritarian rule or afforded to everyone thanks to the ongoing democratic transitions. But nothing could be done as rapidly on the social front: the 60–70 percent of the population in nearly every Latin American country that is poor, devoid of formal employment, decent education, health, and housing, that does not pay taxes, and whose level of consumption is just above the minimum possible cannot be transformed overnight into a European or Canadian middle class.

Hence the *historical* nature of the problem. The gradualism of the nineteenth century and parts of this one is not applicable in Latin America. Indeed, the immediacy of the situation is even worse than just described, if one factors in another contemporary ingredient absent in previous eras. The impoverished masses who can now vote, organize, demonstrate, and demand in Latin America are part of a more informed world than the one their nineteenth-century predecessors lived in. Television, urbanization, literacy, the global flow of information, all enhance the tension between democracy and inequality today as compared to before. The demands generated by the perception of widening social gaps are greater and more intensely felt because there is far more information available today to the destitute and excluded about how desperate their fate actually is.

The "overload syndrome" that characterizes Latin American economic, social, and political life today is thus specific and historical. This also means that the solution to the problem, once accurately described, must also be solidly anchored in the region's traits. An additional effort to circumscribe the issue with greater precision is consequently in order. It implies addressing the exceptions, lags, and alternatives (at least theoretical in nature) that the problem involves.

One apparent exception to the hypothesis whereby Latin American democracy only barely survives under conditions of severe and worsening, or in any case not improving, inequality lies in the more or less prolonged periods following either hyperinflation or authoritarian rule. In both cases, it would seem that, despite growing inequality, poverty, and injustice and the implementation of economic policies that severely concentrate wealth and income, democratic institutions and regimes tend to thrive, enjoy broad popular support, and acquire an enhanced capacity to pursue their agendas. The more well known examples of this are Argentina under Carlos Menem in relation to hyperinflation, Chile under Patricio Aylwin with regard to a return to democracy, as well as Bolivia since Víctor Paz Estenssoro's stabilization experiment began in the early 1980s. Some might conclude, in the light of these examples, that by resorting to the market and establishing democratic rule, a virtuous cycle was set in motion in these countries whereby the two pillars of enlightened societies—democracy and the market—reinforce each other and render matters such as the inequality of outcomes irrelevant because equal opportunity is extended to all.

Actually it can be argued that, in the case of a victory over hyperinflation, the honeymoon that some democratic regimes enjoy despite widespread, standing injustice can be explained by the fact that runaway inflation is precisely inequality-generating par excellence, and thus its elimination provides a respite from, and in some cases an improvement in, overall inequality. The poor and the harassed middle class can come to perceive an easing of inflation as not only improving their lot in absolute terms but even in relation to other sectors of society.

This is particularly true when price stabilization is linked with trade liberalization and local currency appreciation, as was the case in Mexico between 1989 and 1992, in Chile from 1977 through 1981, and in Argentina from 1990 onward. Access to imported goods generally identified with upscale consumption, the possibility of traveling abroad and saving in dollars, all are contributing factors to this sentiment. The popularity of regimes that implement draconian adjustment programs right after serious bouts with hyperinflation does not negate the tension between inequality and democracy. If anything, it reaffirms this tension by showing how a perceived, if only temporary, bettering of the affliction of inequality reinforces democracy. It also does not demonstrate that the success in fighting inflation will forever discourage the tensions discussed here. It is reasonable to expect that, after a certain period of time after which memories of high inflation fade, reality weighs in, and that when unsatisfied demands for other forms of reducing inequality—higher salaries, social spending, jobs—kick in, the enthusiasm for democratic institutions and their elected regimes will begin to wane.

A return to democratic rule is also a motivation for a honeymoon. Often, after lengthy periods of dictatorship and repression, electorates and various social movements are willing to grant newly installed democratic governments a breathing spell. They do not press all their pent-up demands immediately; they do not "overload" the system overnight, particularly if there is a widespread belief that such overloads led to authoritarian rule in the first place. This is clearly relevant to the Chilean case today, where after sixteen years of military dictatorship and sweeping inequalities, the people of Chile did not insist on the prompt satisfaction of their aspirations for justice, higher salaries, and more social spending. The return of democratic rule in Uruguay in 1983 under Julio María Sanguinetti can also be interpreted in this fashion.

But again, appearances can be somewhat deceiving. In fact, the government of Patricio Aylwin in Chile did raise social spending and increased taxes to finance it, and did reduce part of the poverty generated in Chilean society by a decade and a half of radical free market policies. And as time went by, the honeymoon wore off, with the traditional militancy of the Chilean labor and popular movements resurfacing, albeit under new, different forms. This led to a greater emphasis on social spending with the inauguration of the new administration headed by Eduardo Frei. If anything, the social honeymoon in Chile and the relatively rapid, though still incomplete, restoration of Chilean democracy owe part of their existence to the modest but undeniable redistributive policies of the Aylwin-led Center-Left coalition.

A third explanation for certain apparent exceptions regarding the democracy-inequality tension involves the type of countries just referred to. It can be surmised that there is a certain threshold of inequality: below it, tensions are almost always present; above it, they can be avoided or postponed. It may be no coincidence that three of the countries mentioned as exceptions—Argentina, Uruguay, and Chile—are, together with Costa Rica, the least unequal nations of Latin America (despite degrees of injustice that are far greater than those of the industrialized world) and those that suffer from the smallest volume of ethnic, regional, racial, and social disparities. It is true that, in relative terms, the deterioration in at least two of these nations—Chile and Argentina—has been as marked as elsewhere, if not more, and that it is small consolation to the poor of greater Buenos Aires or Santiago that they are "less unequal" than their counterparts in Recife or Mexico City. But there may well be a question of an absolute level here: the starting point for the decline in these nations is clearly higher than in the rest of Latin America, and thus the capacity to absorb broader inequality without "overloading" a newly reestablished democratic system is also greater.

Finally, there is the question of time. On many occasions in Latin America, particularly in the nations with a strong pre-Columbian heritage, time moves differently—some would say more slowly—than in other regions and countries. Immediate reactions, quick responses, rapid cause-and-effect relationships are rarely the case. Time lags, delayed reactions, and an often incomprehensible patience tend to be much more common. The famous Mexican saying "In Mexico nothing ever happens until it happens" is a symptom of this: the quick pace of causes is not always matched by an equally fast rhythm of effects. Where it may seem that a given cause—say, growing inequality—should produce a determined effect rather quickly, the absence of which suggests that there may not be much of a cause in the first place, in fact the explanation for the apparent mismatch is time, not the lack of causality. On many occasions the effect is simply slow in coming: it will happen, in time.

The exceptions, then, are explainable. Nothing in these examples lessens the substantive contradiction between democracy and a given threshold of inequality, and a given evolution of it. This last point is essential: if Albert O. Hirschman is right in positing a "tunnel effect" whereby it is more important for matters to be moving in the optimal direction, and that there be a perception among those affected that things are improving, then the opposite is also true. If there is a reverse "tunnel effect" and people sense that their lot is deteriorating and in reality it probably is, the "overload syndrome" will almost certainly come into play at some stage. The main thrust of this line of reasoning is that, other than under exceptional circumstances such as those outlined above, and in the absence of a "tunnel effect," democracy and the levels of inequality prevalent in Latin America are not compatible, and the tension between the two will become exacerbated. At some point the elastic band will be stretched too far.

The fundamental difficulty in untying this knot lies in another Latin American dilemma, which touches on the heart of the matter, the redistributive question. There are two indisputable premises for reducing inequality in Latin America: producing new wealth and distributing it differently than existing wealth. Without growth, no redistribution is possible. But distributing new growth the same way as before will only ensure that existing disparities are maintained: there is no automatic way of reducing inequality just by generating new wealth. To reduce injustice in Latin America, given growth, implies a redistributive imperative.

There is a growing body of literature suggesting that there are sound economic and political reasons for redistribution in highly unequal societies, in addition to the obvious ethical justifications. The first, mentioned in the previously quoted work by Alesina and Perotti,[8] stresses the countervailing pressures exerted by redistribution. The old approach emphasizes the discouraging effects on investment generated by high taxation, which is still the most efficient instrument of redistribution. But these authors note that redistribution through taxation, if effective, makes for less unequal societies, which in turn makes for more stable political systems that generate certainty, guarantee property rights, and so forth, which finally implies higher levels of investment and thus of growth. Another twist to this same argument is that more just societies permit sounder and more accountable governance because it is more democratic. Any comparison or counterfactual exercise involving higher or lower levels of taxation and redistribution has to take into account the deterrent effect on savings, investment, and growth generated by high degrees of social inequality and the political instability that generally accompanies it. The fundamental question is how to set in motion the trends toward redistribution and lesser inequality in a context where these two trends have been mostly absent.

Here is where the issue of democracy comes into play. In principle, there are several ways of redistributing wealth, income, opportunity, achievement, and ultimately capability, to use Amartya Sen's enumeration. Universal suffrage is not the only one: revolution, command capitalism along Korean lines, or outside intervention—the American factor in Japan, Taiwan, and also Korea in the late 1940s and 1950s—are among them. Unfortunately none of these other ways is quite suitable or viable for Latin America. Revolution has certainly worked from a redistributive perspective: Cuba is the least unequal country in Latin America by any definition, and, until a few years ago, this was not simply equality of the destitute. But that road does not seem to remain open in the post–cold war world, and few in the region today would find it attractive.

Command capitalism, with a strong authoritarian state, an honest civil service, and an agreeable private sector, has been tried too, also with some success as far as growth and reducing poverty are concerned, but with much less to show for itself as far as reducing inequality. The Brazilian model from 1964 onward, and even the case of Mexico, are good examples, up to a point. But here again, given current aspirations for democracy, and the bittersweet taste left by those experiences, it seems unlikely that redistribution from above can truly function in Latin America today. Nor does redistribution from abroad appear to be functional: it has never worked too well in the past—the Alliance for Progress precedent is ambiguous at best—and it is difficult to conceive of conditions under which the United States could actually take charge of land reform or other distributive mechanisms in Latin America, as it did in Japan under the occupation after World War II.

Indeed, there is every reason to believe not just that the only path conducive to some sort of redistribution today—democratic governance—is also the one whose absence explains a fair share of the inequality prevailing in the region today, or even a decade ago, after what Hirschman has called *les trente glorieuses*. We now know that even high levels of economic expansion, such as those Mexico and Brazil enjoyed from the 1940s through the early 1980s, in the context of undemocratic governance does not substantially improve distribution and may have worsened it. Conservative economists or commentators have argued that the explanation for the paradox of high growth and poor distribution lies in the *type* of economic growth that countries like Mexico and Brazil experienced: protected, subsidized, with an overpowerful state-owned sector of the economy that encouraged rent-seeking and concentration of assets and income. While there is no doubt that the type of growth in question was clearly of that nature, it is less evident that therein lies the cause of the inequality. The best counterexample is Chile from the mid-1970s through the late 1980s, a sufficiently extended period to warrant comparisons with other cases. Chile did achieve high growth during this period, particularly after 1984 and before 1981; and the type of growth it enjoyed was precisely the kind that radical free market advocates prescribe: nonsubsidized, unprotected, private sector-driven. Yet by every indication and source, Chile was a far more unequal nation and society in 1990 than in 1970, or in 1975 when the Pinochet experiment truly got under way.

Unfortunately for the perspective suggested here, Chile is not a much more egalitarian society today, after five years of democratic rule, than it was before. Without democracy in Latin America today, it seems nearly impossible to achieve the aim of alleviating gaping disparities. But one should not exaggerate the extent to which democracy alone can accomplish this task; this thesis should be posited only with caution and wide-open eyes.

Since 1988 Chile has negotiated a difficult transition to democratic rule. It has done so successfully, although serious handicaps and restrictions endure. Not only are the former military rulers still in command of the armed forces; not only are several institutions still not subject to any type of democratic accountability; in fact, a not insignificant share of the national budget remains automatically and unmovably allocated to the military. Nonetheless, just about by any standard that is relevant to Latin America, Chile no longer suffers from one of the most atrocious episodes of authoritarian rule the region has ever known. Largely as a consequence of this transformation, the social policies of the dictatorship have been overhauled. Spending on education, health, housing, and the poor has increased. In order to finance this "repayment of the social debt," as it is known in Chile, taxes have been raised, not as much as they should be, but Alejandro Foxley, Aylwin's finance minister, was the only Latin American technocrat in favor of higher taxes, not lower. Chile is, for practical purposes, the only country in the hemisphere pursuing some sort of redistributive effort, chiefly as a result of the drastic shift from authoritarian rule to representative democracy.

The emphasis on social spending has partly paid off. The number of officially poor Chileans dropped between 1990 and 1993 from 5 million to 3 million. But income distribution has barely budged: it remains stuck at roughly the same levels as in 1988, in turn far worse than in the early 1970s. In other words, a significant effort, in a country enjoying high rates of economic growth and an undeniable democratization process, has left in four years a scant trace in terms of redistributing income and thus in reducing inequality. There are, of course, plausible explanations. One is time: four years is simply not enough, perhaps. Another is the locked-in nature of the economic policies of the dictatorship. Despite the social effort, wages remain low and must continue to be in order to attract investment; trade liberalization and the absence of subsidies make it difficult to transfer resources from the rich to the poor. Furthermore, so much ground was lost in this area during the previous fifteen years that simply arresting the decline is an accomplishment; reversing trends is a much more difficult task. Finally, the tax system, given trade policies, capital mobility, and political restraints, has not been stretched very far. The increase in revenues remains low. Yet the Chilean case cannot but make one wonder: is any sort of redistribution possible, even under favorable political conditions?

The Chilean case also opens another line of discussion. Is the main impediment to democratic rule inequality or poverty? Or, conversely, may it be possible to consolidate democracy if extreme poverty is significantly alleviated, even if inequality stays the same (i.e., if the bottom ranks of the income scale improve their lot in absolute terms, even if in relative terms they do not)? This is a central question in Latin America today, precisely because it does seem possible to reduce absolute levels of poverty, at least among the most destitute sectors of society, but it is much more difficult to redistribute wealth and income.

Indeed, many students of the region are suggesting that the new forms of combating poverty—highly targeted programs, the efforts of nongovernmental organizations, philanthropic work, and so on—are the modern equivalent of previous, now obsolete efforts at Keynesian redistribution. It is important to distinguish two issues here. One is that combating extreme poverty does not necessarily alter the income distribution structure of a nation, or, in any case, it mostly affects the bottom rank in the scale by subtracting from the share of the lower middle-class ranks. This is basically what occurred in Chile from the late 1970s through the late 1980s. Poverty and inequality are not the same. As we already saw, India may be poorer than any country in Latin America, but it is less unequal.

A different issue is whether combating poverty can be an adequate and effective substitute for reducing inequality as far as its effects on democracy are concerned. If the key issue is poverty, and not inequality, then the current democratization boom in Latin America might be consolidated simply by following well-planned antipoverty programs, at the same time that income and wealth remain highly concentrated.

The benefit of this alternative is that it does not alienate the wealthier and more powerful sectors of society, alienation that is, after all, the single most prejudicial and counterproductive by-product of traditional redistributive schemes. The problem in Latin America has always been that any attempt at reducing the wealth, power, and impunity of elites, be this attempt democratic or authoritarian, conservative or revolutionary, has inevitably provoked their wrath and reaction. The latter has in turn unleashed a series of uncontrolled forces that either did away with democratic institutions or forced a clampdown on them, leading to exile, plotting, and the *contra* syndrome. Whether the redistributive exercise was accomplished with moderation (Guatemala, 1951–54) or excess (Cuba, 1959–61), democratically (Chile 1971–73) or by the military (Peru, 1968–74), it has systematically brought a negative, antidemocratic, and visceral counterattack by those affected by it. If it were possible simply to reduce poverty—without diminishing inequality in the short term—and the antipoverty effort were to have virtually no redistributive effect, there would be a painless, effective, and democracy-stabilizing solution to the age-old dilemma. No wonder that, in theory, this silver bullet has received the blessing of all the powers that be, from the Washington Consensus to Chicago Boys in Santiago.

There is little empirical evidence yet available in one direction or another in this regard. The new microtargeted antipoverty programs in Mexico, Chile, and Argentina are either too recent or insufficiently studied with proper data to permit any evaluation either of their actual, lasting effects on reducing poverty or on their impact on the stability of the democratic (or not-so-democratic) institutions in the countries in question. It may well be, however, that instead of its being necessary to redistribute income from the rich to the middle class, and transforming the poor in general into a widening middle class in order to stabilize democratic institutions, it is enough to shift the extreme poor into the next higher category—just poor, period—in order for the virtuous cycle of democracy, justice, and so on to be set in motion.

While this possibility cannot be ignored, it seems safer to believe that democracy without reducing inequality can endure only under great stress and given exceptional conditions; at the same time, only democracy can reduce the disparities that make it untenable. It seems safer to say that the only way to consolidate democratic rule in Latin America today is by redistributing wealth and income by combining economic growth—virtually of any type: the variable is not the nature of the growth but its existence and the context in which it takes place—with a sufficiently democratic political system that allows those sectors of society that have been heretofore excluded from most of the fruits of previous growth to fight for and achieve a larger share of the pie.

Federal, state, and municipal elections, tax reform to finance higher expenditures on education, health, and housing, labor rights, a more vigorous civil society, land reform in those regions where it is still relevant, urban reform in other areas: all of these are, among other things, redistributive factors operating through democratic channels. Workers do obtain higher wages if they are allowed to negotiate collectively, to organize unions, and, when useful, to strike. Citizens can vote for parties and measures that raise taxes to finance greater social spending; municipal authorities that do not steal do redistribute wealth from their potential pockets, or those of their predecessors, to society in general.

There is little disagreement here. That democracy can redistribute, even in Latin America, seems a truism. Any sustained alternation in power through elections with the broader trappings of democratic rule will, in Latin America, generate almost unavoidably a redistributive effect. The mechanics of how to proceed are also well known: investment in human capital (education, training, and health), other forms of social spending (housing, child care, and so forth), jobs, and development of infrastructure to promote growth—there is no great mystery about what must be done. The problem always has lain in finding the money to achieve these goals, not in the exact nature of the goals. The fact that today the fiscal option—as opposed to direct public sector involvement in the real economy—is the preferred option does not alter matters greatly, nor does it imply that the taxation avenue does not lead to a certain state presence in the economy in the medium term. Nor does this imply that ideological and policy fads will not shift again, sometime.

The main point is that the trick is political, not technical. The problem lies in the consequences, for both democratic rule and redistribution, of "going too far" and in the difficulty of defining "too far." The scope of the latter phrase is by definition in the eyes of the victim: what is "too far" for a landed oligarch may be acceptable for an ECLA (Economic Commission for Latin America)–born industrialist, whose definition is in turn narrower than that of a telecommunications magnate who got rich in the sobering years of the debt crisis. And all of their estimates of the acceptable breadth of reform may be far less broad than that implicitly or explicitly held by the presumed beneficiaries of the reforms themselves. Normally that is what elections, debate, congressional accountability over the budget, and collective bargaining are for: determining in a democratic, universally accepted fashion what is "too far" and what is not. In Latin America, this has not truly been the case ever, anywhere, with the possible exception of Costa Rica since 1947.

But there are some grounds for being optimistic in this regard. The persistence in time—as opposed to the actual rooting—of democratic institutions makes it more difficult for them to be overthrown; a return to military rule in countries like Brazil, Chile, or even Venezuela (a more complicated case) seems improbable. There is a virtuous gradualism in this. The discredit of the military, the attachment of broad sectors of society to the democratic paradigm, and the international context make a simple destruction of democratic institutions à la Chile or Guatemala more unlikely than ever.

The new international context is also a deterrent to the refusal of the powerful sectors of society to accept some form of redistribution. Short of conspiring and succeeding in overthrowing the institutions of representative democracy, the privileged instrument of resistance to redistribution is capital flight, refusal to invest, or both. Greater capital mobility in the globalized economy of today would seem to make this a more potent weapon and a nearly impossible one to defend against. At the same time, to the extent that there is beginning to be a shift in beliefs in the world regarding the need to reduce inequalities in certain regions, and there are growing possibilities of achieving new forms of international cooperation on taxation of assets abroad, for example, that weapon may begin to lose its effectiveness.

Moreover, if other conditions in the world, the region, and a given country are favorable to investment, the exact behavior of certain domestic private sector members may no longer be as relevant as before. In the same way that speculative capital has flowed in, in nearly identical proportions, to "best students" Mexico, Chile, and Argentina as it has to macroeconomic basket cases such as Brazil, it is quite possible that if the overall fundamentals are kept sound, foreign investment would continue to flow into nations that made a serious redistributive effort, even if domestic investment were to dry up for a time as a form of resistance to that effort.

Finally, there is the greater evil-lesser evil dynamic. There are important sectors of Latin American elites that still believe they have no need to countenance any redistributive intent. Either through ideological windmills, such as what is currently called neoliberalism, or good old-fashioned cynicism, they continue to maintain that under no conditions will they accept any reduction in their wealth, income, privilege, and power. But other sectors are beginning today, as they did in some nations in the aftermath of the Cuban Revolution in the early

1960s, to understand two facts, one of convenience, the other of indifference.

Certain segments of the rich and powerful today realize that their profits are so huge, that the difference between the rates of return on their investments in Latin America and elsewhere is so great, and the gaps between their situation and that of the vast majority of the region's inhabitants are so broad, that there is much room for painless concessions. Accepting higher taxes, paying higher wages, tolerating lower profits is not the end of the world; it might even be a way of making the world as it is somewhat more livable. Other sectors are beginning, once again, to be frightened by the specter of violence, armed uprisings, crime and drug trafficking, and the gaping inequalities from which all these blights ultimately stem. They are beginning—just barely—to acknowledge that while a revolution along Bolshevik, Chinese, or Cuban lines is no longer a realistic threat, armed chaos and popular fundamentalism is, and whatever the final result of such outbursts might be, in the meantime the current way of life of the wealthy and powerful in Latin America would become untenable.

The vicious cycle of democratization, social pressures, reforms, and counterreaction/end of democracy is precisely what has made democratic rule such a sporadic and unlikely feature of Latin American life. The only way to break the cycle is, of course, to attack all its links simultaneously: make democracy deeper and broader, so that it is more firmly rooted and more difficult to destroy; reduce inequalities as quickly and as decisively as possible, so as to defuse social pressures to go "too far"; encourage and implement reforms bold and substantive enough to reduce inequalities and give satisfaction to social demands and moderate enough to bring at least part of the business and foreign elite along, all the while neutralizing the military so they do not act on behalf of those who do not go along; at the same time bring to bear sufficient international cooperation to forestall capital flight or at least obtain some benefit from it, while insisting on welcoming foreign investment with tax rates that are higher than before but still lower, given overall rates of return, than in the wealthier and poorer nations.

The increments in leeway or breathing space one obtains through each of these changes and cautious steps enhance the maneuverability on the next turn around of the cycle: more democracy, in order to channel greater social pressures into more redistribution, thus defusing additional pressures and enabling the continuation of a moderate pace of reforms, consequently allowing the process to maintain allies in the business and international communities. Until this effort is undertaken in this manner, or one similar to it, with a sustained political will to proceed in this direction and at the same time the support and skill to stick to such a course, we will not know if it is simply a naive aspiration or a realistic blueprint for change.

In this way the vicious cycle can become the beginning of a virtuous dynamic that can make the two terms of our tension self-reinforcing instead of antagonistic. If democracy lasts long enough, and is accompanied by at least moderate but sustained economic growth, it can be a fulcrum for redistribution. If so, the institutions and mechanisms that bring about a reduction in inequality will be credited with this success, and will also enjoy the popularity and backing that comes not only from their intrinsic merits and from the evils of authoritarian rule, but from a specific improvement in the lives of millions. If democracy and growth coincide, and the former redistributes the fruits of the latter, democratic rule and inequality can be compatible for a while. If democracy does not coincide with growth or with redistribution, in all likelihood it will not last in Latin America during these last years of our century.

# 4

# *Traditional Power Structures and Democratic Governance in Latin America*

## Frances Hagopian

Among the challenges confronting democratic regimes in Latin America in the 1990s, the persistence of traditional power structures in the region stands out as critical. In an area long plagued by economic inequality, traditional elites historically have denied the fruits of full citizenship to peasants and other lower-class groups through coercive labor systems and various formal and informal political mechanisms that limit mass political representation. Today the power of traditional elites and the economic and political structures buttressing that power gravely threaten what Jorge Domínguez and Abraham Lowenthal urge us in the introduction to this collection to ponder: the capacity of institutions within democratic regimes to govern effectively and with accountability in response to the expressed concerns of the electorate. In those countries in which traditional power structures are strongest, democracy is arguably the most fragile. More specifically, the deficiencies of democratic governance highlighted by the contributors to this collection—weak political parties, incomplete state reform, and ineffective governments—are most in evidence.

This chapter examines the manifestations, causes, and consequences for democratic governance of the persistence of traditional power structures. In several countries where power is narrowly concentrated in closed circles of "traditional elites," or elites related by kinship or personal connections who dominate outside of industrial sectors and the largest cities, agrarian structures are egregiously unequal. "Traditional" parties command a sizable vote in elections and seat delegations to national and provincial legislative bodies large enough to exert a profound influence on public policy. Traditional elites dominate the political arena through blunt coercion exercised in the private sphere, through state institutions, and through more subtle mechanisms, especially the dispensation of state patronage. During the period of transitions to democracy, these elites preserved their access to state institutions and patronage resources, as well as their prerogatives to block constitutional reforms and ordinary legislation inimical to their interests, through negotiations with prodemocratic forces. Democratization has not so much threatened the persistence of traditional power structures as traditional elites have threatened democracy.

This chapter argues that while the electoral participation of "conservative" forces may enhance the stability of elective regimes, the residual power of traditional elites threatens the democratic process by undermining both the *effectiveness* and *accountability* of democratic governments. Patronage politics, the hallmark of governance by traditional elites in an era of mass politics, have driven government deficits sky-high and hampered the ability of states to deliver social services efficiently and on a universal basis. In some cases, traditional elites have even worked to block market-oriented reforms. They have also diminished democratic accountability by deforming democratic institutions and diluting mechanisms for political representation and participation in the decision-making process. Moreover, the limits on political, economic, and social reform they often exact as a price for their tolerance of formal democratic procedures ultimately weakens the attachments of nonelites to democracy. I conclude with the recommendation that political reforms be initiated to eliminate nondemocratic institutional arrangements and ensure that traditional elites compete electorally on a fair basis with other social forces, particularly those on the Left. Democratic governance has been most problematic where the opponents of traditional elites are weakly organized.

## Traditional Elites and Democracy: The Problem Elaborated

A long tradition in the social sciences, most successfully articulated by Barrington Moore Jr., sees ridding the economic and political orders of the "aristocracy" as a necessary prerequisite for successful democratization.[1] Where landed elites were able to resist the erosion of their powers through opportune alliances with rising industrial and commercial elites, the road to democracy in the modern world was blocked. John Johnson's classic 1958 text extolling the political role of the middle sectors in Latin America made the same assumption.[2] Although Johnson's optimism and faith in the potential of the middle classes to challenge the power of the "oligarchy" and bring democracy to the region's most developed countries in the 1950s was in retrospect misplaced, it is true that where "middle sectors" allied with urban lower classes to pry open their political systems, competitive if ultimately unstable democracies were established in this century. Where, on the other hand, revolutionary and populist alliances were unsuccessful, as in El Salvador and Peru before 1968, democracy remained an elusive goal. Most observers agree that it was only after Peru's reformist military regime undermined the power of the country's landed oligarchy that the potential for a fuller democracy to take root became real.[3]

The breakdown of democratic regimes that pushed reform agendas upon recalcitrant elites and the violence of the counterrevolution that swept the region from the mid-1960s to the mid-1980s has led some observers to urge that this traditional view about the desirability of strategies that attempt to defeat traditional elites outright be revised. These observers believe that the strength of traditional elites during the process of redemocratization and in the early years of a democratic regime should be seen as a positive development insofar as it allows those elites to negotiate policies and procedures favorable to their interests that will ultimately secure their attachment to a democratic order.[4] They contend that giving the "Right" an electoral voice and a credible chance to win elections, as long as it is willing to play by the rules, is preferable to more perfectly constructed democracies that may not underrepresent the Right but will surely drive it to extra-electoral means to protect its interests.

Comparative evidence supports the view that compromise with traditional elites can serve to stabilize democracy. In Argentina, conservative elites, sensing the futility of participating in and respecting the outcomes of elections that they were bound to lose, instead enlisted the support of the military in 1955, 1962, 1966, and again in 1976 to remove governments that injured their economic interests. Since the late 1980s, Gibson's tentative conclusion that the growth of the rightist UCEDE (Union of the Democratic Center) had "reduced the uncertainty of democratic politics for Argentina's upper classes and, thus, . . . helped to integrate them into the democratic process"[5] has rung true. Similarly, in Venezuela, an Acción Democrática (Democratic Action) government that "took a direct stance against the traditional authoritarian alliance" lasted only three years, but when the interests of all elites were safeguarded in the political pacts that reestablished democracy in 1958, democracy was consolidated on a more solid foundation.[6] More recently, in Spain, a "third wave" democratizer,[7] a political consensus in favor of democracy was forged through a series of political and economic pacts that purchased the loyalty of the traditional pillars of the Franco regime to the democratic order as well as peace between labor and capital.

The Venezuelan and Spanish precedents in particular have buoyed the hope that negotiated settlements between democrats and conservative political elites will not only purchase a short-term truce permitting fragile democracies to survive but also lay the foundations for a stronger democracy in the medium and long term. Advocates of such a strategy of reconciliation expect that the formerly nondemocratic Right will become more faithful to democracy once it gets better at the game of democratic politics. Most important, they expect that the political generations that follow, socialized into competitive electoral politics, will have a stronger attachment to democracy than their predecessors for whom the acceptance of democracy was conditional upon the preservation of their interests. Such a scenario, it is claimed, unfolded in the postwar German Federal Republic.[8]

After a decade or more during which this advice has been heeded and democracy has been reestablished via negotiations that left traditional elites in power in several Latin American countries, most notably Brazil, Ecuador, and El Salvador, the time is ripe for a reassessment of this new orthodoxy. This chapter undertakes such a reassessment through an examination of the influence of traditional elites on the early phases of democratization. I proceed by first distinguishing traditional power structures and traditional elites from the Right and other conservative economic and political elites (who are capably discussed in the chapter by Edward Gibson in this collection).

## Traditional Power Structures in Latin America

"Traditional power structures" serve as the economic and political foundations of the power of traditional elites. "Traditional elites," sometimes referred to as oligarchs, are most frequently defined socioeconomically as agrarian or rural-based elites and politically as "conservative" and "rightist" forces. They are "rural-based" in that they or their families, at least at one time, enjoyed the concentrated ownership of land, especially in those countries where land is scarce. Also, as Blachman and Sharpe have persuasively argued in the Central American context, they have benefited from coercive labor systems: debt peonage, sharecropping, and other labor-repressive institutions.[9] Today's traditional elites are the "heirs," as Zeitlin and Ratcliffe put it in writing of the Chilean elite, "of their own political families' landed political power and propensity to rule."[10]

Nonetheless, these common definitions of traditional elites often obscure more than they clarify. Many "traditional" rural-based elites, including the coffee oligarchies of Central America and the cattle ranchers and grain producers of the Pampas, have in fact long employed "modern," productive agricultural techniques in large-scale commercial agriculture for domestic and foreign markets. They can no longer be equated with "landed elites," moreover, because they have diversified their economic activities, a step that has allowed them to survive agricultural modernization, urbanization, and industrialization in the postwar period. The overlapping of agricultural and commercial interests makes it impossible to restrict the "traditional" label to rural-based, agricultural elites.[11] Finally, traditional elites are not the only political groups that hold conservative beliefs, promote a conservative agenda, and organize political parties of the Right.

Traditional elites in Latin America today, not readily identifiable purely by a common economic condition, are perhaps most accurately conceived as closed circles of power holders that dominate a range of state institutions and political processes, and that concentrate political as well as economic power within a limited number of families.[12] It is their control of *political* resources that has enabled traditional elites to preserve their economic power and resist the meaningful expansion of political competition and participation. The most important of these political assets was, until recently, their alliance with the military. Historically and in the contemporary period, traditional elites have also effectively used judicial, bureaucratic, and legislative power to win favorable state policies and to deny the extension of a broad range of citizenship rights to the lower classes, most notably the right to organize. Today, exercising tight control over several political parties, they also control political recruitment; membership in or alliance with these families is often key to political advancement.

Although the power base of traditional elites lies in local and regional politics, they have enjoyed ample success in national-level politics. At minimum they have gained sufficient electoral support to gain entry into governing coalitions and, not infrequently, their parties have won outright legislative majorities and even control of the executive branch. Historically Latin American traditional elites dominated the electoral arena through coercion, particularly of dependent peasant populations. Although they still resort to coercion in some places, in recent years they have demonstrated their capacity to survive in increasingly more participatory and competitive electoral systems by employing newer, more subtle forms of political domination, in particular, the distribution of state patronage. Traditional elites use clientelism more than any other method of competing in elections and governing, and they do so more extensively and regularly than any other set of politicians. What distinguishes the "traditional" from the "nontraditional" use of patronage is that it is exercised through highly personalized, family-based, clientelistic networks. Personalism, in fact, is as much a hallmark of traditional politics as is limited political competition.

Although there is considerable overlap between the economic power of the agricultural sector and the electoral success of traditional parties, this correspondence is not perfect. In some countries, the power of traditional elites has been ravaged by social revolution or moderated by the rise of parties of the Left and the cultural predisposition of elites to compromise. In Mexico, Bolivia, Nicaragua, and Cuba, social revolution and the land reforms of revolutionary governments deprived prerevolutionary traditional elites of their principal source of power. A new, postrevolutionary political elite consolidated power to such an extent in Mexico that it is possible to speak of a political oligarchy, but this elite cannot be considered "traditional."[13] In Bolivia the pre-revolutionary white, Spanish-speaking, landed aristocracy was stripped of its landholdings by a sweeping agrarian reform. Minifundismo and military intervention, however, rendered the effects of social revolution less thorough and permanent than in Mexico and Cuba and permitted a new agricultural and mining elite to arise. In nonrevolutionary settings, political reform and economic differentiation sometimes served the same end. In Peru the military-sponsored agrarian reform of 1969, however incomplete, broke the power of the landed elite.[14] As Lowenthal put it, "most of Peru's former oligarchs have fallen from unquestioned authority to oblivion or even ignominy."[15] In Venezuela, agrarian reform finished what the conversion to an oil economy had begun: the shift of power away from traditional, rural elites.[16] In Costa Rica a tradition of small-holder agriculture and a political class that embraced democratic principles made agrarian reform less essential for democratic development than elsewhere on the continent.[17]

In the agriculturally fertile countries of the Southern Cone, the power of traditional rural-based elites was tempered by the successful organization of urban-based competitors, especially those in the popular classes. In both Argentina and Uruguay, highly commercially oriented agrarian elites shared power early in the twentieth century with middle sector groups. In Argentina they irrevocably lost their political hegemony after 1912, but after 1930 they did not hesitate to back extraparliamentary means to remove populist governments that manipulated exchange rates to favor industrial interests over their own. In Uruguay, traditional elites were committed to a democratic order that combined electoral dominance for their two political parties with the most progressive package of social welfare policies in the hemisphere. Traditional elites in Chile accepted democratization as long as their property rights were secure and the peasantry was excluded from political participation. Until the 1960s these elites used their congressional veto to block legislation that would have permitted rural organizing efforts, the dismantling of harshly labor-repressive agricultural systems, and measures to redistribute land. Subsequently, in the early 1970s, they fought to overthrow an elected government that redistributed their assets. In the mid-1970s a "counterreform" reversed much of the agrarian reform of the late 1960s and early 1970s, but did not restore the pre-1962 agrarian system. Nonetheless, today the National Agricultural Society remains a powerful interest group, the Renovación Nacional (National Renovation) remains a powerful political party, and the interests of traditional elites are well represented in the current Congress by a thin majority in the Senate that includes Pinochet appointees and a substantial minority in the directly elected lower Chamber.

Elsewhere the power of traditional elites has been preserved, even after economic modernization, by the ability of traditional elites to

deny outright basic rights of citizenship or to manipulate state resources and representative networks to their advantage. In Brazil, Colombia, Ecuador, El Salvador, Guatemala, and Honduras, traditional
elites control several branches of government: they might occupy the
presidency, command a working legislative majority, or make or ap-
prove appointments to the judiciary and civil service. They also control
important political parties and the policy agenda to such an extent that
a mass democratic politics has hardly taken root. These are countries
in which traditional power structures persist at high rates. In Brazil,
traditional elites exercise a great deal of control over the national congress and state and local governments, several major political parties,
and, to a large extent, the design of political institutions and economic
and social policy. In Honduras and Colombia, "traditional" parties
enjoy virtually uncontested electoral hegemony. The National and Liberal Parties in Honduras have captured at least 92 percent of the vote in
every election held since 1980. With the singular exception of the vote
for the M-19 in the Constituent Assembly elections of 1991, the Conservative and Liberal Parties in Colombia have captured more than
90 percent of the vote in every election since the restoration of democratic rule in 1958, allowing them to control the presidency, the legislature, and all other state positions appointed by these powers. The
leadership of these parties has remained for decades in the hands of the
same families, and even in the 1980s this "patrimony of traditional
elites" had apparently only moderately diminished.[18] In Ecuador a resilient oligarchy based in Guayaquil that "worked closely" with all five
constitutional regimes between 1948 and 1963[19] has survived military
rule and oil-financed industrialization. Even today, it exercises significant influence in the Ecuadorian Congress and Supreme Court.[20]

The persistence of traditional elite power is even more pervasive in
the Central American nations of El Salvador and Guatemala. In El Salvador, the oligarchy has retained control of the judiciary and has organized a formidable political party, ARENA (Nationalist Republican
Alliance), that defeated the reformist Christian Democrats in the 1989
presidential election and captured nearly half of the seats in the Legislative Assembly two years later. Even when out of office during the
Christian Democratic administration of Napoleón Duarte (1984–89),
the coffee elite of El Salvador collectively battled, and ultimately defeated, the establishment of a coffee marketing board, and it also managed to dilute the agrarian reform. More obviously consequential for
democratic consolidation, traditional elites blocked crucial reforms of
the judicial system and civil-military relations that most observers feel
are prerequisites for the full integration of all democratic players in the
Salvadoran political system.[21] In Guatemala the oligarchy has for half a
century used whatever means necessary to fend off the multiclass coalition that would restrain its powers. Increasingly unable to impose a

settlement, it has accepted the protection of the Guatemalan military and military-written constitutions to preserve its hegemony.

In the Dominican Republic, Haiti, Paraguay, and prerevolutionary Nicaragua, personalistic dictatorships and intermittent occupation by U.S. forces served both to prop up and to attenuate the dominance of regionally based traditional elites. Elites in these countries sacrificed absolute domination for economic opportunity, restrictions on mass organizing, and insulation from the pressures to expand the limited opportunities for political participation. In the Dominican Republic where, until the death of Rafael Trujillo in 1961, "the primitive bureaucracy was concerned almost entirely with supporting the personal interests of the ruling oligarchy,"[22] a legacy of the Trujillo dictatorship was the excessive centralization of power and personalism today evident in the persistent political dominance of Joaquín Balaguer. In the late 1970s, in the Dominican Republic, traditional power holders joined with industrial elites to fashion a democratic regime. In Haiti, a decade later, they conspired with military elites to overthrow one. The Paraguayan Colorado Party, which served as the electoral vehicle for the dictator Stroessner and elected two-thirds of the representatives to both chambers in 1983, emerged from authoritarian rule in the 1989 elections with 74 percent of the vote. Its vote total slipped to 40 percent in the 1991 municipal elections, but it is still the largest party.[23]

The remainder of this chapter focuses on the cases of "high" and "medium" traditional elite persistence. The next section elaborates how traditional elites in these countries were able to survive both the reigns of increasingly professional and autonomous militaries that came to power to "modernize" their countries and the transitions to fuller, more participatory democracies to such a degree that it is meaningful to consider their impact on democratic governance today. The experience of these elites with military rule and its demise also contributes to our understanding of how their attitudinal and behavioral predispositions toward democratic government were shaped.

## Traditional Elites, Military Rule, and Democratization

The conventional wisdom used to be that military rule in Latin America benefited traditional elites. As Charles Anderson long ago pointed out, military coups took place precisely to assure the holders of important power capabilities that their position in society would not be endangered,[24] a claim best evidenced by the historic marriage between the ruling families and military establishments of Central America. Alfred Stepan's work on the Brazilian military, which demonstrated a considerable level of military institutional autonomy, perhaps forever shattered the image of the military as the storm troopers of the oligarchy.[25] His thesis was only strengthened when the Peruvian military proclaimed itself "anti-oligarchic" and when militaries in "bureaucratic-authoritarian regimes" subsequently did not relinquish power to civilians. Instead, they empowered technocrats and insulated them from political representatives in order to stabilize economies in crisis and to promote industrial development. These regimes most zealously attacked the interests of labor, but they also were perceived as betraying the traditional and modern upper classes that had supported the overthrow of elected presidents. In many lesser developed countries in the region as well, rifts opened between military establishments and civilian elites.

Whether military regimes were committed to reform or restoration, the effects of their economic policies and political strategies altered the power of traditional forces. In some countries, traditional elites were strengthened, and in others they were weakened by the economic policies adopted by militaries to stabilize or restructure their economies. They were also affected by the political strategies these militaries pursued to maintain themselves in power or fashion the polity to conform to their vision even after their departures. Thus, in Peru, twelve years of military rule eroded traditional power structures and the influence of the traditional landed families and their financial institutions,[26] whereas in Ecuador traditional elites survived a nominally reformist military regime "virtually unscathed."[27] The Ecuadorian regime had a less profound commitment to reform, it was less cohesive, and traditional elites were able to mount an effective opposition to agrarian reform and other military-sponsored programs. Traditional elites also benefited from the marginalization of political parties under military rule. While all parties were weakened, those new parties that were only beginning to make inroads among the country's popular sectors were disadvantaged to a larger degree than already established traditional parties.[28]

Most bureaucratic-authoritarian regimes excluded the political representatives of civilian elites from decision making at the same time that these regimes supported the economic interests of these groups. The result was a variable pattern of influence on the persistence of traditional power structures. In Brazil, agricultural elites benefited from real negative interest rates on loans from the state-owned Bank of Brazil, and agrarian reform was effectively removed from the political agenda for two decades. Agricultural modernization proceeded quickly in the southern parts of the country and on the southern and western frontiers, but traditional elites retained their control of land in the northeast of the country. The Brazilian military regime was also the only bureaucratic-authoritarian regime to offer political protection to the traditional elite. Because the military needed the skill, networks, and support of the traditional political elite to win legislative and local elections, it favored traditional elites who organized politically well-integrated state clientelistic networks and who could effectively dispense state patronage. Traditional elites in Brazil emerged from the period of military rule stronger than they were at its outset, and perhaps stronger than they would have been otherwise.

In the more politically repressive military regimes of the Southern Cone, the effects of military rule on traditional power structures are more ambiguous. In Argentina and Chile these effects may not have been significant. Exchange rates meant to favor exports strengthened the hand of the grain exporters of the Argentine Pampas but, as Edward Gibson argues in his chapter in this collection, civilian elites learned that the military, driven by its own agenda and internal divisions, was an "uncontrollable partner that could not effectively implement policy." In Chile, favorable policies for the "modern" agricultural sector, in particular for "nontraditional" exports that helped to sustain traditional elites, also helped to offset the adverse political consequences that might have followed from the decision of the Chilean military to retire political parties, including the then leading party of the Right and representative of the traditional elite, the Partido Nacional (National Party).

In Uruguay, on the other hand, military rule may have served to weaken traditional power structures. The military governors declared traditional parties, which had competed and governed for decades on the basis of their ability to distribute state patronage to their constituents, to be in "recess." By depriving traditional party leaders of positions in state administration and the opportunity to compete in electoral campaigns in which they typically exchanged pork for votes—in other words, of their ability to practice political clientelism—the military may have eroded their electoral dominance. The leftist Frente Amplio (FA, Broad Front) and Nuevo Espacio (New Space) coalitions increased their electoral representation from 18 percent in the 1971 and 1984 elections to 30 percent in 1989. Nonetheless, despite the improved electoral performance of coalitions of leftist parties, the traditional parties continue to control the presidency.

Most analysts agree that South American militaries experienced a loss of power and prestige as a result of their most recent governing experiences. By contrast, military establishments in Central America have gained power. When he assumed office as the elected president of Guatemala in 1985, Vinicio Cerezo was subject to numerous restrictions on his power by the military.[29] The militaries in Honduras and Guatemala in recent decades have acquired unprecedented levels of autonomy from their traditional allies,[30] and their alliance with economic elites is now an alliance of equals.[31] In a 1991 interview, General Héctor Gramajo spoke of the Guatemalan military's desires for greater autonomy and claimed that "The Army no longer plays an electoral role . . . [nor] are we any longer the redeemers for the right-wing *latifundistas.* . . . They no longer dominate the Army. The Army doesn't ask them for food rations [for the soldiers], but it doesn't do their dirty work for them either. We are not concubines, we are professionals."[32] In Honduras, Guatemala, and Ecuador, independence from civilian elites was achieved to a significant degree because of the active involvement of the military in the economy. The military in Honduras has a hand in public utilities, transportation, and, through its own pension institute, is a major player in financial markets.[33] The Ecuadorian armed forces, as Isaacs reports, "have amassed a vast and diverse economic empire."

The trend toward growing military autonomy in both Central and South America prompted many Latin American traditional elites not to attempt to block the return of civilian rule and, once established, not to support attempts at military coups.[34] Where militaries attempted to govern autonomously, there were two principal reasons for the conversion of traditional elites to the virtues of democratic governance. First, in Peru, Ecuador, Nicaragua, and Panama, authoritarian rulers did not govern consistently in the interests of the elite. Second, in these countries as well as in Honduras, the Dominican Republic, and Argentina, traditional elites wearied of their lack of access to top policymakers. In both cases, they embraced democracy as a means to *expand* their influence. In Argentina, in particular, traditional elites also dropped their customary resistance to democratic governance because, as Gibson notes, the military led the country into a "reckless war," and because they believed that the economic constraints of the 1980s would eliminate any possible reversion to anti-agrarian, anti-exporting, populist policies. In several Central American countries, reigning oligarchies additionally embraced elections in order to win international support in their bid to stave off impending revolution.

Whatever their motives, since the transitions to democracy, traditional elites have by and large made commitments to electoral politics, though to different degrees and for different stakes. In Argentina, for example, the traditional elite invested considerable resources and effort in organizing a credible electoral alternative on the political Right for the first time in fifty years, primarily through uniting the conservative provincial parties of the interior with the Buenos Aires–based UCEDE in the Alianza de Centro (Alliance of the Center).[35] In the late 1980s the modest success of this electoral alliance won for the Right influence in government[36] and, together with the estrangement between civilian and military elites, reduced the potential for an authoritarian regression. In El Salvador, the incorporation of one faction of the traditional right into the ARENA party moved the resolution of political conflict from the military toward the electoral arena. With nearly half the seats in the legislature occupied by ARENA delegates, ex-president Alfredo Cristiani, representing a faction of the traditional Salvadoran elite willing to compromise on democracy, was able to make credible moves toward democratization.[37]

On the other hand, whether traditional elites initiated the transitions to democratic regimes or merely embraced the ideas of civilian rule and competitive elections at some point during the transition process, their role in the democratization process has contributed to the preservation of traditional power structures. Through their participation in coalitions to end authoritarian rule they carved out spaces for themselves in the political arena, which they might have otherwise lost through the "natural" processes of socioeconomic and electoral change. From these strongholds, they exercise veto power over many political and economic reforms at the top of the political agenda in new and newly reestablished democracies. In this respect, recent negotiated transitions to democracy in several Latin American countries—Brazil and Ecuador chief among them—have more closely followed the Colombian precedent than the Spanish one. The consociational agreements forged in Colombia in 1957 in the aftermath of a decade of political violence, praised by many for securing democracy, also fortified traditional power structures *and* limited democracy. In the decades that followed the establishment of the National Front, the "gentlemen" who governed Colombia were able to limit popular mobilization, limit access to higher education, and stymie agrarian reform.[38] These developments were not merely undesirable features of a stable democracy. They have threatened democracy itself, leading to a Colombian state so weak that it cannot respond adequately to challenges to its authority.[39]

Does this mean, then, that the participation of traditional elites in political pacts is bad for democratic consolidation? The evidence suggests that the new common wisdom about broadly inclusive negotiated transitions should not be discarded altogether, but it should be qualified. Advocates of political pacts base their argument that political pacts provide an auspicious beginning for democratic regimes on three assumptions: (1) that key players participate in pacts; (2) that pacts solve procedural questions, and occasionally substantive issues (the former are crucial for strengthening democratic institutions, whereas the latter, Przeworski argues, are binding only on the signatories, not their political heirs);[40] and (3) that each side is strong enough that no one actor can dominate the outcome. Where traditional elites dominate, these assumptions are only partly true.

In model pacted transitions such as those that took place in Venezuela and Spain, political transitions were supported by leaders of established political parties, business, and labor organizations. Backed by their constituents and members, these civilian elites struck a series of political settlements that distributed fair chances for all parties to compete for power in the electoral arena and socioeconomic pacts that reduced the uncertainty of democracy and guaranteed economic "rights" for all actors. In Brazil and Ecuador, by contrast, leaders of corporate groups did not participate in negotiations that were dominated by traditional elites. In these countries as well as the Dominican Republic, democratic regimes were brought into being without class compromise. As Conaghan and Espinal put it in writing of Ecuador and the Dominican Republic, "These democracies did not emerge as a political arrangement to negotiate the relations between labour and capital, but as a vehicle for restructuring domination by economic and political elites."[41] In none of these cases was social peace or institutional reform achieved as a result of pact making.

In those countries where traditional elites reemerged from military rule with substantial reservoirs of economic and political power, they insisted, as a price for their cooperation with the democratic opposition, on limiting policy reform. They also undermined, rather than strengthened, democratic political institutions, including political parties. In Brazil, for example, in exchange for supporting the civilian opposition candidate for president, traditional politicians were able to negotiate their continued access to the high-level state posts and patronage resources that underlay their political power. They also flooded and won seats on the governing bodies of all major political parties except the Workers' Party (the PMDB [Party of the Brazilian Democratic Movement] was transformed from a party posed to represent popular classes into an oligarchical vehicle), thus robbing several of budding programmatic identities. In the early years of the New Republic, social policy and constitutional issues were bartered for personal political gain. The votes of traditional elites to preserve the presidential system of government, for example, were won with generous allocations from the housing and other ministries. In short, the price of constructing a temporary majority for the purpose of accelerating the departure of the military was that traditional clientelistic networks and other antidemocratic modes of political representation were revitalized, and forces that might have challenged military prerogatives were weakened.

A similar chain of events transpired in Ecuador. In Ecuador, the formation of governing coalitions involved "the distribution of an inordinate amount of patronage, which in turn mortgaged the president's ability to govern effectively. . . . The particular way in which patronage politics has dominated bargaining and compromise . . . has served more to undermine than to bolster the democratic process." In short, "tenuous party loyalties, party fragmentation, a surfeit of patronage politics, and persistent conflicts between the president and the congress" continue to plague Ecuador despite the "crafted transition."[42] While it is too soon to assess the outcome of the peace process in El Salvador, its success may depend on whether the negotiations indeed move away from settling who should hold power and resolve what the mechanisms and forms should be for competing for power, as Córdova Macías hypothesizes, in his chapter in this collection, has been the case. The "Forum on Socio-Economic *Concertación*," he reports, to date has not moved beyond defining an agenda.

One feature that may work to the advantage of the Salvadoran transition which was absent in the Brazilian and Ecuadorian cases is the presence of a Left in the negotiations that is strong enough to bargain effectively. If a "too strong" electoral Left—one that can form a government without "centrist" allies to moderate a program of radical reform—is threatening to democracy because the traditional elite is likely to back military force to safeguard its interests (e.g., Venezuela in 1948; Chile in 1973), a "too weak" electoral Left poses different but no less serious dangers to democracy. In both Ecuador and the Dominican Republic, where the lower-class population was not effectively mobilized or otherwise threatening, traditional and modern sector elites created postauthoritarian regimes that Conaghan and Espinal have characterized as "democratic-authoritarian" hybrids.[43] The participation of the Left in the electoral process appears to enhance rather than detract from the prospects for establishing stable, competitive democracies. In Chile the participation of the Socialist Party and the socialist-leaning Party for Democracy in the 1988 "Campaign for the No," in the subsequent negotiations over the establishment of a democratic regime, and indeed, beginning in 1990, government, has contributed to one of the continent's most effective and accountable democracies. The role in the negotiations to bring about the democratic transition and the subsequent electoral success of the Uruguayan Left in the 1980s, after years of frustration at the polls and the military defeat of the Tupamaros, has augmented, not harmed, the prospects for democracy in Uruguay. In one of his last writings on the state of democracy in Uruguay, Gillespie was sanguine that democracy was well on its way toward being reconsolidated.[44]

What the evidence from these examples suggests is that pacts can be valuable under three conditions: (1) when they are negotiated among near political equals, and thus each party must concede something of value; (2) when they resolve economic, social, or cultural conflict (as, for example, between capital and labor, landed and landless, or ethnic or linguistic majorities and minorities); and (3) when they safeguard the opportunity for all segments of society to participate politically. When, instead, they satisfy none of these conditions but preserve traditional elite power, often at the expense of democratic institutions, they can result in defective democracies that govern poorly, as we see below.

## The Impact of Traditional Power Structures on Democratic Governance

The contention that where traditional power structures are strong, democratic governance is the least effective and accountable is supported by an obvious set of correlations. Where traditional elites are strongest, political parties are weakest, executive-legislative relations are at their worst, and economic reforms have lagged. Where the power of traditional elites has been broken or attenuated, economic reform has been made possible or secured under democratic regimes, political parties are healthier, and democratic institutions have been strengthened since the return to democracy, even if they have not made a full recovery from military rule.

The obvious question which these observations raise is whether or not such failures should be attributed to the persistence of traditional power structures or if they could more accurately be viewed as caused by any one of a number of factors frequently cited by other analysts: faulty institutional design; poorly devised electoral laws; and a nondemocratic political culture. Exaggerated federalism, strong presidents, and congresses too weak to govern effectively but strong enough to obstruct executive initiatives (the institutional flaws aptly cited in the chapter by Lamounier in this collection as underlying what he describes as Brazil's "hyperactive paralysis syndrome"), as well as permissive party legislation, have undeniably contributed to governance problems in several countries across the region. But it is problematic to treat deficient institutions and electoral systems as the *independent* source of the most acute of these governance problems.

If faulty institutional design were the foremost cause of the disappointing performance of democratic government, then how is it to be explained that some countries with otherwise similar institutional features exhibit different governance problems? All Latin American countries, for example, have presidential systems of government, but presidents in Brazil and Ecuador are more often vulnerable to the lack of adequate support in congress and less effective than are their counterparts in Chile, Argentina, and Costa Rica. Electoral and party laws that discourage party discipline and allow the number of political parties to proliferate, moreover, are not equally damaging in all countries. Party discipline is surely eroded in Brazil by the unique combination of open list proportional representation and large, multimember districts.[45] Yet Uruguay's "double simultaneous vote," which by design should be just as threatening to party unity and the programmatic integrity of its parties, has not weakened Uruguay's parties to nearly the same extent. Uruguayan parties are able to retain their leaders and voters and frame accountable policies. The harm done by permissive party legislation per se is also unclear. While the proliferation of parties to feed the ambitions of politicians has undoubtedly fragmented many party systems, "political entrepreneurs" such as Luis Inácio "Lula" da Silva and Fernando Henrique Cardoso in Brazil and Carlos "Chacho" Álvarez in Argentina that have founded new parties based on programmatic alternatives have enhanced the representativeness of their party systems without necessarily diminishing the effectiveness of their governments.

There are in fact several reasons to believe that where the institutional and cultural problems highlighted by many analysts as threatening many Latin American democracies do tend to coincide with a specific cluster of governing problems—such as congressional inaction, fragile governing coalitions, and a rapidly declining public faith in democratic institutions—these institutional defects are themselves epiphenomenal, brought on by traditional elite power. Behind weak presidents, ineffective legislatures, and unfulfilled popular expectations most often lay weak parties with volatile bases of public support and undisciplined congressional delegations that are generally associated with high levels of traditional elite power. "Government gridlock" and policy immobilism can be attributed to traditional elites using their power base in the legislature to check the executive, often when they have failed to control the presidency, although it would be inaccurate to view traditional elite-dominated congresses as uniformly ineffective. Congresses in countries in the grip of traditional elites are readily able to pass legislation in areas that do not affect the power base of traditional elites, but stall measures that would redistribute wealth and income or redesign institutions along lines that would make democratic governments more accountable to mass electorates and less accountable to traditional elites. Similarly, the "consociational" pull away from the center highlighted by Lamounier, embodied in governmental federalism and parties with strong provincial governing bodies, are themselves in the Latin American context creations of strong, preindustrial regional elites seeking to maximize their power. Federalism has persisted where traditional elites are strong, as in Brazil, and declined to the advantage of the center where they are not, as in postrevolutionary Mexico.

Aspects of political culture that are deemed unsupportive of democratic governance, too, are shaped by the beliefs and political practices of traditional elites. Historically, the dominant strains of the political cultures of Brazil, Ecuador, and Colombia were personalism, clientelism, and regionalism. Today mass publics breaking out of traditional patterns of deference not surprisingly hope that democracy will bring material rewards as well as freedom from fear of repression, but the reason why the Brazilian and other electorates expect an "unreasonable" amount from their democracies is probably because parties that can neither frame nor pursue a coherent program of government raise rather than discipline popular expectations. When they fail to satisfy public appetites for government outputs, they also erode public confidence in democratic political institutions.

In what specific ways, then, have traditional elites with high levels of political power, either directly or through parties, undermined the performance of democratic government? First, because these elites depend on distributing patronage resources to compete in democratic political systems, they have fueled patronage inflation, politicized the delivery of social services, inhibited policymaking, and strained government budgets with their profligate spending patterns.[46] In the first few years of democratic government in Brazil, regionally based political elites, most of them traditional, went on a spending spree that resulted in a debt of U.S.$57 billion that the federal government was later forced to assume. The inefficient delivery of scarce social resources such as education and health might also be attributed to the excessive clientelism practiced by traditional elites. In the Dominican Republic, Rosario Espinal points out that the education, health, and agricultural ministries, as well as the judiciary, have been grossly underfunded in recent years.

A second way in which traditional politicians have reduced the effectiveness of democratic government has been to either slow or block market-oriented reforms, or to negotiate even more patronage resources in exchange for supporting reform in areas that affect them least, such as systems of wage and salary compensation, trade liberalization, and the regulation of foreign investment. This has occurred more often than market-oriented economic reforms have undermined the power base of traditional elites. In Brazil the earliest portion of an economic reform program that has lagged by regional standards to be completed was trade liberalization, and traditional politicians readily lent their support in the Congress to anti-inflation legislation that restrained wages in exchange for the government "opening its coffers."[47] These same politicians, however, have most stubbornly and to date effectively resisted state reform that would reduce the state payroll, restrain the spending of state governments, and reform the social security system, all of which most experts feel are required to complete Brazil's fiscal stabilization. In Colombia, according to Matthew Shugart, elites of the traditional parties posed such an obstacle to economic liberalization that former president Virgilio Barco lent his support to a referendum initiative to stage an extraordinary election of a Constituent Assembly that would otherwise not have been held. The new constitution promulgated in 1991 was designed to reduce the clientelistic basis of economic policymaking.[48] In Ecuador the president has lacked support for his economic program in the Congress and most significantly from within his own party. According to Anita Isaacs, all other legislation, including judicial reform, has been postponed pending the passage of economic reforms. The legislature has not even produced a budget in fifteen months.

Where traditional power structures persist at high levels, moreover, democratic accountability is limited at best. In Guatemala, Honduras, and El Salvador, the forces of the traditional Right are so strong that they have twisted democracies into what critics have called "façade democracies" in which, despite the staging of elections, ruling groups do not lose power.[49] The most blatant distortion of democracy has been a lack of constitutional guarantees for those segments of the population that elites would prefer to exclude from the electoral process. Opponents of traditional elite dominance have been denied equal access to the media and public during electoral campaigns, and they have even been physically intimidated. In El Salvador, in 1993, the United Nations estimated that close to 800,000 eligible voters, or 27 percent of voting-age Salvadorans, were without electoral identification cards. The unregistered, as Córdova Macías points out, were overwhelmingly from two zones: the largest urban areas and the rural areas that had formerly experienced high levels of armed conflict. Although the UN believes that today the largest obstacles to voter registration are lack of citizen mobilization and technical inefficiencies, the hypothesis cannot be discounted that for some time opponents of traditional elite power were systematically disenfranchised.

Elsewhere, democratic accountability is undermined by distortions of electoral law. While it may be customary in democracies to over-represent underpopulated regions in one chamber (usually the upper), the state of São Paulo is grossly underrepresented in the *lower house* of the Brazilian Congress (the Chamber of Deputies) as well as the Senate. A deputy needs only 14,000 votes to be elected in Amapá, 180,000 in Rio Grande do Sul, and 300,000 in São Paulo.[50] The underrepresentation of São Paulo, designed by the military to give electoral advantage to its supporters among the traditional elite in Brazil's northeast, persists to this day because those who benefit, a majority in the Congress, can block any attempts to redress this inequity.

Even when these political systems appear to be operating according to democratic rules, democratic accountability is limited by the appropriation by traditional power holders of mass political parties. In an era of mass politics, the strategies that parties representing traditional elites employ to compete with one other and nonelite parties, mobilize their electoral supporters, and even govern—all based on clientelism—weaken political party programs, deny mass political representation in the political and policy arenas, and almost always underrepresent the collective interests of the mass electorate. The country studies in this collection attest to the fact that, in those countries in which traditional elites are strongest, political party attachments in the electorate are weak; parties have short lives; they do not readily distinguish themselves from one another by program; and they are the least effective in fulfilling their interest-aggregating functions.

Weakened parties are especially evident in Brazil, Ecuador, and Guatemala. In both Brazil and Ecuador, analysts have employed the same metaphor of "shirt-changing" to describe the frequency with which traditional politicians move from one party to another.[51] In Brazil, once the opposition elected the president in 1985, state and local politicians deserted the pro-military PDS (Democratic Social Party) en masse for the ranks of the newly created PFL (Party of the Liberal Front) and the former opposition party, the PMDB; in the early 1990s, the fortunes of the PRN (Party of National Reconstruction) similarly rose and fell with the star of Fernando Collor de Mello. In Ecuador, according to Isaacs, by April 1994 one-third of those elected to Congress had deserted the party for which they ran, many lured away by the promises of government patronage. The problem for democratic governance when politicians frequently change parties is that they can be held accountable only for their constituency service, not for the passage or blockage of issue-based legislation. When parties are extremely short-lived, this problem is exacerbated. In his chapter in this collection, Edelberto Torres-Rivas decries that parties in Guatemala have only a "precarious temporal existence" (eight of the sixteen parties contesting the 1984 election for a Constituent Assembly had been created within one month of the election, and another five were less than one year old); their programs are vacuous; and they lack roots in the electorate. It is little wonder that in Guatemala political parties do not represent the social and economic interests of the political community and have little say in actual governance. As another observer of contemporary Guatemala has written, "since 1954 the political realm has not been where accords are defined and solutions sought to the fundamental problems of the nation. . . . The ruling authority negotiates directly with special interests and establishes political accords with them. Thus, the power dynamic of personal authority has replaced the power of the political party. Parties merely bless decisions already made in the political black market, decisions made beyond any legal authority or regulatory process."[52]

Finally, more often than not, traditional elites extract as a condition for their support for democratic regimes limits on policy reform. Agrarian reform, scuttled in Colombia in the 1960s, Ecuador in the 1970s, and El Salvador and Brazil in the 1980s, is only the most obvious of a longer list of impermissible public policies. Such limits threaten democracy because the absence of anticipated reform weakens the attachment to democracy of potential beneficiaries whose support for democracy is often instrumentally based.[53]

Where weak parties have not effectively represented popular interests and policy reform has been limited—precisely in those countries in which the persistence of traditional power structures is most pronounced—there are apparent declining rates of electoral participation and shallow commitments on the part of the masses to democracy.[54] In Brazil, voter turnout in only four years (1986–90) plunged from 95 percent to less than 70 percent, and the number of blank and spoiled ballots cast rose sharply in 1990 to 31.5 percent, a level even higher than that registered at the height of the dictatorship in 1970, when the opposition was encouraging such symbolic protest. In the 1993 plebiscite to choose a form of government, less than 55 percent of the population cast a valid vote for either presidentialism or parliamentarism.[55] In Ecuador voter absenteeism exceeded 25 percent in the 1984 presidential elections.[56] In Honduras, 35 percent of voters abstained from casting a ballot in the 1993 presidential elections, compared with just 6 percent in the 1985 election.[57] In El Salvador, voter absenteeism was 67.4 percent in the 1989 presidential election.[58] In Guatemala, turnout for the runoff election for president in 1990 was 42.9 percent of registered voters,[59] and in the 1993 municipal elections abstentions rose still higher to 70 percent of registered voters.[60] These tendencies toward declining voter turnout conform to a longer trend in Colombia where, according to Kline, rates of participation have been low since the 1950s. With the exception of the presidential election of 1970, they have fallen within the range of 34–50 percent of the electorate. In the March 1994 congressional election, abstention rates reached 70 percent.[61]

Public opinion in these countries also explicitly evaluates the performance of democracies and democratic institutions poorly. In 1989, ten years after the transfer of power to civilians, public opinion in Guayaquil and Quito was sharply divided about the desirability of democracy and its ability to solve problems. Less than a majority of respondents to polls conducted by the Institute of Social Studies and Public Opinion in Guayaquil found democracy preferable to, and better at solving problems than, dictatorship.[62] Five years later, in April 1994, 64 percent believed democracy was not the best form of government for Ecuador, and 80 percent felt that political parties did not serve the public interest.[63] Eighty percent of respondents in Quito were without strong party loyalties (up from 38 percent in 1989).[64] In Brazil in late 1993, in the midst of a corruption scandal, according to Lamounier, 55 percent of a national sample interviewed by DataFolha rated the Congress as "bad" or "very bad," 31 percent as "fair," and only 8 percent as "good" or "excellent." The proportion saying that the country "could do well without the Congress" had climbed to 43 percent. The failure to make progress on economic and political inclusion has, moreover, fueled rebellions in Guatemala, El Salvador, and even Colombia that certainly threaten democracy. Less dramatic but also potentially destabilizing protest has also been registered in Paraguay, according to Diego Abente Brun, in his chapter in this collection, as a result of long-repressed social demands.[65]

In sum, if securing the attachment of politically powerful traditional elites to the democratization process has accelerated the timetable of transition to democracy and in essence solved "the Argentine problem," it has also hindered democratic governance by undermining the effectiveness and accountability of democracy. With traditional elites retaining positions of preeminence as a result of military rule and the democratization process, and exercising that preeminence in the political parties and the legislature, a new series of problems has been created: "façade" democracies (the "Central American problem"); policy immobilism (the "Colombian problem"); the conversion of political parties into vehicles for the private use of oligarchies (the "Brazilian problem"); and the concomitant alarming reduction in popular political participation.

## Conclusions and Recommendations

This chapter has suggested that the challenges of democratic governance are qualitatively different and immeasurably more severe in countries that exhibit "high" levels of traditional political elite persistence than in those with "medium" and "low" levels. In the former set of countries, expedient alliances formed between democratic oppositions and traditional elites to exit from military rule that often postponed or abandoned outright the reform of social policy, agrarian structures, political institutions, and constitutions and that awarded the perquisite of filling government posts to the forces of the traditional right, have temporarily quieted the real divisions between elite and nonelite and rural and urban citizens. However, these simmer beneath the surface. Without sufficient guarantees to participate in the electoral process and a credible expectation of sharing power, the Left could turn to open rebellion, as it did in Guatemala since the 1950s, in Colombia in the 1970s and 1980s, and in El Salvador in the 1980s. The attachment of the Right to democracy is no less secure.

Democratic regimes in Latin America today inevitably find themselves attempting to navigate a treacherous course between the Scylla of confrontation and the Charybdis of accommodation. Confronting traditional elites surely risks the familiar military coup, or what O'Donnell has called a "sudden death" for democracy.[66] However, the persistent strength of traditional forces permitted by accommodationist strategies also poses a risk that democracy will expire via the steady erosion of its effectiveness and accountability, leading ultimately to the rejection of democratic institutions on the part of mass publics—a "slow death" different from that envisioned by O'Donnell but just as final. Is there a way out of this dilemma? Can the power and antidemocratic tendencies of traditional political elites be attenuated without pushing them to adopt antisystem behavior as they did so often in the past in response to developmental-populist coalitions?

A probing examination of the role played by traditional elites in the early years of democratic rule suggests that where political institutions and procedures are relatively unfettered by negotiated settlements and where the nonelite democratic opposition is strong, and traditional elites must learn to defend their interests in competition with a credible Left in the electoral arena, the prospects are much improved for their positive contribution to the process of democratization. Where, on the other hand, traditional forces are relatively unrestrained and their hegemony uncontested, they pose grave threats indeed to democracy. This is especially true where they are still closely allied with military establishments. If this argument is correct, negotiation and delayed or gradual reform is not a panacea to consolidate democracies plagued by traditional power structures. More important than pacing reform to conform to a gradual schedule is to strengthen the forces with which they must negotiate.

I conclude with two sets of recommendations for reform. The first is to reduce the economic power of traditional elites and strengthen nonelite groups through poverty alleviation, not asset redistribution. The recent history of Latin America shows that measures that threaten to harm the economic interests of traditional elites are the first that will provoke them to antisystem behavior, but that traditional power holders will not today bring down Center-Left governments that respect their economic interests. Although the government of Peronist Carlos Menem in Argentina has done little that a government of the Right would not have, that of the Concertación in Chile has. Since the transition to civilian rule, the governing Center-Left coalition of Christian Democrats and Socialists in Chile has pursued policies that have not redistributed assets but that, through taxation (and sound fiscal policy) have improved social services and reduced poverty. With the economy growing, there is little basis for traditional elite discontent. Such a strategy could serve as a model for reform in other countries in which traditional elites can be electorally defeated but not discounted.

The second proposal is to curb traditional power structures through political reform. My recommendation here falls into three parts. The first is to pursue whatever steps are politically feasible to deepen the wedge between militaries and traditional elites created by the most recent episodes of military rule. This proposal may ultimately be as important as the more frequently sounded ones to reduce military budgets and assert civilian control over both military and police forces.

Second, priority should be assigned to enacting ordinary and constitutional legislation that guarantees formal democracy. Most obviously, legislation that supports coercive labor systems and that limits the ability of popular classes to organize for either economic or political goals should be repealed. In many countries, a fuller democracy will require substantial judicial reform and guarantees of physical safety, as most of the authors of the country studies in this collection have stressed. In other countries, a revision of electoral laws may be required. What makes sense in contexts of electoral dominance by traditional power holders is to revise electoral laws in such a way as to expand the opportunities for political representation of other social groups in decision-making arenas. Where the opportunity still presents itself, it is important to represent the Right, but not to overrepresent it. If traditional elites exercise their strongest authority at the regional and local levels of the political system, extreme caution should be exercised before proceeding with reforms that would *decentralize* power and decision making. The best chance to advance democratizing reforms may be at the national level.

Third, once formal institutional rules are made more democratic, the most important task is to strengthen the avenues for political participation and representation, in particular political parties that speak to the issues and defend the interests of their constituents, whether defined by social class, ethnic group, gender, or neighborhood, in ways that enhance democratic accountability. The corollary to this recommendation is to decrease, by whatever means, the strains of personalism, clientelism, and corruption that prevail in precisely those countries in which traditional elites are strongest. Contrary to the oft-heard claim that clientelism and democracy are perfectly compatible and that clientelism can even be a means by which disadvantaged classes gain access to state resources, recent trends toward rising voter disillusion in Brazil, Ecuador, and elsewhere in Latin America have shown that the excessive resort to patronage politics has weakened parties, damaged the competence of governments to manage the economy, and eroded public faith in democratic institutions. It is no longer only the naysayers who ask if democracy can survive such distortions of political representation and governance.

Traditional political elites are certainly not the only ones who dip their hands into public coffers to buy votes. But this practice, a prop of the traditional order in the modern polity, has been the only basis upon which they have created parties, run electoral campaigns, and governed in the formal democracies in which they enjoy their greatest strength, and it has gravely threatened democratic governance. Alternative methods of representation that can safeguard, to a reasonable degree, the interests of elites without sacrificing the form and substance of democracy are urgently needed at this time. If adopting these reforms jeopardizes a quick death for democracy, it may be the case that probability will increase rather than decrease over time, and there may be no better time to strike than now.

# 5

# *Indigenous Protest and Democracy in Latin America*

## Deborah J. Yashar

On New Year's Day 1994 the Chiapas rebellion captivated Mexico and the rest of the Americas. Shocked by the well-planned and executed military maneuvers, analysts were left wondering where this movement had come from, whom it represented, and what it wanted. Yet, from a comparative perspective, the Chiapas uprising represents perhaps only the most dramatic and internationally followed example of organizing within indigenous communities. Indeed, in the 1980s and 1990s, there has been a rise in indigenous organizing and mobilizing in Latin America, including international campaigns for the five hundred years of resistance and the 1993 Year of Indigenous People, the emergence of Indian organizations in Ecuador, Bolivia, Colombia, and Guatemala, the rise of autonomy movements in Panama and Nicaragua, the 1993 election of Víctor Hugo Cárdenas, a prominent indigenous leader, as vice-president of Bolivia, and the awarding of the 1992 Nobel Peace Prize to Rigoberta Menchú, a Mayan Indian leader from Guatemala.

The codevelopment of the increasing organization of indigenous communities and the hemispheric embrace of political democracy in the 1980s and 1990s present the opportunity and responsibility to reevaluate the relationship between ethnic cleavages and democracy in Latin America.[1] Why have indigenous communities become increasingly politicized along ethnic lines in recent years? What are the conditions under which strong ethnic identities are compatible with, and even supportive of, democracy?[2]

This chapter argues that these movements are primarily a response to the twin emergence of delegative democracies and neoliberal reforms.[3] Democratization in the 1980s provided greater space for the *public* articulation of ethnic identities, demands, and conflicts. Nonetheless, indigenous communities have experienced a new stage of political disenfranchisement as states fail to uphold the individual rights associated with liberal democracy just as neoliberal reforms dismantle state institutions that had previously extended legal corporate class rights, representation, and social welfare. Building on social networks left in place by prior rounds of political and religious organizing, indigenous groups have mobilized across communities to demand rights and resources denied them as Indians.

Confronted with the lost momentum of traditional leftist parties and popular movements that have yet to define a political vision that resonates in indigenous communities, newly mobilized indigenous communities have organized and gained a new domestic and international presence. Yet, in contrast to the examples of the former Yugoslavia, Sri Lanka, Rwanda, and Burundi, indigenous mobilization in Latin America has rarely been a prelude to civil war struggles to capture the state; Sendero Luminoso, the guerilla movement in Peru, is the obvious exception, although even here the combatants do not see their struggle as part of an ethnic conflict. Rather, Latin America's indigenous movements have largely demanded greater democracy, including greater political representation in and access to national political institutions as well as greater local autonomy.

This chapter constitutes, therefore, a springboard for preliminary ruminations and discussions about a topic that has received scant attention within the Latin American context. It is sure to overgeneralize and misrepresent, particularly given the multiple meanings associated with ethnicity and democracy. These are problems associated with delineating ethnic identities, boundaries, and relations in the different Latin American countries, and analyzing the intersection of ethnic and democratic politics from a macrocomparative perspective when very little work to date has explored these issues in a systematic, reliable, and crossnational framework. Yet, against the history of exclusion, denial, and repression of Latin American indigenous peoples coupled with the knowledge that the failure to address ethnic cleavages elsewhere has unleashed a politics of xenophobia and a xenophobia of violence, it is important to begin addressing the future of democracy in pluri-ethnic states in Latin America. I begin with two descriptive overviews of the ways in which Latin American states have interpreted ethnic relations, followed by a discussion of the recent mobilizations within and by indigenous communities. The final two sections explain why these movements have emerged and how to bridge ethnic cleavages in a way consonant with greater indigenous representation and the deepening of democracy.

## The "Indian Question" in Latin America

The history of ethnic relations in Latin America has been one of violence, subordination, denial, and assimilation.[4] With the arrival of Columbus and the ensuing conquest by Spanish and Portuguese settlers, indigenous communities were subsequently subordinated to the political authority of newly created Latin American states and the spiritual authority of the Catholic Church.[5] Military expeditions against the indigenous population were particularly brutal in Uruguay, Argentina, Chile, and to a lesser degree in Brazil.[6] These same countries, like many others in Latin America, enacted legislation to attract European immigration, arguing that this would improve the racial composition and therefore the economic and political prospects of the new states. Latin American states treated indigenous peoples as heathens, a threat to security, an impediment to economic development, and a source of cheap, if not free, labor. The various states enacted corresponding, if at times internally contradictory, policies to address these fears, perceptions, and goals. They killed those perceived as a threat to an emerging nation-state, isolated or denied the existence of those in remote areas, coerced populations for their labor, and promoted a policy of assimilation.

Indeed, in the twentieth century, goals of assimilation informed educational programs and state policies designed to construct a homogeneous nation.[7] Most politicians and scholars assumed that the existing state was legitimate but that the construction and identification of primary identities, be they around the mestizo nation or class, needed fixing. To this end, Latin American governments created Indian institutes to study indigenous populations—much as one would analyze national folklore—and to create the mechanisms to assimilate them into the national (read modern mestizo) population. While Brazil formed an Indian office in 1910, other Latin American countries founded these offices in the 1930s and 1940s.[8] Moreover, in 1940, the first Interamerican Indigenista Congress was held and led to the founding of the Interamerican Indigenista Institute. This policy was designed in places like Mexico, Guatemala, Peru, and Bolivia to incorporate people perceived as backward into the ranks of a new, presumably more civilized nation.[9] States encouraged indigenous men and women to discard any public display of indigenous identity, encouraged the adoption of a mestizo identity, and thus publicly encouraged miscegenation to "whiten" the population.[10]

Latin American states, therefore, promoted ethnic assimilation (and often miscegenation) to arrive at a mestizo national identity where population reflected ideology. According to positions articulated by state officials and intellectuals, mestizaje allowed for social mobility as one's ethnic status changed from indigenous (other) to mestizo (us); this process presumably depoliticized ethnic cleavages. Yet, if ideologically, ethnic identity became fluid, states and landlords often continued to repress these same communities (particularly when rebellious in the face of state colonization, development plans, and repressive rural labor relations) according to a rigid understanding of the appropriate ethnic and class rights of the assimilated population.[11] Consequently, economic mobility of the newly assimilated rarely advanced beyond a relatively low ceiling.[12]

The dominant paradigms in the social sciences after World War II tended to reinforce nineteenth-century liberal discourse in Latin America regarding the primordial, transitory, and atavistic nature of indigenous groups. The social sciences, in general, tended to devalue the salience and contemporary character of ethnicity in Latin America and elsewhere. While anthropologists conducted invaluable ethnographic work in the region, much of this work drew from paradigms that assumed that ethnic identities, particularly among indigenous groups, were an expression of a past world. Whether informed by traditions as diverse as modernization or Marxist theory, scholars tended to reduce ethnic identity to primordialism. They often assumed that, with economic development and the further integration of ethnic groups into an industrializing capitalist economy, presumed atavistic identities would and should subside.[13] One anthropologist, writing in the early 1970s, stated that "Ecuador is not a country inhabited by white folk, for as an ethnic minority they only add up to scarcely one-tenth of the total population. Neither is it a country of Indians, for in that case its history would be one of regression, or else, of stratification . . . the nation is Mestizo. . . . Once the Indians enter civilized life . . . the Mestizo part of the population will be more homogeneous."[14]

Modernization theorists posited that, with economic growth, the proliferation of technology, and social mobilization, individuals would transcend ethnic ties and become, among other things, more individuated, secular, and eventually more committed to the nation-state. Marxists, however, tended to argue that, with the increasing impoverishment associated with capitalism and the increasing integration of ethnic groups into the labor market, primary ethnic identities would subside as economically exploited individuals realized that the more salient and liberating corporate identity would revolve around class.[15] In short, the expression of ethnic identities was seen as a problem. In practice and ideology, states and intellectuals identified ethnicity and the ethnic problem as coterminous with the indigenous and the indigenous problem. From this perspective, getting rid of Indians (through assimilation or repression) was necessary to arrive at and sustain modernity on the basis of a mestizo nation.

## The Rise in Indigenous Organizing and the Articulation of New Agendas

Against this backdrop, indigenous men and women seem to disappear, responding passively to the incursion of new states, markets, and clerics whose very purpose to undermine the political structures, economies, and cosmologies of indigenous groups remains unchallenged. Yet these assumptions regarding the passivity and obsolescence of indigenous peoples have been repeatedly challenged, particularly in the 1980s and 1990s. First, while economic development has often occurred at the expense of indigenous communities, and while many indigenous men and women outwardly assimilated into mestizo culture—severing or weakening ties with their local communities and practices—self-identified indigenous communities have survived, albeit as with all communities, they have changed over time.

While current, reliable, crossnational data is hard to find, it is commonly stated that approximately four hundred ethnic groups live in Latin America, composing 35–40 million people, 6–10 percent of the total Latin American population, and an estimated 10 percent of the world's more than 300 million indigenous peoples. The Andean region and Mesoamerica claim 90 percent of Latin America's indigenous peoples. These populations, which have been largely agricultural and sedentary, are the ones that the colonists made the greatest effort to incorporate and dominate in Latin America. By contrast, the other 10 percent of indigenous peoples are located in Orinoguia, Amazonia, Mato Grosso, Gran Chaco, Araucania, and Patagonia. Their economies have historically revolved largely around hunting, gathering, fishing, and occasionally small-scale agriculture. This great diversity of regions and economies coincides with great cultural and numerical differences between indigenous communities within and across regions.[16]

It is commonly argued that indigenous peoples constitute the majority of the population in Bolivia and Guatemala, followed by substantially large populations in Ecuador, Mexico, and Peru. In absolute terms, the largest numbers of Indians reside in Mexico, followed by Peru, Guatemala, Bolivia, and Ecuador (see Table 2). The estimated, though not terribly reliable, figures in Table 2 do not reveal the ways in which indigenous communities have changed with respect to the meaning, content, scope, and form of identities, practices, or goals of indigenous peoples. Nor do these figures intend to stipulate a shared identity among indigenous peoples. Indeed, the very idea of an "indigenous people" is predicated on the arrival of "settlers" against whom indigenous peoples identify themselves and are identified. Hence there is a dual image that needs to be kept in mind. While indigenous peoples differ substantially among themselves with respect to primary identities, practices, and so on, often leading to conflict or competition, they have often shared common opposition to those who have tried to dominate them as a people.

By the mid-1980s, indigenous organizations had emerged in almost every country and had begun developing nationally and internationally recognized personas. Particularly important examples of these first organizations included the Shuar Federation of Ecuador, the Regional Council of Cauca in Colombia, and the Kataristas in Bolivia.[17] From the outside looking in, the most striking pattern seemed to be the increasingly public and vocal position articulated by indigenous leaders and

*Table 2* Estimates of Indigenous Peoples in the Americas, 1979–1991

|  | Estimated Population | % of Total Population |
| --- | --- | --- |
| Argentina | 477,000 | 1.5 |
| Belize | 15,000 | 9.1 |
| Bolivia | 4,985,000 | 71.2 |
| Brazil | 325,000 | 0.2 |
| Canada | 892,000 | 0.8 |
| Chile | 767,000 | 5.9 |
| Colombia | 708,000 | 2.2 |
| Costa Rica | 19,000 | 0.6 |
| Ecuador | 3,753,000 | 37.5 |
| El Salvador | 500,000 | 10.0 |
| French Guyana | 1,000 | 1.2 |
| Guatemala | 5,423,000 | 60.3 |
| Guyana | 29,000 | 3.9 |
| Honduras | 168,000 | 3.4 |
| Mexico | 10,537,000 | 12.4 |
| Nicaragua | 66,000 | 1.7 |
| Panama | 194,000 | 8.0 |
| Paraguay | 101,000 | 2.5 |
| Peru | 8,097,000 | 38.6 |
| Surinam | 11,000 | 2.9 |
| United States | 1,959,000 | 0.8 |
| Uruguay | 0 | 0.0 |
| Venezuela | 290,000 | 1.5 |

*Source:* Stefano Varese, "Think Locally, Act Globally," in North American Congress on Latin America, *Report on the Americas: The First Nations, 1492–1992* 25, no. 3 (1991): 16; computed from Enrique Mayer and Elio Masferrer, "La población indígena en América en 1978," *América Indígena* 39, no. 2 (1979), World Bank, *Informe sobre el desarrollo mundial 1991*, and United States and Canada census. A slightly different set of numbers is provided in James W. Wilkie, Carlos Alberto Contreras, and Christof Anders Weber, eds., *Statistical Abstract of Latin America*, vol. 30, pt.1 (Los Angeles: UCLA Latin American Center Publications, 1993), table 662, 150; data also derived from Mayer and Masferrer, "La población indígena," quoted in *Intercom, International Population News Magazine of the Population Reference Bureau* 9, no. 6 (1981).

the increasing scope of indigenous networks and mobilization outside of state- or party-initiated mobilization. Indeed, the organizations of largely indigenous communities were new insofar as the emerging movements generally emerged from within and across indigenous communities; publicly articulated demands in opposition to state-defined national (assimilationist) and development goals (that seemed to be taking place at the material and cultural expense of the communities); and began challenging the failure of class-based parties or peasant movements and coalitions to address the demands, practices, and identities of indigenous members.

From the inside looking out, however, the emergent organizations are quite diverse with respect to goals, strategies, representativeness, and scope of networks. These differences are played out within and between indigenous organizations over the primacy of material versus cultural orientation of the organization and its demands, alliances with popular movements and political parties, and tactics for change.

Despite the diversity within coalitions of indigenous peoples, one can discern an emerging agenda. In what follows, I discuss four inter-related demands[18]: land rights, human and civil rights, spaces for greater political participation, and rights to political and cultural autonomy. It is important to reiterate that not all indigenous groups work toward each of these goals addressed here, nor are all indigenous groups working in coalition. Indeed, as with any political organization, there are internal debates over goals, allies, strategies, tactics, and related conflicts. Rather, in what follows, I paint a canvas in broad brush strokes to highlight issues that have emerged in one form or another in various parts of the region.

One of the most pressing and pervasive issues articulated by indigenous groups has revolved around land or property rights. Demands have included agrarian reform, land titling, and territorial demarcation.[19] In Mexico, Guatemala, and Peru, for example, a number of indigenous groups have mobilized for agrarian reform. Associated demands also include access to credit, technology, and other agricultural resources. In each of these three countries, the state alienated land from the indigenous population and coerced indigenous communities into providing labor for plantations, mining, and so on. Subsequent land reforms did not have a lasting effect on these communities. In Guatemala the 1952 land reform was largely reversed with the 1954 counterreform. In Mexico the land reform of the 1930s seems to have had the least effect in regions with the largest indigenous populations, amply documented in the discussions of the Chiapas rebellion. In Peru the 1960s land reform was not implemented evenly in all regions.[20]

Land reform in these cases has historically been articulated and understood largely as a class issue—to redistribute land to peasants or small farmers—even if "objectively" the beneficiaries have included a large number or even a majority of indigenous men and women. Moreover, traditional land reform projects have looked at land reform as a way to distribute private property to individuals rather than to indigenous corporate communities.[21] More contemporary indigenous movements, however, have demanded land on the basis of ethnic, community, and class-based identities.

Indigenous movements in Argentina, Chile, Costa Rica, and Panama, which are considerably smaller in both absolute and relative terms to those in Mexico, Guatemala, and Peru, have largely demanded land titling. For example, in April 1993 approximately 7,000 Kuna and 15,000 Embera Indians in Panama organized to protest the slow deliberations of a land titling bill by blockading the highway and briefly taking hostage the governor of the province of Panama. While the Kuna and Embera are each demanding around 180,000 hectares of land, the Guaymí and Buglé are demanding title to around 11 million square kilometers.[22]

Land reform and titling defer to the state to arbitrate and regulate property rights. However, other demands for land rights have emerged which challenge the state's right either to influence all political relations within a certain territory or to assume property rights to natural resources. Demands for territorial demarcation, as in Brazil, Colombia, and Panama, and for rights to natural resources within a given territory, ultimately refer to issues of political and cultural autonomy in addition to material well-being. With these ideas in mind, the 1991 Colombian Constitution referred to indigenous lands as "territorial entities" in article 286; according to this article, existing political authority structures assume governing capacity, including criminal and civil jurisdiction, in these territories; moreover, the territories are responsible for determining their own development strategy and for administering public resources as if they were municipalities. At the time of this writing, complaints have emerged within the Colombian indigenous community that the actual distribution of these territories remains undecided and that the regulation of disputes between the national government and the future territorial entities remains unclear.[23]

These demands for a clearly demarcated territory and for control over the resources contained within those boundaries have become particularly salient as developers, ranchers, settlers, poachers, and the like increasingly penetrate areas that previously had been the de facto home of indigenous communities, as in the Amazon. In Ecuador and in Chiapas, Mexico, indigenous groups have protested the acquisition of titles over land and resources acquired by foreign oil companies. This increasing encroachment on Indian lands has not only resulted in the decline in indigenous-held territories but also in the decline of populations as violence, environmental destruction, and new diseases threaten indigenous people residing in these areas. The human rights commission of the American Anthropological Association, referring to the Awa-Guaja Indians in Amazonia, forecasts that they face extinction.[24]

In addition to land-related demands, a second set of demands implores the existing government to uphold and protect human and civil rights. In Mexico, Guatemala, and Peru, the governments have often orchestrated or turned their back on human rights abuses targeting indigenous peoples. Human rights groups have documented nationwide abuse of indigenous communities in Guatemala and Peru. In these two countries, military and paramilitary practice have tended to suspect indigenous communities as sympathetic to, if not members of, the guerrillas. In Mexico, human rights abuses occur in regions with large indigenous populations, as in Chiapas and Oaxaca.[25] Stavenhagen notes that while the constitutions of many Latin American countries have stipulated the juridical equality of its citizens, that in fact indigenous men and women do not experience a continual respect for human rights.[26] These human rights abuses obviously mock the rights constitutive of democracy.

A third set of demands addresses issues of political representation in national politics. The constitutions of Latin America, in fact, do not directly discriminate against Indians as individuals (although they have been discriminated against historically through literacy requirements for suffrage). However, legislation has often treated Indians as wards of the state. For example, despite comparatively liberal Brazilian legislation, indigenous men and women are often discussed in statutes referring to legal minors and the juridically handicapped.[27] Pedro Balcúmez, a Mayan Indian leader with the Consejo de Organizaciones Maya stated: "We do not want protection but effective participation in society and the economy."[28]

In the 1990s there have been scattered albeit important advances in indigenous participation in national positions. Indigenous leaders have assumed prominent national positions including the 1993 election of Bolivian vice-president Víctor Hugo Cárdenas;[29] the Guatemalan minister of education, Celestino Tay Coyoy, as the first Mayan cabinet appointment in that country; and indigenous representation in Colombia's Constituent and Legislative Assembly.[30] The inclusion of indigenous representatives has been a significant advance over the near, if not total, exclusion in the past of indigenous participation at the national level. However, electoral participation has served to highlight the diversity of ethnic groups (in countries such as Ecuador and Bolivia) and the salience of often conflicting agendas. Indeed, in the significant example of the Bolivian vice-president, he was able to win office by forming an electoral alliance with the MNR (National Revolutionary Movement), leaving some to question the integrity and endurance of the vice-president's party.

Finally, indigenous communities have called for autonomy and self-determination, widely used concepts that in fact mask a diversity of demands from cultural to political to developmental. Calls for cultural autonomy and self-determination are reacting against the assimilationist policies discussed earlier. They are reacting against the image projected abroad by tourist offices of quaint Indians marketing ethnic artifacts. Against pressures to assimilate and folkloric images presented by tourist offices,[31] many indigenous leaders have begun to define their own culture, both for themselves and others. Hence, in Guatemala, for example, a number of indigenous groups have emerged to promote cultural autonomy, integrity, and respect that the state has traditionally denied them. Mayan priests have come forth to announce and to celebrate Mayan cosmology and history, as illustrated by the 1990 gathering at Iximché; projects promote indigenous language study; women who had stopped wearing indigenous clothing have begin to wear *traje*. These demands and actions highlight the changing boundaries of identity that are transcending localized communities to embrace a broader Mayan identity. Hence women who have chosen to wear *huipiles* again now often do so irrespective of the community from which their families originate. This seems to be the case particularly for women who now live in the city.

Demands for political autonomy present, along with demands for territory, the most dramatic challenge to Latin American states as some communities want indigenous jurisdiction over a given territory, as in the Nicaraguan case of the Miskito and the Colombian case of territorial entities. Finally, calls for increased autonomy over and input into development projects have taken place through international and national forums. Throughout the region, indigenous communities have applied for and some have received funding from international nongovernmental organizations committed to local development projects. Moreover, indigenous communities have called for increased access to participation in state development agencies.

In Chile, for example, indigenous communities have attempted to increase access to state programs and funding for the increased economic, political, and cultural autonomy of the Mapuche (160,000), Aymara (170,000), and Easter Islanders (3,000). According to the *Latin American Weekly Report* (February 11, 1993), Chilean Indians acquired "a national development corporation of their own, a fund for land and water, and a fund for 'ethno-development,' to help them preserve their language and their culture. Already one Mapuche organization is pressing for more official recognition that they are a 'people,' not just another sector of society."

Demands for recognition as a people have raised legal eyebrows, for fear that recognition as a people is the first step toward secession or a threat to the power of the national state.[32] This might be the case among a few groups, but it appears to be uncommon. Miguel Sucuquí, a Mayan organizer in the governing board of the Council of the Ethnic Communities "We Are All Equal" (CERJ), a largely indigenous human rights organization, for example, said:

> So our most immediate task is organization and unification, and this must be done on the basis of our culture and our traditions. With that unification, we Mayans would have an enormous capacity to build our own life within the Guatemalan state. We are not forming a state within another state—we want that to be well understood. But were there freedom of organization, of expression, of religion, the Mayan people could unite, strengthen ourselves, and create the proper institutional expressions for sustaining our lives as a people.[33]

This set of demands around land, human and civic rights, political representation, and political autonomy has been articulated at the national as well as international level. Indigenous groups have gained access to international forums where they have influenced political agendas. The United Nations, for example, created in 1983 a working group on indigenous peoples that has included representation from member states and indigenous organizations to draft a declaration of indigenous rights; this working group declared 1993 the Year of Indigenous People. Indigenous peoples have formed transnational organizations such as the South American Indian Council, the International Indian Treaty Council, and most dramatically for the Campaign for Five Hundred Years of Indigenous, Black, and Popular Resistance that culminated in 1992. And they have gained a presence in international environmental movements, displayed with fanfare at the 1992 Earth Summit in Rio de Janeiro, Brazil.[34] Indigenous communities have also found an institutional space within transnational environmental groups, which have worked in coalition to promote equitable and sustainable development.[35]

## Why the Increase in Indigenous Mobilization?

Why have indigenous communities mobilized in increasing numbers and scope in the past decade? Given the widely divergent types of groups that we have discussed and the as yet limited comparative information available on ethnic relations in Latin America, the following comments are initial observations that form part of an ongoing research project.

### Ethnic and Class Conflict

It is a given in Latin America that indigenous populations experience ethnic discrimination, marginalization, material deprivation, and economic exploitation. "World Bank and other development agencies indicate that Indians remain the poorest and most destitute of the region's population, with the highest rate of infant mortality and childhood malnutrition and the lowest rates of literacy and schooling."[36] Carlos Fuentes, speaking of the inextricable fusion of ethnic and class identities among the Mayas in Chiapas, said: "What has an extremely long lifespan is the sequence of poverty, injustice, plunder and violation in which, since the sixteenth century, live the Indians who are peasants and the peasants who are Indians."[37]

These structural conditions have disadvantaged indigenous communities for centuries and constitute a constant source of conflict and object of change. Resistance has assumed multiple forms from sporadic rebellions to everyday forms of resistance embedded in dances, stories, and rituals that are an integral part of indigenous communities.[38] The dance of the conquest, for example, has been amply studied by anthropologists who have highlighted the ways in which the dance is a vivid reminder of an ongoing process of colonization, anger toward the landlord, and expression of resistance. Similarly, the Popul Vuj weaves many complex tapestries of meaning, one of which is the oft-repeated phrase: "May we all rise up, may no one be left behind." Violent resistance and everyday forms of resistance against these conditions will continue so long as sharp discrepancies between ethnic and class communities continue to be delineated so sharply.

Yet, looking at these structures alone cannot explain why in recent years there has been a continentwide rise in indigenous organizing along ethnic-based demands. Indeed, if we want to explain the recent increase in indigenous organizing, we need to look beyond these constant causes to the new conditions that have led these dominated groups to resort to what Albert O. Hirschman has called voice (in its legal and violent forms), as opposed to exit or loyalty.[39]

## Democratic and Neoliberal Reforms: The Changing Role of the State

The recent round of democratization has created the legal space for the expression of new identities as the resort to repression has become more problematic, although certainly not altogether absent. Indigenous groups have occupied these legally sanctioned spaces, which are not always respected by the militaries of the different countries. Indigenous groups have assumed this space particularly in the wake of popular movements and leftist political parties, many of which had played an important role in anti-authoritarian struggles but rarely succeeded in proposing viable political and economic alternatives.[40]

Yet, if indigenous communities have largely applauded the recent wave of democratization and efforts at demilitarization, they have remained wary of other efforts to dismantle the state in response to neoliberal reforms.[41] Indeed, the 1980s and 1990s have witnessed a change in state-society relations in ways that have affected indigenous communities in contradictory and often adverse ways. As Latin American states dismantle many of the social programs, they take away corporate benefits and representation that had previously defined state relations with indigenous communities. The move toward privatization, for example, has affected de jure and de facto indigenous lands. In Mexico the state's decision to withdraw protection of *ejidos* has generated anxiety, and rightfully so, over indigenous communities' loss of previously communal lands to large agribusiness. In Brazil the opening up to foreign direct investment has resulted in an increased number of developers (and illegal poachers) who have encroached on Amazonian lands that had (often by default) effectively been the domain of indigenous communities. In Ecuador, austerity measures, agrarian development laws, and oil exploration threaten indigenous land tenure and the environmental standards of the region.

Many indigenous leaders, alongside others in the popular movement, therefore, interpret the consequences of neoliberal reforms as an assault on physical, material, and cultural well-being. For example, efforts by Ecuadorian president Sixto Durán-Ballén to pass an agricultural development law prompted widespread protests by the National Confederation of Indigenous Nationalities of Ecuador (CONAIE), which opposed the law on the grounds that it would break up communally owned land and that it sold water rights. The threat of nationwide protests led the government to amend the law to limit the sale of land by communities and to allow for the expropriation of private property if carried out for a social reason, among other things.[42] CONAIE has also participated in coalitions with workers in general strikes to protest neoliberal reforms and the granting of further oil exploration licenses. They have called for study of the environmental impact of any future oil exploration and for research into alternative development strategies.[43]

With the implementation of neoliberal reforms, the corporate basis of state-society relations is being renegotiated. Rather than finding economic interests articulated through corporate laws and through more populist parties, indigenous peasants (and workers alike) are facing a situation in which social welfare issues are not being addressed by the state or through political parties. This has weakened representation for indigenous communities that had previously articulated demands (however feebly) with the state as peasants, as in Mexico and Bolivia.

Finally, the neoliberal concern for the individual in theory has not always translated into concern for the individual in practice. O'Donnell has analyzed this phenomenon in his discussions of the uneven ways in which democracy is experienced in Latin America. This is in large part because efforts to downsize an overbearing and inefficient state have often neglected to strengthen those parts of the state that are necessary for the effective functioning of democracy. Indeed, the uneven practices of judicial and bureaucratic branches of the state have been particularly disadvantageous to indigenous peoples who often remain subject to the political power of local and regional elites.[44]

In the absence of state reforms, individuals cannot necessarily practice their theoretically state-sanctioned civil and political rights that the new democratic regimes claim to uphold; unsurprisingly, the excluded tend to include the indigenous, the impoverished, and women. In this sense, the dismantling of corporate forms of representation and protection, without establishing more effective forms of individual representation and mediation, has left many indigenous communities and individuals without effective access to state resources and with an unreliable judicial and bureaucratic state apparatus. This has proven particularly disadvantageous for the poor, indigenous, and women.

## Building upon Existing Organizational Networks

Indigenous organizations appear to have mobilized against changes in state and social relations by building upon and drawing strength from existing institutional networks left by groups that had previously organized in rural areas. The Catholic Church, followed by peasant union and leftist parties, has left a particularly significant institutional legacy.[45] The church, alongside the military, has traditionally been seen as one of two institutions that most successfully penetrated rural areas and historically attempted to control indigenous areas. As is now well known, following Vatican II and inspired by liberation theology, representatives of the church promoted new forms of organization within and across urban and rural communities.

Indigenous lay leaders, drawing on consciousness raising, community networks, strategizing, and the legitimacy and resources of the church, emerged to promote community organizations. These originally revolved around material struggles within a Christian framework and were often subsumed within class-based popular movements and leftist parties. They also provided a forum for subsequently strengthening indigenous networks and developing a generation of indigenous leaders with authority often within and beyond traditional community-based authority structures. This was clearly the case in Guatemala and Mexico and likely played a role in other countries inspired by liberation theology or with previously strong leftist movements or parties. I suggest that indigenous communities particularly capitalized on these institutional legacies with the recent wave of democratization and neoliberal reforms.

## The New International Moment

While international communication among organized indigenous groups began in the early 1970s, it accelerated in the late 1980s with the approach of 1992 and with the increased concern of transnational organizations and lending agencies for equitable and sustainable development, environmental protection, and human rights.[46] On the one hand, the struggles to redefine 1992 as five hundred years of resistance rather than five hundred years of celebration sparked continentwide conferences that grew in size and scope with each meeting. The meetings provided the forum for indigenous leaders to gather together and in the process appears to have both heightened and deepened awareness of an "Indian" identity *shared* by indigenous groups throughout the Americas. Moreover, it increased networks between and within indigenous communities. In response to a question as to whether Mayan rites had become more widespread or more public in recent years, Miguel Sucuquí of the CERJ said:

Actually, it is both. . . . But when Spain and the Latinamerican countries started to make a lot of noise about celebrating the Columbus Quincentenial [*sic*], this caused a restlessness, a curiosity, in our people, and an investigation of the Mayan religion began, and more people began to consult with priests and elders about what had happened. The message of these leaders has been received by the people with great interests, and our Mayan religious practices are being revived publicly, and are being accepted by our people.[47]

On the other hand, international organizations and lending agencies have become more receptive to and supportive of indigenous groups and their demands. Indigenous people have gained an increased presence within the United Nations and its working groups. International coalitions with nongovernmental organizations and advocacy groups have significantly increased access to material resources, information, and the media. Moreover, international lending agencies have created and strengthened new programs that have increased funding possibilities for indigenous groups. Lending programs that include environmental and democratic conditionalities have also created new political opportunities for indigenous groups to pressure their respective governments.[48] Alison Brysk notes, however, the very severe limitations for promoting domestic citizenship when work is focused on the international arena.[49] Local- and national-level organizing continues to be an essential component in indigenous struggles for more equitable citizenship rights.

## Deepening Democracy as Part of Bridging Ethnic Cleavages

Increased indigenous mobilization coincided with the hemispheric transition from authoritarian rule. However, by the end of the 1980s and the beginning of the 1990s, many of the countries that had ethnically heterogeneous societies experienced political closure. Witness, for example, the successful coup attempts in Peru and Haiti and failed ones in Guatemala and Venezuela.[50] Yet it would be foolhardy to conclude that ethnically heterogeneous societies and political democracy are incompatible.[51] Indeed, if we assume that a strong civil society is important to democracy, then we should embrace many of these mobilizations while thinking about the creation of institutional arenas for expressing dissent and conflict as well as consent and compromise.

To return to the final question raised at the beginning of this chapter, what are the conditions under which this increased articulation of indigenous communities is compatible with, and even supportive of, democratic practices and consolidation? The following suggests ways in which we need to reconceptualize citizenship in Latin America while looking at institutional mechanisms for creating more participatory, representative, and durable political democracies in ethnically heterogeneous societies.

### Reconceptualizing the Nation

First, at an ideological level, Latin American states need to begin by reconceptualizing the very idea of a homogeneous mestizo nation. As Stefano Varese has noted, the emergence of indigenous movements and their denunciation of assimilationist policies challenge the conception in Latin America that a mestizo nation does or should correspond to the existing states.[52] Indeed, the very process of nation building in the late nineteenth and most of the twentieth century is being fundamentally questioned as people begin to talk about difference and equality. The challenge becomes to articulate a way in which democracy can emerge and endure in multi-ethnic states.

Rustow, in his pathbreaking essay, argued that one needs a sense of national unity to achieve democracy: it provides the sense of loyalty that glues the pieces together in the face of societal conflict.[53] Yet it is questionable if one needs "national" loyalty or loyalty to a "state" to achieve and sustain democracy. If Latin American indigenous communities are to develop or sustain commitment to democratic regimes, then multi-ethnic states need to revise the ideology of a mestizo nation to account for the more diverse composition of a given country's citizenry. This is particularly the case given that citizenship rights in practice are often derivative of whether one is conceived of as part of the nation. In some countries, such as Colombia, Paraguay, Mexico, and momentarily in Peru, constitutional changes have been made.[54] These are important steps.

### Rethinking the Institutions of Political Representation

A discursive and constitutional recognition of a pluri-ethnic population is an important beginning. However, without institutional changes, it remains a symbolic advance. Indeed, the new Latin American governments need to redesign political institutions in creative ways to allow for greater and more effective political representation. In this spirit, I tentatively highlight issues of institutional design that merit additional research and analysis.

How does one provide for democratic representation and governance in ethnically divided societies in which ethnic cleavages seem increasingly politicized? This is largely a question of who is to be represented and how. In the case of indigenous communities, this question encompasses the dilemma of how to balance respect for individual and corporate representation.

A first and older set of arguments originally called for consociationalism. The simplified argument was that elite representation of the major ethnic groups needed to be institutionally guaranteed; the ensuing "cartel of elites" would defuse conflict over who controls the state while increasing the spaces for discussion and compromise over issues that had been particularly contentious. In recent years, this approach has been criticized on the following grounds.[55] First, this political arrangement assumes the primordial nature of ethnic identity and institutionalizes these very differences. Second, a political cartel of elites can and does lead to antidemocratic behavior; in turn, it inhibits democratic participation by groups whose identities and interests are assumed rather than expressed. The cases of Venezuela and Colombia, which implemented consociational-like solutions (although ones that revolved around partisan rather than ethnic identities), have highlighted the limits of this kind of institutional approach, as has Lebanon. Finally, it assumes that ethnic conflicts are vertically organized with varying ethnic groups vying for state power. Yet in Latin America, as we have seen, ethnic groups overwhelmingly remain horizontally organized and geographically concentrated, often seeking input or power over more local or regional politics rather than control over national politics.

A different set of arguments has highlighted the need to redesign district boundaries to increase indigenous electoral representation. The mechanisms for doing so vary according to the district magnitude of electoral regions, whether and how these regions coincide with ethnic groups, and the methods for calculating representation (proportional representation versus plurality voting). Redesigning electoral boundaries to coincide with indigenous territories or majority indigenous populations should compel politicians, be they indigenous or not, to begin to respond to varied demands as they are articulated by communities in a given district.

An alternative way of envisioning increased representation and participation within ethnically heterogeneous societies, therefore, is to decentralize political control. Decentralization can accommodate calls for more localized control and cultural autonomy while maintaining centralized decision making over issues that affect the country as a whole. While this boundary between local and national issues is clearly a source of tension itself, a more decentralized system at least allows for a more heterogeneous and changing vision of identity, provides more control over regional political economies, and might increase local participation.[56] This type of system would require tax reform to protect against the increasing economic disparity between regions and to ensure relatively comparable provision of social services. However, for this system to function differently than it already does, say in Mexico, we need to look at reforming clientelist control over regional politics that occurs through corrupt party systems, privatized power holdings, and inefficacious state apparatuses.

## Reforming the State

In many of the countries, reforming the military institution to prevent human rights abuses, particularly in the countryside, is a necessary measure for consolidating democracy and bridging ethnic cleavages. On the one hand, human rights abuses are clearly inimical to democracy. On the other hand, military repression itself often compels groups to resort to violence as they find limited legal spaces for organizing and confront democratic practices subverted by the military's presence and practices in the countryside.

Moreover, the issue of state capacity has to be further problematized in Latin America. At the very moment that Latin American regimes are negotiating the retreat of the state from the economy, fairly little is being done to increase the transparency, efficiency, and legal practices of such central state institutions as the courts, the bureaucracy, and the police—all essential to the rule of law and one's rights as a citizen.[57] The absence of more pervasive and functional courts and bureaucracies has particularly affected indigenous sectors as they are located in areas in which political power is often exercised independently of and often in disregard for the law. As O'Donnell and Lehmann have both indicated, constitutional political equality is symbolically meaningful but substantively meaningless without the state capacity to make it a reality for sectors that have been marginalized along class, ethnic, and gender lines.[58]

Indeed, in the absence of the functioning of the rule of law, responsive bureaucracies, and military and police forms subordinated to democratically elected civilian rule, it is difficult to practice the rights of political citizenship. From this perspective, political order is not just a question of the organization and representation of social groups but also about creating states with the capacity to carry out their respective functions in the presence of competing private power centers. In the absence of effective reform, participation remains what O'Donnell has called low-intensity citizenship, contributing, I contend, to the increasing politicization of ethnic cleavages in cases such as Guatemala, Mexico, and Peru.[59]

## Material Conditions and Citizenship

T. H. Marshall, echoing a refrain from Tocqueville, argued three decades ago that the political equality associated with liberal democracy was at odds with the social and economic inequalities associated with class/capitalism. The welfare state was the response. In Europe and parts of Latin America, political coalitions sought to alleviate the poverty and conflict produced by capitalism and articulated an ideology in which the state was responsible for ensuring that its citizens sustained a certain standard of living.

With the move toward market-oriented macroeconomic reforms, and fiscal and political limits of social welfare spending, many countries have cut back on social programs originally intended to alleviate poverty. While these reform programs are associated with macroeconomic growth in some countries, they have also coincided with increasing impoverishment among the poor, a pattern that has particularly affected indigenous communities. In each of these states, this dramatic retreat of the state has compounded already serious problems related to property relations and living standards within indigenous communities.

If this increasing impoverishment continues (particularly if government measures are seen as a threat to land access or sustainable development) *and* indigenous communities conclude that they are left without legally assured and functioning state channels to influence policy and access resources, more indigenous communities will be left with little option but to take to the streets in protest, as in Ecuador and Guatemala, or turn to violence as in Mexico. From this angle, it is essential to address those "constant causes" mentioned earlier and to redress conditions of poverty and political marginalization as part of a respect for and pillar of democratic citizenship (as opposed to an explanation of rising mobilization, per se).

Here, of course, the issue of land—its distribution, titling, and political jurisdiction—reemerges as the central issue and dilemma. Where indigenous groups demand land, traditional elites are sure to bristle, and in the past this bristling has never been good for the maintenance of democracy. At a minimum, therefore, countries with strong elites need to find creative fora to address these issues directly, involving both indigenous communities and elites in the process of developing political solutions. Moreover, more integrated development strategies are needed that allow not only for local participation in their design, but that promote economic sustainability, credit, investment, training, and infrastructure. With this thought in mind, we return to the Chiapas uprising. As the Indigenous Revolutionary Clandestine Committee of the Zapatista General Command stated in a January 6, 1994, communiqué, its central goal after all is "making known to the Mexican people and the rest of the world the miserable conditions in which millions of Mexicans, especially we indigenous people, live and die."[60] At a minimum, governments need to democratize politics and promote an idea of citizenship in which the provision for basic economic needs is seen as a right and not a privilege.

# Notes

## Chapter 1   Incorporating the Left into Democratic Politics (Angell)

1. From an interview with José Aricó, in NACLA (North American Congress on Latin America), *Report on the Americas: The Latin American Left* 15, no. 5 (1992): 21.

2. This theme is brilliantly developed in Jorge Castañeda, *Utopia Unarmed: The Latin American Left after the Cold War* (New York: Alfred A. Knopf, 1993). The merit of this book is not only that it is an acute and perceptive account of the development of the Left in a number of Latin American countries, but that it is also a thoughtful presentation of a social democratic alternative for the Left in Mexico. For a shorter, more historical account and an extensive bibliographical essay, see Alan Angell, "The Latin American Left since the 1920s," in Leslie Bethell, ed., *The Cambridge History of Latin America*, vol. 6 (New York: Cambridge University Press, 1994).

3. Even Cuba arouses little enthusiasm on the Latin American Left any more, except as a kind of residual anti-Americanism. The exception to this statement is in Central America, where solidarity with Cuba is a much stronger force. But even here there is no longer any desire to emulate the "Cuban model."

4. Defining the Right is no less difficult. A recent authoritative book on the Right defines it as including "many different elements of society and many different political agendas. The term refers to different combinations in different contexts, but they would usually include, among others, the holders of traditional wealth in land and minerals, anti-populist businessmen and economists, the conservative wing of the established Church, anti-communist international elites and, in most countries, much of the military." Douglas Chalmers et al., eds., *The Right and Democracy in Latin America* (New York: Praeger, 1992), 4. As a working definition, this is vague and ambiguous and begs as many questions as it answers, but it does highlight the difficulty of trying to define such imprecise terms as *Left* and *Right*.

5. Marxism as an ideological force has been very influential in Mexico, for example, even at the level of government during the presidency of Cárdenas, while Marxism as an organized party has been weak and mostly marginal. As Barry Carr writes: "It would be unwise to equate the left only with formal political parties and currents. . . . There is a broader Mexican left wing tradition comprised of contradictory positions. This tradition, embracing radical nationalism, statism, syndicalism and a history of struggles against corruption and for popular democracy, is not easily identifiable with the actions of particular parties. Non party, and sometimes anti-party manifestations of these tendencies have always been present in the union movement. . . . Since the late 1960s radicalized variants of this tradition have also come to dominate the ideology and practice of social movements outside organised labour." Barry Carr, "Labor and the Left," in Kevin Middlebrook, ed., *Union Workers and the State in Mexico* (San Diego: Center for U.S.-Mexican Studies, 1991).

6. An interesting suggestion for the Left in Europe, but that could be applied to Latin America, comes from the *Economist*: "Social democrats may be better equipped with lots of small ideas than with a few big ones, so long as those ideas offer an alternative to the ideas of the right—essentially by upholding the

belief that societies should be judged not by the well-being of their richest members but by the fate of the less well off." *Economist,* July 11, 1994, 25.

7. The growth of evangelical movements can be seen as part of this same process of rejection of the traditional forms of social organization, whether it be the political parties or the Catholic Church. In Peru an important base of support for Fujimori came from the evangelical churches.

8. I am grateful to Carol Graham for raising this point.

9. Although to describe these parties as populist begs many questions, it does point to features that differentiate them from the orthodox parties of the Left. They had a stronger desire for power, enjoyed broader social appeal, and had more flexible and politically astute leaders. Examples of such parties include APRA, Acción Democrática (Democratic Action) in Venezuela, the Partido Peronista (Peronist Party) in Argentina, the Colorados (Colorados) in Uruguay, the Partido Trabalhista Brasileiro (PTB, Brazilian Workers' Party) of Vargas in Brazil, and the Liberal party of Colombia.

10. Haya de la Torre had written about Chilean socialists in 1946 that "they have contempt for democracy because it has not cost them anything to acquire it. If only they knew the real face of tyranny." After 1973 they did indeed know the real face of tyranny. Quoted in Jorge Arrate, *La fuerza de la idea socialista* (Santiago: Ediciones del Ornitorrinco, 1989), 23.

11. Figures from the chapter by Michael Coppedge in this collection. This chapter explains very well the loss of popularity of what had been a very stable two-party system, giving rise to support, on the one hand, for a new Left party, Causa R, and on the other, for an old-style populist now campaigning against the parties, Rafael Caldera.

12. But as Juan Rial points out in his chapter in this collection, the union movement in Uruguay is less centralized and disciplined than it was, and is divided between a radical and moderate faction.

13. Rial (ibid.) describes the former guerrilla movement, the Tupamaros as fully—if negatively—integrated into the democratic system and as the "bearers of a high voltage discourse that defends the main tenets of the ideology of the extreme left."

14. Quoted in an interview with Lula in *Adelante* (London) (January 1981): 6.

15. It is perhaps too easy, in a rather bleak panorama, for the Left overall to praise the PT. A cautionary note is sounded by Bolivar Lamounier: "The PT is neither a disciplined party of the old Soviet-inspired variety, nor an European style labor or social-democrat party. It is not even a relative of Argentine justicialismo, ready to follow any president as long as he comes from the peronista ranks and seems to be succeeding. Unlike the rank-and-file of these other left of center varieties, the PT's dedicated militancy is characterized by a diffuse and somewhat messianic intent of substituting a 'good' for the now defunct 'bad socialism.'" Bolivar Lamounier, "Brazilian Democracy from the 1980s to the 1990s: The Hyperactive Paralysis Syndrome" (paper for the Inter-American Dialogue, Washington, D.C., 1994), 52.

16. In the words of Denise Dresser, writing about the 1994 campaign: "Cárdenas is attempting to shed his statist image and reinvent himself as a modernizer with a social conscience. He has vehemently disavowed suggestions that he would nationalize the banks, and return to the protectionist policies of the past. What he does propose is the need for a revised role of the government in the promotion of economic growth, employment and the design of an industrial policy. Cárdenas offers continuity with 'revisions.'" Denise Dresser, "Mexico: Twilight of the Perfect Dictatorship" (paper for the Inter-American Dialogue, Washington, D.C., 1994), 10.

17. Lewis Taylor, "One Step Forward, Two Steps Back: The Peruvian *Izquierda Unida* 1980–1990," *Journal of Communist Studies* 6, no. 1 (1990): 74.

18. Quoted in James Dunkerely, "The Pacification of Central America," Institute of Latin American Studies, Research Paper no. 34 (University of London: 1993), 103.

19. Christopher Abel and Marco Palacios, "Colombia since 1958," in *The Cambridge History of Latin America* (Cambridge, 1991), 8:655.

20. Marc Chernick and Michael Jimenez, "Leftist Politics in Colombia," in Barry Carr and Steve Ellner, eds., *The Latin American Left* (Boulder, Colo.: Westview Press, 1993).

21. James Dunkerely describes the current political situation in Central America as pacification rather than democratization. He makes the point that the Left's exclusion from previous elections works to its disadvantage: "It is worth noting that even parties such as the Guatemalan Christian Democrats that have participated in deeply flawed electoral systems have thereby acquired operational skills and systems lacking in excluded organisations. Age and the attendant familiarity and loyalty have been core assets for established parties even where failure to win office has precluded the distribution of rewards or threatened a sense of impotence and exhaustion." Dunkerely, "Pacification of Central America," 48. It remains to be seen, then, how the Left in Central America will react to persistent electoral defeat if that occurs.

22. Successful stabilization policies can bring immediate popularity to an incumbent government, whatever its politics. But crucial to the long-term success of those measures are widespread poverty alleviation programs. If governments can combine both, then the outlook for the Left is poor. For a detailed and illuminating account of the Bolivian ESF (Emergency Social Fund), see Carol Graham, *Safety Nets, Politics and the Poor: Transitions to Market Economies* (Washington, D.C.: Brookings, 1994).

23. In discussion, Alex Wilde pointed out that the democratic agenda in Latin America is incomplete in the sense that some issues are not included in the debate on democracy, notably those involving distributional issues. One function of the Left, then, should be to ensure that issues elite pacts prefer not to address are put on the political agenda.

## Chapter 2 Conservative Party Politics in Latin America (Gibson)

I thank Jeanne Giraldo for her very helpful comments on the first draft of this chapter.

Parts of this article are taken from my book, *Class and Conservative Parties: Argentina in Comparative Perspective* (Baltimore: Johns Hopkins University Press, 1996).

1. Guillermo O'Donnell and Philippe C. Schmitter, *Tentative Conclusions about Uncertain Democracies*, part IV of *Transitions from Authoritarian Rule: Prospects for Democracy*, ed. Guillermo O'Donnell, Philippe C. Schmitter, and Laurence Whitehead (Baltimore: Johns Hopkins University Press, 1986), 62–63.

2. For the purposes of this analysis, conservative parties are defined as parties that draw their core constituencies from the upper strata of society and are thus defined by their social base rather than by their ideology. This helps to distinguish this type of party from other parties or movements that are often considered to be part of "the Right." In this chapter, "the Right" refers to one end of a Left-Right ideological continuum that conservatism might well share

with movements of different sociological bases. Fringe groups on the Right, quasi-fascists, or paramilitary party groups are thus excluded from this analysis unless they are characterized by this strategic relationship with socioeconomic elites. For a more detailed theoretical discussion of this issue, see Gibson, *Class and Conservative Parties: Argentina in Comparative Perspective.*

3. The phrase "lost decade" refers to the 1980s, which is known in common parlance as Latin America's lost decade of development. This period, which saw the region's most impressive historical wave of democratization, also represented its worst and most generalized socioeconomic crisis since the Great Depression.

4. For the Colliers' argument about the pivotal importance of state-labor relations in the evolution of political regimes in Latin America, see Ruth Berins Collier and David Collier, *Shaping the Political Arena: Critical Junctures, the Labor Movement, and Regime Dynamics in Latin America* (Princeton: Princeton University Press, 1991).

5. See, for example, Collier and Collier, *Shaping the Political Arena;* Dietrich Rueschemeyer, Evelyn Stevens, and John Stevens, *Capitalist Development and Democracy* (Chicago: University of Chicago Press, 1992); and Karen L. Remmer, *Party Competition in Argentina and Chile* (Lincoln: University of Nebraska Press, 1984).

6. The figures for Costa Rica skew the average for the first group of countries considerably. In this case, the median ratio is probably a fairer measure. The median ratio for the group of countries with strong conservative parties is 4.2, while the median ratio for countries with weak historical legacies of conservative party organization is .55. If only the South American cases are taken into account (the Central American cases providing the extreme values on both ends), the average ratios are 3.43 and 0.9. Whatever measure is chosen, however, the conclusion remains the same: countries with viable national conservative parties in place at the start of democracy experienced far greater democratic stability throughout the twentieth century than countries that did not.

7. For an exploration of this question by a prominent member of the Brazilian Left, see Francisco Weffort, "Why Democracy?" in Alfred Stepan, ed., *Democratizing Brazil: Problems of Transition and Consolidation* (New York: Oxford University Press, 1989), 327–50.

8. For an account of Belaúnde's strategies on his return to power, and the symbolic strength of his campaign as a repudiation of the experience of military rule, see Julio Cotler, "Los partidos políticos y la democracia en el Perú," *CEDES/CLACSO Grupo de Trabajo de Partidos Políticos, Documento de Trabajo 9* (Buenos Aires: 1989).

9. This phenomenon was not limited to the above-mentioned countries. It was also present in such countries as Ecuador and Bolivia, where a profound deterioration in business-state relations occurred, even without the drama of bank nationalizations. As Catherine M. Conaghan, James M. Malloy, and Luis A. Abugattas point out, business concern over the unpredictability of military rule was a major factor shaping postauthoritarian politics in all Central Andean countries. See their article, "Business and the 'Boys': The Politics of Neoliberalism in the Central Andes," *Latin American Research Review* 25, no. 2 (1990): 3–30. For Argentina see also Carlos Acuña, "Intereses empresarios, dictadura, y democracia en la Argentina actual (O, sobre porqué la burguesía abandona estrategias autoritarias y opta por la estabilidad democrática)," *Documento CEDES* 39 (Buenos Aires: Centro de Estudios de Estado y Sociedad, 1990).

10. See Roberto Tirado, "Los empresarios y la política partidaria," *Estudios Sociológicos* (Mexico City: El Colegio de México) 15 (1987).

11. The evolution of business-government relations during the García government is analyzed in detail by Francisco Durand in *Business and Politics in Peru: The State and the National Bourgeoisie* (Boulder, Colo.: Westview, 1993).

12. See Blanca Heredia, "Can Rational Profit-Maximizers Be Democratic? Business and Democracy in Mexico," paper presented at conference of "Business Elites and Democracy in Latin America," Kellogg Institute, the University of Notre Dame, May 3–5, 1991, p. 2. See also Leticia Barraza and Ilán Bizberg, "El Partido Acción Nacional y el régimen político mexicano," *Foro Internacional* 30, no. 3 (1991): 418–45.

13. Mirko Lauer, "Adios conservadurismo, bienvenido liberalismo: La nueva derecha en el Perú," and Francisco Durand, "The National Bourgeoisie and the Peruvian State: Coalition and Conflict in the 1980's," in *Business and Politics in Peru: The State and the National Bourgeoisie* (Boulder, Colo.: Westview, 1993).

14. Heredia, "Can Rational Profit-Maximizers be Democratic?"; Barraza and Bizberg, "El Partido Acción Nacional."

15. Gabriel Gaspar Tapia, *El Salvador: El ascenso de la nueva derecha* (San Salvador: CINAS, 1989).

16. Soledad Loaeza, "Derecha y democracia en el cambio político mexicano, 1982–1988," conference paper no. 24 (New York: Columbia University–New York University Consortium, April 1990), 47.

17. For an analysis of factors behind ARENA's performance in the 1994 elections, see Liesl Haas and Gina M. Perez, "Voting with Their Stomachs: 'Las Elecciones del Siglo' in El Salvador," *LASA Forum* (Latin American Studies Association) 25, no. 3 (1994): 3–6.

18. For an analysis of recent developments in Bolivian politics, including policymaking and coalition building by the MNR under presidents Paz Estenssoro and Sánchez de Lozada, see the chapter by Gamarra in this collection.

19. I am indebted to Jeanne Giraldo for this point.

### Chapter 3 Democracy and Inequality in Latin America (Castañeda)

1. Fernando Benítez, "Desigualdad," *La Jornada*, January 8, 1994.

2. Nora Lustig, "Introduction," in *Coping with Austerity: Poverty and Inequality in Latin America* (Washington, D.C.: Brookings, 1995).

3. Rafael Rodríguez Castañeda, "El reparto de la riqueza en tiempos de Salinas de Gortari," *Proceso* 971 (July 12, 1992): 6–9.

4. Alberto Alesina and Roberto Perotti, *Income Distribution, Political Instability, and Investment* (Cambridge, Mass.: National Bureau of Economic Research, October 1993).

5. Sebastian Edwards, *Latin America and the Caribbean: A Decade after the Debt Crisis* (Washington, D.C.: World Bank, 1993), 118.

6. *World Development Report 1992* (Oxford: Oxford University Press, 1992): 236.

7. Thomas E. Skidmore, *Politics in Brazil* (Oxford: Oxford University Press, 1970): 192.

8. Alesina and Perotti, *Income Distribution.*

### Chapter 4 Traditional Power Structures and Democratic Governance in Latin America (Hagopian)

I am grateful for the helpful comments I received from Jorge Domínguez and Jeanne Giraldo on an earlier version of this chapter.

1. *Social Origins of Dictatorship and Democracy* (Boston: Beacon Press, 1966).

2. John Johnson, *Political Change in Latin America: The Emergence of the Middle Sectors* (Stanford: Stanford University Press, 1958).

3. Cynthia McClintock, "Peru: Precarious Regimes, Authoritarian and Democratic," in Larry Diamond, Juan J. Linz, and Seymour Martin Lipset, eds., *Democracy in Developing Countries: Latin America* (Boulder, Colo.: Lynne Rienner, 1989), 355, advances the argument that changes in social structure— of which expropriating virtually all the major interests of the oligarchy stands out—were advantageous to the establishment of democracy in Peru. Although democracy is weak in Peru today, the threats to democracy in the early 1990s are attributable to causes other than a rebellion of the traditional Right.

4. John Higley and Richard Gunther's *Elites and Democratic Consolidation in Latin America and Southern Europe* (New York: Cambridge University Press, 1992), for example, assumes that democratic consolidation and ulti- mately the stability and survival of democratic regimes depend critically upon a broad elite consensus concerning the rules of the democratic political game and the worth of democratic institutions. See the volume's introduction by Mi- chael Burton, Richard Gunther, and John Higley ("Introduction: Elite Transfor- mations and Democratic Regimes"), p. 3. In his contribution to the volume ("Spain: The Very Model of the Modern Elite Settlement"), Gunther applauds the participation of members of the Franco regime in the construction of a new democracy in Spain, judging it preferable that they play "active roles in the reform process, rather than sitting on the sidelines as embittered opponents of change or as vengeful victims of a political purge" (p. 52).

5. Edward L. Gibson, "Democracy and the New Electoral Right in Argen- tina," *Journal of Inter-American Studies and World Affairs* 32, no. 3 (1990): 213.

6. Terry Lynn Karl, "Petroleum and Political Pacts: The Transition to De- mocracy in Venezuela," in Guillermo O'Donnell, Philippe C. Schmitter, and Laurence Whitehead, *Transitions from Authoritarian Rule: Latin America* (Baltimore: Johns Hopkins University Press, 1986), 203.

7. Samuel P. Huntington, *The Third Wave: Democratization in the Late Twentieth Century* (Norman: University of Oklahoma Press, 1991).

8. Ibid., 264–65.

9. Morris J. Blachman and Kenneth E. Sharpe, "The Transitions to 'Electoral' and Democratic Politics in Central America: Assessing the Role of Political Parties," in Louis W. Goodman, William M. LeoGrande, and Johanna Mendelson Forman, eds. *Political Parties and Democracy in Central America* (Boulder, Colo.: Westview Press, 1992), 35.

10. Maurice Zeitlin and Richard Earl Ratcliffe, *Landlords and Capitalists: The Dominant Class of Chile* (Princeton: Princeton University Press, 1988), 207.

11. The Guayaquil-based "agroexport" oligarchy in Ecuador controls im- porting and even industrial interests; see Osvaldo Hurtado, *Political Power in Ecuador* (Albuquerque: University of New Mexico Press, 1989), 176, 178–79. In Guatemala, El Salvador, Nicaragua, and Honduras, traditional, agriculturally based elites had commercial and financial dealings; see Blachman and Sharpe, "Transitions," 33. In Chile, an interlocking web of agricultural, industrial, and financial interests within families led Zeitlin and Ratcliffe, *Landlords and Cap- italists,* to refer to them as "landed capitalists" rather than traditional elites.

12. A long tradition narrowly identifies as the nucleus of the "traditional elite" of El Salvador a limited number of governing families that range from fourteen to twenty. Elsewhere I have argued that political elites in Brazil who

are descended from a small number of governing families might be considered "traditional" even if they no longer base their power primarily or exclusively on land or agricultural activities; see my *Traditional Politics and Regime Change in Brazil* (New York: Cambridge University Press, 1996). Writing of the Chilean agrarian elite, Zeitlin and Ratcliffe, *Landlords and Capitalists*, 206, asserted that "to belong to a landed capitalist family is to be marked for political prominence."

13. Peter H. Smith, *Labyrinths of Power: Political Recruitment in Twentieth-Century Mexico* (Princeton: Princeton University Press, 1979).

14. For the effect of the 1952 revolution on the power of the landed aristocracy in Bolivia, see James M. Malloy, *Bolivia: The Uncompleted Revolution* (Pittsburgh: University of Pittsburgh Press, 1970), 188–215; and Antonio García, "Agrarian Reform and Social Development in Bolivia," in Rodolfo Stavenhagen, ed., *Agrarian Problems and Peasant Movements in Latin America* (Garden City, N.Y.: Anchor, 1970), 301–46. In the Peruvian case, McClintock, "Peru," 355–58, has argued that even if it fell short of its distributional goals— land reform reached only between one-fifth and one-fourth of the potential beneficiaries—military-sponsored agrarian reform broke the back of the landed oligarchy and created new classes of small farmers and wealthy rural workers. See also Abraham F. Lowenthal, "The Peruvian Experiment Reconsidered," in Cynthia McClintock and Abraham F. Lowenthal, eds., *The Peruvian Experiment Reconsidered* (Princeton: Princeton University Press, 1983); and Laura Guasti, "Clientelism in Decline: A Peruvian Regional Study," in S. N. Eisenstadt and René Lemarchand, eds., *Political Clientelism, Patronage, and Development*, Contemporary Political Sociology 3 (Beverly Hills: Sage, 1987), 217–48.

15. "The Peruvian Experiment Reconsidered," 425.

16. John Duncan Powell, *The Mobilization of the Venezuelan Peasant* (Cambridge, Mass.: Harvard University Press, 1971); Karl, "Petroleum and Political Pacts," 199–203.

17. John A. Booth, "Costa Rica: The Roots of Democratic Stability," in Diamond, Linz, and Lipset, eds., *Democracy in Developing Countries*, 387–95.

18. John D. Martz, "Party Elites and Leadership in Colombia and Venezuela," *Journal of Latin American Studies* 24, no. 1 (1992): 96, 99.

19. Hurtado, *Political Power in Ecuador*, 179.

20. Appointments to the Supreme Court, which, according to Anita Isaacs, in this collection, are highly politicized, are made by the Congress.

21. Jeffrey M. Paige, "Coffee and Power in El Salvador," *Latin American Research Review* 28, no. 3 (1993): 7–40.

22. Richard C. Kearney, "Spoils in the Caribbean: The Struggle for Merit-Based Civil Service in the Dominican Republic," *Public Administration Review* 46, no. 2 (1986): 145.

23. Carina Perelli and Juan Rial, "Partidos políticos y democracia en el Cono Sur" (Montevideo: PEITHO, September 1991), 15.

24. Charles W. Anderson, *Politics and Economic Change in Latin America: The Governing of Restless Nations* (Princeton: D. Van Nostrand, 1967), 96–97.

25. Alfred Stepan, *The Military in Politics: Changing Patterns in Brazil* (Princeton: Princeton University Press, 1971).

26. Lowenthal, "The Peruvian Experiment Reconsidered," 425.

27. Anita Isaacs, *Military Rule and Transition in Ecuador, 1972–92* (Pittsburgh: University of Pittsburgh Press, 1993), 60.

28. Ibid., 124–26.

29. Richard L. Millett, "Politicized Warriors: The Military and Central American Politics," in Goodman, LeoGrande, and Mendelson Forman, eds., *Po-*

*litical Parties*, 67. In a press conference at the Carnegie Endowment in Washington, D.C., Cerezo estimated that he entered the presidency with 30 percent of the power, a figure he hoped to increase to 70 percent by 1989.

30. Mark Rosenberg, in this collection, speaks of a forty-year tradition of military autonomy in Honduras.

31. According to Millett, "Politicized Warriors," 64–65, modernization of these militaries, U.S. assistance, and the emergence of divisions within the officer corps all contributed to these developments.

32. Jennifer Schirmer, "The Guatemalan Military Project: An Interview with Gen. Héctor Gramajo," *Harvard International Review* 13, no. 3 (1991): 12–13. It is worth quoting Gramajo at length: "This generation of military officers is more professional. . . . The success of Guatemala depends on wresting power from the economic elite. In 1954, groups from the economic elite and the Army overthrew the government with a counterrevolution. A new Army was created and joined forces with the right wing. With the rise of the insurgency in 1960, this alliance drew even closer together, such that between 1970 and 1978, they were almost one and the same. . . . In 1982, the money of the right staged a coup against Lucas to replace him with Ríos Montt, who then brought in his own people, and the two split apart once again. General Mejía tried to bring the two groups together again between 1983 and 1986, but the economic situation was bad and the right treated him badly, as they remained separated. . . . Now . . . the structure [of our autonomy] is in place."

33. See the chapter by Rosenberg in this collection.

34. An example would be the failure of civilian elites to support the attempted military coup in Guatemala in 1993.

35. Gibson, "Democracy and the New Electoral Right," 197.

36. Ibid., 185, 187–88, 189–92, 198.

37. The coffee millers (represented by ABECAFE [Salvadoran Association of Coffee Cultivators and Exporters]) and two factions contesting the leadership of the association of coffee growers (ASCAFE [Salvadoran Coffee Association], or La Cafetalera) are not; see Paige, "Coffee and Power in El Salvador," 7–40. According to Paige, from 1984 to 1989, la Cafetalera was directed by a faction led by Orlando de Sola that shunned any notion of compromise and democratic development in El Salvador; a more moderate faction now holds power, yet still has little commitment to the steps that would be required to bring a stable democracy to El Salvador.

38. The characterization of the political oligarchy of Colombia as "gentlemen" is from Alexander Wilde, "Conversations among Gentlemen: Oligarchical Democracy in Colombia," in Juan J. Linz and Alfred Stepan, eds., *The Breakdown of Democratic Regimes: Latin America* (Baltimore: Johns Hopkins University Press, 1978), 28–87. The view of the consequences of the National Front is that of R. Albert Berry and Mauricio Solaún, "Notes toward an Interpretation of the National Front," in R. Albert Berry, Ronald G. Hellman, and Mauricio Solaún, eds., *Politics of Compromise: Coalition Government in Colombia* (New Brunswick, N.J.: Transaction Books, 1980), 439–45.

39. See Jonathan Hartlyn, "Colombia: The Politics of Violence and Accommodation," in Diamond, Linz, and Lipset, eds., *Democracy in Developing Countries*, 329–30.

40. Adam Przeworski, "Some Problems in the Study of the Transition to Democracy," in O'Donnell, Schmitter, and Whitehead, *Transitions from Authoritarian Rule: Comparative Perspectives*, 59–60.

41. Catherine M. Conaghan and Rosario Espinal, "Unlikely Transitions to Uncertain Regimes? Democracy without Compromise in the Dominican Re-

public and Ecuador," *Journal of Latin American Studies* 22, no. 3 (1990): 555; also cf. Isaacs, *Military Rule*, 120.

42. Isaacs, *Military Rule*, 128–29.

43. Conaghan and Espinal, "Unlikely Transitions," 554–55.

44. Charles Guy Gillespie, "The Role of Civil-Military Pacts in Elite Settlements and Elite Convergence: Democratic Consolidation in Uruguay," in Higley and Gunther, eds., *Elites and Democratic Consolidation*,

45. This argument has best been made by Scott Mainwaring, "Politicians, Parties, and Electoral Systems: Brazil in Comparative Perspective," *Comparative Politics* 24, no. 1 (1991), 23–28.

46. Barry Ames ("Electoral Strategy and Legislative Politics in Brazil, 1978–1990: A Progress Report," Washington University, a paper circulated at the International Congress of the Latin American Studies Association, April 1991, 6) has also linked the fact that in Brazil "electorally successful parties embrace distant, hostile portions of the ideological spectrum, and many if not most deputies spend the bulk of their time getting jobs and pork-barrel projects for their constituents" with the fact that "the national congress is weak and ill-suited for policy making on issues of national concern." He anticipates that in the long run "the ability of Brazil's congress to grapple with social and economic issues could be hindered—perhaps crippled—by the inability of the parties to organize around national-level issues."

47. The expression is that of the powerful former governor of Bahia, Antonio Carlos Magalhães.

48. "Economic Liberalization with Constitutional Reform in Colombia," in Leslie Elliott Armijo, ed., *Conversations about Democratization and Economic Reform: Working Papers of the Southern California Seminar* (Los Angeles: Center for International Studies, University of Southern California, 1995), 248–49.

49. Blachman and Sharpe, "Transitions," 34, 43. These features distinguish what the authors refer to as "pseudo" and "limited" democracies.

50. *Visão*, January 20, 1993, 6.

51. For the case of Brazil, see David Fleischer, "O Congresso-Constituinte de 1987: Um Perfil Sócio-Econômico e Político," paper presented at the University of Brasília, 1987. For the case of Ecuador, see the chapter by Isaacs in this collection.

52. Héctor Rosada Granados, "Parties, Transition, and the Political System in Guatemala," in Goodman, LeoGrande, and Mendelson Forman, eds., *Political Parties*, 105.

53. Evidence of such views on democracy can be found among sugar workers in Brazil (Anthony Pereira, "Regime Change without Democratization: Sugar Workers' Unions in Pernambuco, Northeast Brazil, 1961–89" [Ph.D. diss., Harvard University, 1991]), and also among residents of coastal cooperatives in Peru (McClintock, "Peru," 360).

54. Perhaps for a lack of reform, though not due to traditional elite persistence, a similar disturbing pattern is evident in Peru. Despite rather consistent support for democratic governance in public opinion polls in Lima for much of the decade of the 1980s, in April 1992, two days after President Alberto Fujimori rolled out the tanks and closed Congress for its refusal to back his proposed economic reform, 73 percent of those surveyed in the capital by the Peruvian Enterprise of Public Opinion supported the president's usurpation of power. Reported in *Folha de São Paulo* (Brazil) April 8, 1992, sec. 2, 1.

55. A higher percentage cast valid ballots in the 1994 presidential elections (67 percent), but the number of valid votes was less than had been cast in 1989.

56. James Wilkie, Carlos Alberto Contreras, and Christof Anders Weber, eds., *Statistical Abstract of Latin America*, vol. 30, pt. 1 (Los Angeles: UCLA Latin American Center, 1993), table 1051, 301.

57. See the chapter by Rosenberg in this collection.
58. Wilkie et al., eds., *Statistical Abstract*, 305.
59. Rosada Granados, "Parties, Transition, and the Political System," 107.
60. See the chapter by Torres-Rivas in this collection.
61. See the chapter by Kline in this collection.
62. Isaacs, *Military Rule*, 134.
63. Ibid., 21.
64. See the chapter by Isaacs in this collection.
65. See the chapter by Abente Brun in this collection.
66. Guillermo O'Donnell, "Transitions, Continuities, and Paradoxes," in Scott Mainwaring, Guillermo O'Donnell, and J. Samuel Valenzuela, eds., *Issues in Democratic Consolidation: The New South American Democracies in Comparative Perspective* (Notre Dame: University of Notre Dame Press, 1992), 25–33.

## Chapter 5  Indigenous Protest and Democracy in Latin America (Yashar)

I thank Jorge I. Domínguez and John Gershman for their constructive criticism on an earlier version of this chapter, Donna Lee Van Cott for sharing her work in progress, and Daniela Raz for her research assistance.

1. The rise in indigenous organizing coincided with the rise in the black consciousness movement, particularly in Brazil. However, given significant historical and contemporary differences between the black consciousness movement and the varied indigenous movements, I limit the scope of this chapter to indigenous organizing and its relationship to democracy. Hence all references here to ethnic identity or organizing refer to the politicization of indigenous organizing alone.

2. See Donald L. Horowitz, *Ethnic Groups in Conflict* (Berkeley: University of California Press, 1985) and "Democracy in Divided Societies: The Challenge of Ethnic Conflict," *Journal of Democracy* 4, no. 4 (1993): 18–38. In his earlier work, Horowitz noted that in Africa and Asia increasing ethnic conflict tended to rise in tandem with the decline of democracy. While indigenous groups in Latin America did emerge in the early 1970s under authoritarian conditions, they have grown in size and reputation under the period of democratization. Horowitz later noted that, in fact, there is a more ambiguous relationship between the articulation and politicization of ethnicity and democracy.

3. See Guillermo O'Donnell, "Delegative Democracy?" *Journal of Democracy* 5, no. 1 (1994): 55–69, for his suggestive discussion of delegative democracies and the retreat of the state in Latin America. In characterizing the former he notes (ibid., 59–60): "Delegative democracies rest on the premise that whoever wins election to the presidency is thereby entitled to govern as he or she sees fit, constrained only by the hard facts of existing power relations and by a constitutionally limited term of office. The president is taken to be the embodiment of the nation and the main custodian and definer of its interests. The policies of his government need bear no resemblance to the promises of his campaign. . . . Typically, winning presidential candidates in DDs [delegative democracies] present themselves as above both political parties and organized interests. How could it be otherwise for somebody who claims to embody the whole of the nation? In this view, other institutions—courts and legislatures, for instance—are nuisances. . . . Accountability to such institutions appears as a mere impediment to the full authority that the president has been delegated to exercise."

4. Ethnicity, like democracy, is a highly contested concept and would require a lengthy monograph to explore and delineate its meaning(s). Nonetheless, for the sake of clarity, I follow the definition articulated by Esman and

Rabinovitch who "define ethnicity in its broadest meaning—as collective identity and solidarity based on such ascriptive facts as imputed common descent, language, custom, belief systems and practices (religious), and in some cases race or color." See Milton J. Esman and Itamar Rabinovitch, *Ethnicity, Pluralism, and the State in the Middle East* (Ithaca: Cornell University Press, 1988). Individual members do not have to possess the bundle of characteristics associated with an ethnic identity, nor does an ethnic group have to possess a "true" or "unchanged" heritage. Rather, following the work of scholars such as Benedict Anderson, *Imagined Communities: Reflections on the Origin and Spread of Nationalism* (London: New Left Books, 1980); Howard Winant, "Rethinking Race in Brazil," *Journal of Latin American Studies* 24 (1992): 173–92; and Arturo Escobar and Sonia Alvarez, eds., *The Making of Social Movements in Latin America* (Boulder, Colo.: Westview Press, 1992), it is important to see these identities as a construction of group solidarity coincident with a belief of shared peoplehood, historical lineage, and customs; it is as much "imagined" as "real." For the sake of this chapter, it differs from the idea of the "nation" insofar as the latter coincides with a state or a struggle for a state.

5. See Florencia E. Mallon, "Indian Communities, Political Cultures, and the State in Latin America, 1780–1990," *Journal of Latin American Studies* 24, quincentenary suppl. (1992): 35–53, and David Maybury-Lewis, "Becoming Indian in Lowland South America," in Greg Urban and Joel Sherzer, eds., *Nation-States and Indians in Latin America* (Austin: University of Texas Press, 1991), 207–35, for a discussion of the varied ways in which nineteenth-century states set out to control indigenous communities through violence, isolation, and assimilation. See Steve J. Stern, "Paradigms of Conquest: History, Historiography, and Politics," *Journal of Latin American Studies* 24, quincentenary suppl. (1992): 1–34, for a sobering discussion of the need to adopt a more nuanced understanding of the colonization of the Americas and the multiple roles and actions of the colonizers and indigenous peoples in this process.

6. See Rodolfo Stavenhagen, *Derecho indígena y derechos humanos en América Latina* (Mexico City: El Colegio de México, Instituto Interamericano de Derechos Humanos, 1988), 29, and Maybury-Lewis, "Becoming Indian."

7. European elites viewed mestizos in the nineteenth century as low life, just a rank above Indians. By the twentieth century, intellectuals had created a mythology around the mestizo who came to symbolize the Latin American nation in countries with multi-ethnic populations.

8. Stavenhagen, *Derecho indígena*, 105, and Maybury-Lewis, "Becoming Indian."

9. See Rodolfo Stavenhagen, "Challenging the Nation-State in Latin America," *Journal of International Affairs* 45, no. 2 (1992): 421–40, for an overview of Latin America. See Mallon, "Indian Communities," for a discussion of the varied contexts and forms that this policy took in Mexico, Peru, and Brazil. This attempt to create a more homogeneous population contrasted with U.S. history where more rigid social lines were drawn between the Indian, black, and white population.

10. Ethnic relations in Latin America have played out historically in quite different ways from African and Asian countries that gained independence almost a century and a half later than in Latin America. Because Latin America gained independence more than a century earlier than Africa, independence and national liberation became associated in the historiography with the European settlers who subsequently set out to construct a nation-state coincident with the ethnicity of the conquerors (i.e., themselves). In Africa and parts of Asia, where many countries maintained colonial status through the 1950s and 1960s, independence movements developed within indigenous communities

against settler populations. National liberation movements set out not only to capture state power but also to refashion a "truer" national identity to coincide with the postcolonial state. Following independence, any semblance of national unity within many African countries broke down and gave way to ongoing conflict between ethnic groups, as in Nigeria, Rwanda, and Burundi. Hence, while pluri-ethnic states compose both Latin America and Africa, ethnic relations and conflict have played out on different terrains.

In Latin America, ethnic conflict has tended to occur between horizontal groups, in which it is seen as conflict between white/mestizo groups that effectively occupy the state and indigenous groups that do not. In Africa, excluding important examples such as South Africa and Eritrea, ethnic conflict since independence has tended to play out between more vertically integrated groups competing, when democratic conditions prevail, to gain political power. For this reason, Horowitz's important 1985 study of ethnic groups in conflict (Horowitz, *Ethnic Groups*) does not apply to Latin America, for he limits his analysis to vertically integrated ethnic groups.

11. Pierre Van den Berghe, "Ethnicity and Class in Highland Peru," in David L. Browman and Ronald A. Schwarz, eds., *Peasants, Primitives, and Proletariats: The Struggle for Identity in South America* (The Hague: Mouton, 1979), 264–65.

12. Pierre-Michel Fontaine, *Race, Class, and Power in Brazil* (Los Angeles: University of California Press, 1985). Fontaine's volume on race relations finds a common pattern for Afro-Brazilians.

13. Given the scope of this chapter, I have simplified the approaches developed to address ethnic identities and conflict. Clearly, both modernization and Marxist approaches dominated intellectual discourse but did not wholly define it. Moreover, both approaches were more complex and varied than I have indicated here. For example, different theorists operating within the modernization paradigm argued that modernization would overcome ethnic primordialism, be impeded by ethnic primordialism, and produce ethnic conflict; in all cases, however, the progress and future of modernization was assumed to rest on transcending and/or controlling ethnic conflict. For a more detailed overview, see, in particular, John Stack, *The Primordial Challenge: Ethnicity in the Contemporary World* (New York: Greenwood Press, 1986). See also Horowitz, "Democracy in Divided Societies" and *Ethnic Groups in Conflict*, chap. 3; and Stavenhagen, "Challenging the Nation-State" and his *The Ethnic Question: Conflicts, Development, and Human Rights* (Tokyo: United Nations University Press, 1990).

14. Norman E. Whitten Jr., "Jungle Quechua Ethnicity: An Ecuadorian Case Study," 240.

15. Through the 1970s and 1980s, many academics and politicians alike tended to reduce discussion of indigenous peoples in Latin America to a discussion of economic issues. Indeed, if one sets out to gather basic demographic information on Latin America, there are a host of economic indicators, broken down by country, class, and sex. Yet it is virtually impossible to gather reliable, continuous, contemporary, and crossnational data on indigenous populations. With the increased awareness of the socially constructed nature of ethnic identity, one could argue that this is actually advantageous. But, within the positivist assumptions held by many of the demographers throughout the 1980s, this absence of information highlights the insignificance attributed to race and ethnicity. For example, the 1984 *Statistical Abstract of Latin America*, suppl. ser. 8, *Latin American Population and Urbanization Analysis: 1950–1982*, ed. Richard W. Wilkie (Los Angeles: UCLA Latin American Center, 1984), does not even make reference to the fact that there is an indigenous population in Latin

America. The statistical abstract on Latin America as a whole does not include ethnicity as one of its main variables; indeed, the 1993 abstract includes only one table, drawing from late 1970s data, that refers to the Amerindian population.

16. See Browman and Schwarz, eds., *Peasants, Primitives, and Proletariats*, 251; Stavenhagen, *Derecho indígena*, 32, 145; Urban and Sherzer, eds., *Nation-States and Indians*; Wilkie, ed., *Statistical Abstract*, 150; NACLA (North American Congress on Latin America), *Report on the Americas: The First Nations, 1492–1992* 25, no. 3 (1991): 16; and *Latin American Weekly Reports*, June 10, 1993.

17. For an overview of these movements, see collections of essays in Donna Lee Van Cott, ed., *Indigenous Peoples and Democracy in Latin America* (New York: St. Martin's Press, 1994).

18. See also Stavenhagen, "Challenging the Nation-State" and *The Ethnic Question*; Van Cott, ed., *Indigenous Peoples*, 11–21; and Urban and Sherzer, eds., *Nation-States and Indians*.

19. In particular, see Stavenhagen, "Challenging the Nation-State," 435. According to Manuela Tomei of the International Labor Organization, Latin American states have adopted new legislation to address indigenous peoples and rights, particularly with respect to land rights. She notes that Colombia and Ecuador are in the forefront but that legislative developments have also occurred in Bolivia, Brazil, Chile, Guatemala, Paraguay, and Peru. Of course, legislation and implementation are two separate issues. See *Latin American Weekly Reports*, June 10, 1993.

20. Cynthia McClintock, "Peru's Sendero Luminoso: Origins and Trajectories," in Susan Eckstein, ed., *Power and Popular Protest: Latin American Social Movements* (Berkeley: University of California Press, 1989).

21. In either case, land reform is not just about gaining access to land; by definition, it is also about decreasing resources of the landed elite and therefore changing rural relations. This raises an interesting dilemma. On the one hand, many studies have shown that a strong landed elite is inimical to democracy as it exercises nondemocratic control over regions. On the other hand, efforts to weaken the latter's control have also proven inimical to democracy, as landed elites have often moved to undermine the democratic regimes that create the political opportunities upon which land reform proposals are often articulated and at times implemented. See Moore's classic statement to this effect: Barrington Moore Jr., *Social Origins of Dictatorship and Democracy: Lord and Peasant in the Making of the Modern World* (Boston: Beacon Press, 1966). Hagopian's chapter in this collection notes that where traditional elites (read landed elites) are strong, democracy appears most fragile.

22. *Latin American Weekly Reports*, May 13, 1993.

23. See U.S. Department of State Dispatch "Colombia Human Rights Practice in 1993" (Washington, D.C., 1994).

24. Information from the American Anthropological Association and Amnesty International, reported in *New York Times*, Week in Review, January 2, 1994.

25. See Amnesty International Reports, Minnesota Advocates for Human Rights 1993 report on Chiapas, and *Boston Globe*, January 16, 1994.

26. Stavenhagen, *Derecho indígena*, 343.

27. See ibid., 344–45, and Maybury-Lewis, "Becoming Indian," 218–26.

28. *Latin American Weekly Reports*, February 2, 1993.

29. Of course, the Bolivian case is ambiguous. On the one hand, it highlights the achievement of high office by a Bolivian indigenous man who has specifically organized around ethnic issues and demands. On the other hand, he and his party have had an extremely low electoral success, highlighting the

limited success of indigenous leaders and parties in mobilizing the Bolivian electorate at the polls.

30. Information from Van Cott, ed., *Indigenous Peoples*, 14–19, and *The Report on Guatemala* 14, no. 3 (fall 1993).

31. Indigenous women do seek to sell textiles and wares to tourists and do benefit materially in the short run from tourism. Nonetheless, the production of daily household clothing and goods for a tourist market has distorted the domestic market for indigenous consumption. In Guatemala, for example, many indigenous women can no longer afford to wear or buy the *huipiles* produced for the international market.

32. For example, upon discovering a document from the Confederation of Indigenous Nationalities of Ecuador (CONAIE), Mariano González, the agriculture minister of Ecuador, claimed that the indigenous organization hopes to set up a state within a state; reported in *Latin American Weekly Reports*, February 18, 1993.

33. Reported in *Report on Guatemala* (fall 1993), 11.

34. See Stavenhagen, *The Ethnic Question*, 35, for a discussion of the United Nations.

35. For a discussion of indigenous participation in transnational nongovernmental organizations, see Alison Brysk, "Acting Globally: Indian Rights and International Politics in Latin America," in Van Cott, ed., *Indigenous Peoples*, 29–54.

36. Shelton Davis and William Partridge, "Promoting the Development of Indigenous People in Latin America," *Finance and Development* 31 (March 1994), 38–40.

37. *New York Times* op-ed article, reprinted in *Boston Globe*, January 11, 1994.

38. For example, see James Scott, *Domination and the Arts of Resistance: Hidden Transcripts* (New Haven: Yale University Press, 1990).

39. As I discuss in the final section, if the terms of class and ethnic subordination do not explain the recent rise in ethnic mobilization, one cannot begin to respond to the demands of these communities without redressing these very structures.

40. As the social movements literature has highlighted, traditional popular movements proved incapable of maintaining their momentum in the new democracies as political parties displaced them in the political arena and as they failed to articulate a politics of proposition rather than protest. See, for example, the final three chapters of Arturo Escobar and Sonia Alvarez, eds., *The Making of Social Movements in Latin America* (Boulder, Colo.: Westview Press, 1992). Similarly, leftist political parties have generally fared poorly in the political arena.

41. Chile appears to be the exception here in two respects. Pinochet implemented comprehensive neoliberal reforms under authoritarian rule, that is, prior to the democratic governments of Aylwin and Frei. Moreover, the Mapuches, as noted, have been able to manage their resources and to channel their profits into a foundation. However, further research is needed to determine why and how this foundation was founded; if and how it is related to the timing and/or the consequences of the neoliberal reforms; if this recourse to international lending is part of a broader pattern to develop autonomous organizations with international funding in the absence of state support; and how the response of indigenous groups in Chile to the neoliberal reforms compares to that of other indigenous communities in Latin America.

42. See *Latin American Weekly Reports*, June 30, 1994, 277; July 14, 1994, 309; and July 28, 1994, 335. Also reported on the British Broadcasting Corpora-

tion, summary of world broadcasts, on June 22, 1994, and Reuter Textline from BBC Monitoring Service, June 24, 1994.

43. See the chapter by Isaacs in this collection and *Latin American Weekly Reports*, February 10, 1994, 52.

44. O'Donnell, "Delegative Democracy?"

45. A related hypothesis suggests that the failure of the Left to articulate and organize around ethnic concerns led indigenous communities to mobilize new ethnic-based organizations. At this stage, however, this hypothesis cannot explain why the Left was able to mobilize indigenous communities along material demands in earlier periods; when ethnic identities appear to have gained more political salience than other types of demands; and why contemporary indigenous organizations predated the decline of the Left.

46. See Brysk, "Acting Globally."

47. *Report on Guatemala* (fall 1993), 7.

48. Davis and Partridge, "Promoting the Development of Indigenous People," 39–40. Note that the World Bank and other international lending agencies have held regular meetings with one another as well as with El Fondo Indígena, The Indigenous Fund (founded by a number of Latin American countries in 1992) to address issues of land regularization and resource management, technical assistance and training, and access to credit and investment.

49. Brysk, "Acting Globally," 45.

50. Note that it is difficult to assess the success of a coup attempt. It is often unclear what coup plotters intended or what they gained in backroom negotiations.

51. Indeed, it appears that the origins of the two coup attempts had less to do with ethnic conflict and more to do with political paralysis resulting from the election of a president without any partisan support in the legislature, a legislature that did not legislate but was beholden to corrupt political parties, and the military's fear of the escalation of the civil war. Under these conditions, in both countries, the respective presidents (Fujimori in Peru and Serrano in Guatemala) created an alliance with the military to get rid of the legislature.

52. See Stefano Varese, "Think Locally, Act Globally," in North American Congress on Latin America, *Report on the Americas: The First Nations, 1492–1992*: 25, no. 3 (1991): 13–17.

53. Dankwart Rustow, "Transitions to Democracy: Toward a Dynamic Model," *Comparative Politics* 2, no. 3 (1970): 337–63.

54. See Van Cott, ed., *Indigenous Peoples*, 15–16.

55. See Hans Daalder, "The Consociational Democracy Theme," *World Politics* 26 (October 1973): 604–21, and Ian Shapiro, "Democratic Innovation: South Africa in Comparative Context," *World Politics* 46 (October 1993): 121–50, among others.

56. Bolivia passed a law on decentralization and popular participation on April 21, 1994. According to *Latin American Weekly Reports* (May 12, 1994, 196): "The participation law enables the central government to share out revenues between municipalities, provinces, and departments in accordance with their populations, and thereby favor traditionally neglected regions and groups. Responsibility for maintaining the physical infrastructure of schools, clinics, roads, and services is transferred from central government to the 301 municipalities. The law has also given legal recognition to Indian communities and other local organizations."

57. See O'Donnell, "Delegative Democracy?" and David Lehmann, *Democracy and Development in Latin America: Economics, Politics and Religion in the Postwar Period* (Philadelphia: Temple University Press, 1990), whose arguments regarding state-society relations and citizenship in Latin America have largely informed this discussion.

58. Guillermo O'Donnell, "On the State, Democratization and Some Conceptual Problems: A Latin American View with Glances at Some Postcommunist Countries," *World Development* 21, no. 8 (1993): 1361, and Lehmann, *Democracy and Development.*

59. O'Donnell, "On the State."

60. *New York Times*, January 17, 1994.

# Index

# III

# Conclusion: Parties, Institutions, and Market Reforms in Constructing Democracies

## Jorge I. Domínguez and Jeanne Kinney Giraldo

While discussing local events, some younger would-be reformers of Ilhéus (in Jorge Amado's novel *Gabriela: Cravo e canela*) observed that the traditional elites "support a state government that plunders us and then practically ignores us. While our local government does absolutely nothing . . . [and] in fact it actually places obstacles in the way of improvements." The reformers resolved to make changes; as one said to another, "you'll earn twice as much if you get into politics and change the existing situation."[1]

Though Amado wrote this forty years ago, his fictional characters still identify key themes in the political experience of a great many ordinary people in Latin America and the Caribbean in the mid-1990s. Government is unresponsive and at times an obstacle, traditional political leaders deserve no support, and political reform is an illusion because those who promise change are likely to change only the beneficiaries of corruption. The record reviewed in this book offers much justification for political cynicism and despair.

In the late 1980s and early 1990s, voters in many countries elected to office politicians who promised change but then disappointed the electorate. Elected on platforms committed to change, Fernando Collor de Mello in Brazil and Carlos Andrés Pérez in Venezuela were impeached for corruption and removed from office. Never before had a constitutionally elected president been removed from office in this manner and for this reason in either country.

More generally, the late 1980s and early 1990s was a time of troubles in many Latin American and Caribbean countries, a period when social, economic, and political circumstances were redefined. One sign of disaffection was the pattern of electoral outcomes. In those years, incumbent political parties were defeated at least once in Argentina, Uruguay, Brazil, Bolivia, Peru, Ecuador, Venezuela, Guyana, Barbados, Trinidad and Tobago, Jamaica, Panama, Costa Rica, Nicaragua, El Salvador, Honduras, and Guatemala, as were the incumbent politicians associated with the authoritarian government in Chile in 1989 and in Haiti in 1991.[2] The voters in these countries were unhappy with long-standing rulers and with would-be reformers.

Voters have blamed governing parties for the region's prolonged economic crisis. Dire living conditions still prevail years after the great depression that hit this region in the 1980s. By the end of 1994, on average and in real prices, the gross domestic product (GDP) per capita of the countries of Latin America and the Caribbean had yet to surpass the 1981 level. Among the Latin American countries, only Argentina, Chile, Colombia, Costa Rica, the Dominican Republic, Panama, and Uruguay had surpassed the 1981 level. In the Anglophone Caribbean, the record was better: the Bahamas, Belize, Guyana, Jamaica, and the countries that belong to the Organization of Eastern Caribbean States (OECS) had exceeded the 1981 level.[3]

Latin America and the Caribbean, in short, have been battered by the winds of change, anger, hope, and dissatisfaction. One might expect voter apathy and alienation from political parties to rise, politicians and civic leaders to redesign basic national institutions, market reforms to fail, and political regimes to fall.

In this chapter we advance four propositions that run somewhat counter to these expectations. Though there is much voter anger, new and many old parties have continued to mobilize support. Several new political parties have become credible opposition contenders even in countries where no "new" party has seriously challenged the political establishment in decades. In other cases, long-established political parties have "reinvented" themselves.

Second, while an orgy of constitutional reform-mongering designed to improve democratic governance has occurred, it has had little impact. Attempts have been made to redesign the relationship between executive and legislative branches, improve the performance of the judiciary, and decentralize certain tasks of government, but these attempts have either not gone far enough or proven counterproductive. In too many countries, the performance of state institutions remains poor and democratic governance is weak.

Third, contrary to the expectations of many in years past, democratic regimes in Latin America have proven more effective at introducing market reforms than had been the case with authoritarian regimes. Even more surprising to certain skeptics, in several cases these governments have effectively used the procedures of democracy to advance and secure such reforms.

And fourth, although the stability of constitutional government in the region is still a matter of concern—especially in view of the coup attempts that took place in the 1990s, some sponsored by constitutionally elected presidents—barriers against *successful* coup attempts have gradually been constructed. Since 1976, outside of Suriname, Haiti, and

Peru, all attempts to overthrow a constitutional government chosen through general fraud-free elections have failed. Important changes within the armed forces, in the relationships between the armed forces and the rest of the society, and in the international community have decreased the likelihood of successful military coups.

## Crises and Opportunities for Representation

Latin American countries are facing a crisis of representation linked to the challenges of two major transitions: from authoritarian to constitutional governments, and from statist to more market-oriented economies. This second transition also affects most of the countries of the Anglophone Caribbean. Representative networks were battered by the authoritarian regimes; in some countries, they broke down. In nearly all new democracies, parties face a mass electorate that is larger, more urbanized, more educated, and more exposed to mass media than was the case under past constitutional governments. Moreover, the economic depression of the 1980s and the nearly simultaneous transition toward a more market-oriented economy strained old networks of representation and created demands for new forms of representation. Many parties have reconsidered their long-held adherence to statist ideologies. Labor union power has weakened nearly everywhere, while business and "liberal" ideologies have gathered strength. The cutbacks in government consumer subsidies and in funding for many public services have hurt the poor and weakened the political allegiances of many middle-class sectors.

As a result of these changes, organizations that seek to represent the interests of citizens have been simultaneously destroyed, created, and recreated. Many of these organizations have been political parties, but a wide array of social movements have also been involved, and many parties have drawn strength from such movements.[4]

This section examines four kinds of representational challenges facing countries undergoing the dual transition from authoritarianism and statist economies. In countries where the transition from authoritarian regimes to constitutional governments coincided with the end of civil war, new democracies face the challenge of incorporating parties that have been formed out of guerrilla and paramilitary groups. Second, in countries where parties have historically been strong, democratizing pressures and efforts to undertake economic reform have led to the creation of new parties that challenge the monopolies or oligopolies on representation that one or two parties have long held. In other countries where parties have been historically weak, such as Brazil, the major representational challenge is the construction of more programmatic and responsible parties. And fourth, older political parties in many countries have scrambled to adapt to changed circumstances, with varying degrees of success. On balance, the transformation of old parties and the appearance of new parties may improve the prospects of effective representation in the medium to long term.

### Explaining the Defeat of Parties

One manifestation of the crisis of representation is the defeat of parties on election day. The most common reason for the defeat of parties at moments of transition from authoritarian rule has been the perception that they are "tainted." In elections that found a democratic regime, parties associated with, or conciliatory to, an outgoing military regime are punished at the voting booth. With the ambiguous exceptions of Mexico[5] and Paraguay, whose elections in the 1980s and early 1990s have been marred by irregularities that protected the incumbents from the full wrath of the voters, the parties most closely identified with an authoritarian regime lost the elections that marked the transition toward constitutional government. This fate befell parties as different as those of the Chilean Right, which lost the 1989 elections at the end of the dictatorship of Augusto Pinochet despite an excellent record of economic growth in the late 1980s, and the Sandinistas in Nicaragua in 1990.

In countries where no major parties supported the military regime, voters chose the opposition party most distant from the unpopular incumbents. This was one important reason why in 1983 Argentina's Radical Civic Union (UCR) beat the Peronistas for the first time since the latter political movement was founded in 1946; why in 1980 Fernando Belaúnde beat the APRA Party (American Popular Revolutionary Alliance) in Peru; and why in 1982 Hernán Siles Suazo became president of Bolivia at the head of a leftist political coalition.

Elections have also punished political parties that were elected as the standard-bearers of political reform but sinned through corruption once in power. The defeats of the Dominican Revolutionary Party (PRD) in 1986, the Christian Democrats (PDC) in El Salvador in 1989 and in Guatemala in 1990, APRA in Peru in 1990, and Acción Democrática (AD) in Venezuela in 1993 can be seen at least in part as voter retribution for such perceived failures.

A third source of electoral defeat for parties has been the response to bad economic conditions.[6] This was certainly a factor in the defeat of the Radical Party in Argentina in 1989, as well as in the defeats of the Christian Democrats in El Salvador in 1989 and in Guatemala in 1990, of APRA in Peru in 1990, and of Acción Democrática in Venezuela in 1993. The economic issue weakened every incumbent Brazilian president since the end of military government in 1985, though Itamar Franco's popularity rose at the very end of his presidency thanks partly to the successful inflation containment policies of his finance minister and eventual successor, Fernando Henrique Cardoso. It also weakened

Guillermo Endara's presidency in Panama, paving the way for the 1994 election victory of the Democratic Revolutionary Party (PRD) once associated with deposed General Manuel Antonio Noriega.

Given the overlap between these three explanations, which is most important to explain the defeat of parties? We believe that "association with authoritarian governments" has more explanatory power than the response to bad economic conditions. Except for the two ambiguous cases already noted (Paraguay and Mexico), no incumbent party tainted by association with prolonged authoritarian rule won an election during the transition from such rule. In contrast, some parties associated with incumbent governments have been defeated despite managing the economy well (in Chile and Jamaica in 1989 and in Uruguay and Costa Rica in 1994), and not every government that has mismanaged the economy has been defeated (Acción Democrática retained the presidency in the 1988 elections). Association with authoritarian rule has been punished more systematically than bad economic outcomes, while good economic management has not always been rewarded.

With the evidence available, however, it is more difficult to determine the relative importance of corruption and bad economic conditions. In Argentina in the early 1990s, for example, the positive economic results under President Carlos Saúl Menem meant more in the public opinion polls than the numerous charges of corruption leveled against people in or close to the administration. In Venezuela, in contrast, the positive performance of the economy under President Pérez during the same years did not bolster his popularity as much as Menem's. It did not save him from later impeachment and conviction on the grounds of corruption, nor did it save his party from election defeats that were also caused in part by the economy's eventual downturn.

The defeat of incumbent parties for any of these three reasons is understandable. Indeed, it is the essence of democratic politics that voters should turn out those officeholders of whose conduct or performance they disapprove. If the reasons why these parties have been defeated give cause to worry about the fate of constitutional government in the region, then the way these parties were defeated gives reason for hope that the instruments of constitutionalism can serve the people's needs.

However, another manifestation of the crisis of representation in the 1990s is the decline of electoral participation in the Anglophone Caribbean and in Venezuela, countries with well-established constitutional governments where such participation had been high historically. Citizens find no electoral vehicle that responds to their concerns to bring about meaningful change. In the early 1990s, as Trevor Munroe notes, voter turnout declined in ten of the thirteen Anglophone Caribbean countries in which general elections were held compared to the average for the 1980s. Voter turnout declined as well in Venezuela, a country with a once consistently high voting rate; its electoral abstention rate rose to 44 percent in 1993, a time of peril for its constitutional life.

### Explaining the Birth of New Parties: From Warrior to Peacemaker

By definition, all new parties are born in dissent. Their leaders and followers claim that existing parties no longer represent them. The revolt against established parties has at times begun literally in rebellion. Never before in Latin America's twentieth-century history have so many political parties been spawned by paramilitary or guerrilla organizations. The new parties examined in this section differ in many ways but share one important trait: their founders once used violence to attempt to overthrow the government or dispose of their adversaries. The transformation of military movements into political parties is best explained as a slow, rational process in which exhausted leaders and followers conclude that politics is more cost-effective than war as a way to gain power.

On the Left, Venezuela's Movimiento al Socialismo (MAS) traces its origins in part to the Venezuelan Communist Party's decision to abandon the guerrilla warfare conducted against Venezuela's governments in the 1960s, after which some key leaders of that effort founded the MAS. By the 1980s and 1990s, as Alan Angell makes clear, the MAS had won a respected place among Venezuela's political parties, and it played an important role in Rafael Caldera's 1993 presidential election victory.

In Colombia the M-19 guerrilla group agreed to demobilize in 1989. Its leaders founded Alianza Democrática (AD) M-19, which won 12.5 percent of the vote in the 1990 presidential elections, the largest share of the vote for any party of the Left in Colombian history, as Harvey F. Kline notes. This party went on to win the second largest bloc of seats in the elections for the Constituent Assembly that met during the first half of 1991, though it had weakened greatly by the time of the 1994 national elections.

Revolutionary victory in Nicaragua in 1979 and the Sandinista defeat in 1990 gradually permitted and eventually required the transformation of the Sandinista Front for National Liberation (FSLN) from a military force into a political party. As Rose Spalding shows, the FSLN as a party has had a tumultuous history since 1990, but it has remained within the framework of constitutional politics.

In El Salvador the FMLN (Farabundo Martí National Liberation Front) began its transformation into a political party upon the signing of the peace agreement in 1992; allied with others on the political Left, as Ricardo Córdova Macías shows, it became the country's second-largest political force in the 1994 elections.

On the Right, it is only a slight exaggeration to argue that El Salvador's Nationalist Republican Alliance (ARENA) was born from a wedding between death squads and a segment of the business community. Roberto D'Aubuisson was the key figure in death squad activities in the late 1970s and early 1980s, and he would become ARENA's equally key leader until his death.

In Argentina, Colonel Aldo Rico led an unsuccessful military mutiny against the constitutional government in April 1987. When national congressional and gubernatorial elections were held in 1991, as Liliana De Riz shows, Rico's Movement for National Dignity and Independence (MODIN) won three seats in the Chamber of Deputies and 10 percent of the vote in the crucial province of Buenos Aires; its subsequent strength has varied but remained generally modest. Moreover, provincial parties in Chaco, Salta, and Tucumán nominated retired military officers who had served as governors during the previous military government; these candidates won the governorships.

The fate of these parties depends in part on their ability to resolve the often bitter internal debates over electoral strategy that occur frequently among new participants in the democratic process. In Colombia the M-19's decision to pursue electoral coalitions with traditional parties instead of focusing on party building seems to have backfired; by 1994 its electoral weight was insignificant. In El Salvador the FMLN split over these issues after the 1994 elections, as did the FSLN in Nicaragua in 1995. The importance of the new parties should not be underestimated, however. In the mid-1990s, the MAS was part of the governing coalition in Venezuela. The FSLN and the FMLN remained among the largest political forces in Nicaragua and El Salvador. And ARENA governed El Salvador.

Why did former military combatants lay down their arms to compete in elections? The general reason is *not* the end of the cold war, which had nothing to do with the creation of the MAS, ARENA, or MODIN, or the M-19's decision to end the armed struggle. Nonetheless, international factors did affect the costs and benefits of war for both the rebels and the government. The decision of some guerrillas in Venezuela in the late 1960s to abandon the armed struggle was part of a wider international debate within the political Left about the proper means to contest power. And the turn away from war by the FMLN and the FSLN was indeed framed by the end of the cold war in Europe.

Apart from these lesser considerations, a familiar but powerful explanation serves best.[7] In Thomas Hobbes' *Leviathan*, political order is established as exhausted individuals recoil from a state of war that is "nasty" and "brutish." In all the cases under review, terrible experiences of prolonged war eventually led the combatants to a rational decision to lay down their arms. Through prolonged war they learned that they could not win. The end of warfare in Latin America led, however, not to Leviathans but to constitutional governments. In the logic of stalemate, neither side could dictate its preferences to the other. Each settled for the second-best solution: to contest each other peacefully.[8] Putting something on the negotiating table became a more effective route to achieve their goals.

Latin America's warriors-turned-peacemakers stumbled unknowingly onto Robert A. Dahl's axiom that, from the government's perspective, "the more the costs of suppression exceed the costs of toleration, the greater the chance for a competitive regime."[9] From the perspective of the armed opposition, the axiom might be rewritten: "The more the costs of rebellion exceed the costs of participation, the greater the chance for a competitive regime."[10] Moreover, governments changed their strategies to provide institutional guarantees and other incentives for guerrillas to make peace and participate in politics. Lawful political space expanded; the insurgents responded rationally. Where the terms for peaceful participation remained insufficiently attractive, as in Guatemala and for some guerrilla forces in Colombia, the war staggers on.

### Explaining the Birth of New Parties: A Protest against Partyarchy and Ideological Betrayal

In recent years, new parties have been more likely to be born and to attract nationwide support when two processes converged: (1) the preexisting party establishment gave signs of seeking to strengthen its ruling monopoly or duopoly, reducing the space for alternative political forces to express themselves within these parties; and (2) the key political party that had received support from the Left abandoned its prior policies and veered sharply toward promarket or other right-wing policies, seemingly "betraying the public trust" and generating a secession on its Left. Political entrepreneurs acted when space on the party spectrum was abdicated through ideological betrayal ("pull factor") and when they no longer found room to play a role within the existing parties ("push factor"). Facing blocked opportunities to voice dissent, the would-be founders of new parties and their followers exited.[11] The new parties gained electorally as citizens expressed their discontent with the status quo by voting against establishment parties.

Argentina, Mexico, Uruguay, and Venezuela exemplify these trends. In these four cases, the emergence of new parties has been in part a response to what some perceived as the arrogance of the national parties and the predominance within older parties of an apparently self-perpetuating leadership—a classic crisis of representation. Writing about Venezuela, Michael Coppedge uses the word *partyarchy* to describe this phenomenon. In Coppedge's analysis of partyarchy, parties fully penetrate organizations in civil society. We use the term a bit more loosely, simply to identify countries where the number of parties long perceived as capable of winning a presidential election is either one (Mexico) or just two (Argentina, Uruguay, and Venezuela), and where party leaders made use of this monopoly or duopoly to create a "cartel of party elites" (in Mexico, Uruguay, and Venezuela) or were perceived to be attempting to create such a cartel (in Argentina in 1994). Under partyarchy, party leaders and organizations seek to regulate electoral competition within each party and between the two dominant parties, to enforce party discipline in legislative assemblies and executive posts, and to rely on intra-elite negotiation to address various important issues.[12]

In Uruguay the constitution was modified in the late 1960s to concentrate greater powers in the presidency and to constrain political rights. Under President Jorge Pacheco Areco, the governing faction of the Colorado party turned to the Right. The government became generally repressive in response to the Tupamaro urban insurgency and began to adopt market-oriented economic policies. Because Uruguay's labor movement had been independent of the traditional parties, it served as a key vehicle to launch a third-party challenge to an entrenched duopoly (the Colorado and Blanco parties) long protected by the electoral law. In 1971 the law-abiding Left reorganized into a broad coalition, the Frente Amplio (FA), to capture 18 percent of the national vote, most of it from the city of Montevideo. By the 1994 national election, the Frente Amplio had made significant gains in the interior provinces; its share of the national vote rose to just under one-third, in a virtual three-way tie with the Blanco and Colorado parties.

In Argentina, President Menem led the governing Peronista Party toward promarket policies in the 1990s, dismantling the legacy of Juan Perón on which Menem had run for the presidency. Critics responded in various ways. Argentine provincial parties acquired a new lease on life.[13] Historically they had done well in gubernatorial and legislative elections, but in 1994 they also obtained important representation in the Constituent Assembly at the expense of both the Peronistas and the Radicals, as De Riz shows. Support for provincial parties, MODIN, and the left-leaning Frente Grande (FG) coalition blossomed in response to the 1994 agreement between President Menem and former president Raúl Alfonsín to modify the constitution, which was widely perceived as an effort to advance their own ambitions. To prevent the continuity of such a duopoly, many voters turned to third parties.

Something similar happened in Mexico, where national elections became much more competitive in the 1980s and 1990s, as Denise Dresser reminds us. After 1982 the long-ruling Institutional Revolutionary Party (PRI) abandoned decades of statist policies to shift toward promarket policies, but it was still reluctant to recognize opposition election victories. In response, the center-right National Action Party (PAN) ran on a platform calling for democratization and was able to increase its national appeal beyond its historic bases of support in various states of northern Mexico. Within the PRI, party elites raised the barriers to internal dissent even as they were abandoning decades of statist policies; denied a voice within the party they had called home, dissenters exited to form a new party. The new center-left Party of the Democratic Revolution (PRD), led by Cuauhtémoc Cárdenas, combined these dissidents from the PRI with supporters drawn from other small parties of the Left (including Mexico's communist party). The PRD considered itself a national party though it obtained disproportionate support from central and southern Mexico.[14] Both the reinvigoration of the PAN and the rise of the Cardenista opposition can be traced to protests against the PRI's monopoly on public office.

In Venezuela in 1989, President Carlos Andrés Pérez shifted away from his populist and statist past toward promarket policies markedly different from those that Acción Democrática had normally espoused. For the most part, the hitherto main opposition party, COPEI (Christian Democratic Party), supported the new economic orientation. In the early 1990s, opposition to these economic policies merged with a revolt against partyarchy that had been gathering strength during the previous decade. Opponents felt that they had no choice but to look outside the two long-dominant parties or to abstain; abstention rates in Venezuelan elections, historically very low, rose significantly. A plurality elected former president Rafael Caldera to the presidency in December 1993 after he had denounced the party establishment and its economic policies, broken with COPEI, and founded the National Convergence (CN), which aligned with the MAS and other parties. Another noteworthy result was the explosive growth of Causa R, a new political party that rose from a social and regional base and quickly became a national party. Causa R emerged in the labor movement of the State of Bolívar, led by union leader Andrés Velásquez, who was elected as state governor and served as the party's presidential candidate in 1993. By the 1993 national elections, Causa R had built a strong presence in the Venezuelan labor movement nationwide and drew support from other regions of the country to capture just under a fourth of the votes cast, a virtual tie with Acción Democrática and COPEI.

The combination of partyarchy and doctrinal abandonment set the stage for the rise of new parties. If partyarchy alone were the explanation, similar challenges should have developed in Colombia (see Kline's chapter) and Honduras (see the chapter by Mark B. Rosenberg and J. Mark Ruhl), where the Liberal and Conservative and the Liberal and National parties, respectively, enjoyed duopolies of representation and where party programs did not typically differ much in ideological content. In these countries, however, the question of "ideological betrayal" never arose. Parties remained reliable: once in office they did not change the behavior displayed in the pre-election campaign.[15] In these countries, despite discontent with the party establishment, no strong new parties emerged in the absence of ideological betrayal.

In the same vein, merely dropping previous programmatic commitments does not suffice to trigger the emergence of a third party seeking to represent interests within civil society. Third parties did not gain much support in Costa Rica in the 1980s, when Liberación Nacional (PLN) governments under presidents Luis Monge and Oscar Arias veered away from the party's historic statism toward freer market policies but did not seek simultaneously to increase barriers to representation. As Lowell Gudmundson tells us, court litigation became the channel for dissent from the new economic policies.

In Argentina, Carlos Menem ran for office without hinting that he planned to abandon decades of Peronista commitment to statist economic policies, but he did. In response, the Frente Grande coalition was formed on the Left to claim the political space that the Peronistas had ceded, but voting support for the Peronistas (though it declined slightly in 1991 relative to the 1989 elections) remained strong in the two nationwide congressional elections following his policy about-face. As De Riz shows, the Peronista share of the vote dropped only in response to the Menem-Alfonsín pact to modify the constitution. The Frente Grande had received only 3.6 percent of the vote in 1993 (before the Menem-Alfonsín pact), but it gained 13.6 percent in 1994 (after the pact), when it also carried the capital city of Buenos Aires; the MODIN's share of the vote rose from 6 percent before the pact to 9 percent after it. In the 1995 presidential elections, the Frente Grande transformed itself into the Frente País Solidario (FREPASO). Its candidate, former Peronista senator and governor José Octavio Bordón, won 28 percent of the votes, finishing second to Menem and ahead of the Radicals—the first time in a century that the Radical Civic Union had failed to come in first or second in a presidential election. (The MODIN's share of the votes fell below 2 percent.)

In short, neither a change in economic policy commitments nor the existence of partisan monopolies or duopolies suffices to trigger the emergence of new parties or party coalitions. Together, however, these two factors greatly increase the likelihood that such parties or coalitions will arise and grow.[16] A hypothesis to explore in the future is the following: when parties are formed around groups organized in civil society (Frente Amplio in Uruguay, PAN in Mexico, Causa R in Venezuela), they are more likely to endure and succeed than parties that are formed principally by dissidents who find their paths blocked within existing parties (Convergencia Nacional in Venezuela, FREPASO in Argentina), with Mexico's PRD exhibiting traits of both processes. There is preliminary support for this view in the December 1995 gubernatorial elections in Venezuela, in which Causa R received 13 percent of the votes cast, the MAS 10 percent, and Convergencia Nacional less than 9 percent.

## Explaining the Birth of New Parties:
## Constructing Political Society

In other countries, representation has suffered not because of the tight grip of one or two strong parties on public office but because of the predominance of many weak parties. Brazil, for example, has been bereft of "real" political parties. As Bolívar Lamounier and Frances Hagopian explain, the combination of powerful traditional elites, entrenched regional interests, the incentives created for politicians by the electoral laws, and the norms and habits of politics have left Brazil with weak, incoherent, unprogrammatic, undisciplined, and fractious parties. In contrast, as Lamounier put it at the Inter-American Dialogue's conference on democracy, "real" modern parties should be internally democratic, pragmatic, and able to recruit cadres and respond quickly to problems with well-defined initiatives.

Since the late 1970s, two real parties have been founded in Brazil. The PT (Workers' Party) grew out of the militant unionism developed in the late 1970s in the metallurgical industries of the highly urban state of São Paulo in protest against the ruling military dictatorship and in search of better economic conditions. It has become the largest explicitly socialist party in Latin America, incorporating a variety of small Brazilian left-wing parties within its midst and providing a partisan home for many social movements that arose in connection with Roman Catholic ecclesiastical base communities, neighborhood associations, and women's movements. In Brazil's 1990 and 1994 presidential elections, the PT's candidate, Lula (Luis Inácio da Silva), came in second. The PT's formal members have genuine opportunities to engage in internal party life and debate and choose party programs and policies. The PT has what Lamounier has called "a definite *esprit de corps.*" It is Brazil's first-ever large mass political party that does not depend on just the popularity of its leader or the efficacy of a patronage machine.

The second real party is the Brazilian Social Democratic Party (PSDB). Founded in 1988 from a schism in the Brazilian Democratic Movement Party (PMDB)—a classic incoherent combination of traditional clientelism, patronage, and factions—the PSDB sought to formulate a centrist "modern" alternative to other parties, with strong appeal to the urban middle class. The PSDB designed a program for effective democratic governance to which its officeholders were ordinarily bound. In 1994 PSDB founding leader Fernando Henrique Cardoso was elected president of Brazil in large part because of his previous success as finance minister. Like the PT, although to a lesser extent, the PSDB is characterized by programmatic coherence, officeholder discipline, and internal party life.

Since the 1994 elections, then, Brazil for the first time has had "real" parties in government and in opposition, in addition to the traditional clientelistic patronage machines. Nonetheless, the strength of those traditional machines was also evident in that election. In order to elect Cardoso to the presidency, the PSDB had to form an alliance with the Liberal Front Party (PFL), a classic patronage party. Thus it remains to be seen how much long-term impact the PT and the PSDB will have on the traditional style of politics in Brazil, especially because skewed electoral laws still limit their representation in Congress.

## Explaining the Reinvention of Old Parties

The region's crisis of representation and its economic depression of the 1980s did not overwhelm every preexisting political party, nor was the creation of new parties the sole response to these problems, however. Many existing parties have made efforts to adapt to changed circum- stances, a strategy of reinvention. In most cases, defeat—either of the party or of democracy as a whole—permitted challengers within the party to marginalize discredited factions and leaders, at times relieving them of their power. Defeat also made it easier to reexamine old dog- mas and discard failed policies. Defeat alone is insufficient, of course, for the successful reinvention of parties. A reinvented party's program- matic reorientation can be consolidated only if the party is rewarded with electoral victory.

During the 1980s, as Timothy R. Scully demonstrates, the Chilean Christian Democrats and the socialists (including the socialist offshoot PPD, the Party for Democracy) rebuilt and repositioned themselves, and forged an alliance (the Concertación Democrática, CD) to win the 1988 plebiscite that ended the dictatorship and then to win the next two presidential elections in 1989 and 1993. The breakdown of democ- racy in 1973, the failure of the protests of the mid-1980s to unseat the military government, and the collapse of heterodox economic policies in neighboring countries affected the balance of forces within the par- ties of the Center and the Left and eventually resulted in the ascen- dance of new leaders who embraced a market-conforming political platform.

Also during the 1980s, the People's National Party (PNP) in Jamaica reconstructed its program and renewed its cadres, after the party's failed statist economic policies led to a crushing electoral defeat in 1980. The reinvented party won the parliamentary elections of 1989 and subsequently effected a transition of the prime ministership from Michael Manley to P. J. Patterson. The party recognized that its statist economic policies during the 1970s failed and had also resulted in its election defeat in 1980.

In Argentina, in response to their 1983 presidential election defeat, the Peronistas reinvented themselves. Founded in the mid-1940s by Juan Perón as what he called a "movement" more than a party, the Peronistas (Partido Justicialista, PJ) at last held internal party elections

in the 1980s to choose candidates for office. These new internal procedures made it easier to remove many old-time leaders who had lost the
support of the rank and file. In the early 1990s, in addition, the Menem
government adopted an entirely new profile of economic policies.

In Panama in the early 1990s the PRD successfully recovered from
its long cohabitation with General Noriega. As Richard L. Millett indicates, after its 1989 defeat the PRD modified its policies toward the
United States, dropped its support for reestablishing the armed forces,
adopted less confrontational stands toward other political forces, and
adopted a market-friendly economic program. It won the 1994 presidential elections.

In Chile, Jamaica, Argentina, and Panama, the reinvention of the
parties rested on a shift from statist to promarket economic policies, a
shift made possible by the shock of defeat, which in turn permitted the
removal of discredited leaders. In many cases a comfortable margin of
victory for the reinvented parties in a later election facilitated the consolidation of the reinvention and the policies associated with it. Leaders who changed the historical policy commitments of their party were
likely to lose some part of their previous constituency; the larger the
victory, the less risky was this change. In Jamaica the margin of victory
of the People's National Party in 1989 meant that the "renovating"
leadership did not need to rely on the vote-mobilizing capabilities of
the more radical wing of the party. In Chile the weakening of the Communist Party removed the incentive for leaders of the Center-Left to
back away from their commitment to more market-oriented economic
policies. In Argentina and Panama the Peronistas and the PRD, respectively, faced ineffectual opposition parties. In short, a significant victory over the opposition was as important to party renewal as the prior
defeat of the party itself.

### Representational Challenges to the Party System
Many of the new parties under review have been linked to social movements, but the relationship between political and civil society remains
problematic in many countries. In Brazil, Chile, Mexico, Nicaragua,
and Venezuela, for example, many groups in civil society have sought
to increase their autonomy with regard to parties in order to avoid partisan manipulation. In Venezuela and Colombia, new social movements
have pressed for the decentralization of the state as a way to weaken
central party leaderships, and new local leaders have run for office successfully as independents. Though understandable, these combined
trends may well make it more difficult to secure both effective political
representation and sustained political cooperation on a nationwide
basis.

In addition, there remain important representational voids that not
even the new parties have begun to fill sufficiently and that are just as

important for effective democratic governance. We call attention to three of them.

As Deborah J. Yashar points out, the representation of indigenous peoples has been woefully inadequate throughout the region. Organized ethnic protest has been emerging since the 1970s in countries with large indigenous populations. In Bolivia, new, small political parties have so far been able to channel these energies and provide some means for representation. But, as Eduardo A. Gamarra indicates, Víctor Hugo Cárdenas, the Aymara leader elected in 1993 as Bolivia's vice-president, may be more popular outside Bolivia than in his own country. He can obtain considerable international sympathy and support on behalf of those whom he claims to represent, but his actual backing within Bolivia, even among indigenous peoples, remains modest for a variety of reasons, including the internal diversity of the indigenous community and the limited accomplishments of his administration. Bolivia has also witnessed the phenomenon of Palenquismo, not organized ethnic protest but populist appeals to indigenous peoples by television and radio personality Carlos Palenque.

In the southern Mexican state of Chiapas, the Zapatista National Liberation Army (EZLN) combines ethnic and regional grievances with a larger national program and the disposition to use armed violence to advance its ends. Because of its reliance on violence, this insurgency has been the most worrisome example of ethnic protest.

In Ecuador the Confederation of Indigenous Nationalities (CONAIE) organized and spearheaded important nationwide protests in the 1990s in opposition to proposed land tenure law changes and other measures that, in its judgment, adversely affected the interests of indigenous peoples. CONAIE also learned to collaborate with some labor unions to organize general strikes. This may well be Latin America's strongest indigenous-based social movement independent of a political party.

Until the 1980s, nationwide political protest by indigenous peoples had been extremely rare in Latin America. To understand the change leading to the rise of such protest, Yashar highlights four features that apply with special force during the 1980s and 1990s: (1) the political opening associated with democratization; (2) the erosion of existing avenues of representation and the increase in material hardship that often accompany the implementation of neoliberal economic policies; (3) the nurturing and enabling effects of institutions such as the changed Roman Catholic Church and other religious communities; and (4) the growth of an international movement of foundations, scholars, and activists to provide support for indigenous organizations in Latin America. There is still the need to explain further, however, why Quechua speakers in Ecuador organize on behalf of the rights of indigenous peoples who happen to be poor, while Quechua speakers in Peru organize on behalf of the rights of poor people who happen to be indigenous.

Why does the likelihood of organized protest on behalf of ethnocultural and linguistic goals vary so much?

A second problem of inadequate representation is evident with regard to gender.[17] Universal suffrage came later to Latin America than to Western Europe and North America, and women's effective participation in politics has continued to lag. In the 1980s and 1990s, some women politicians have emerged on the national scene, but they are still rare. Some of the new and renovating political parties on the Left, such as Brazil's PT, the Chilean socialists, and Nicaragua's Sandinistas, consciously design their internal rules to attempt, with varying degrees of success, to create an active role for women in discussions and leadership.

A third problem of inadequate representation is the oldest and best known: the question of social class and democratic politics. In this collection, Jorge G. Castañeda examines the compatibility between new promarket economic policies and the distributive pressures that, he argues, inevitably emerge in democratic regimes. Latin American and Caribbean countries have not been good at meeting these goals in the past. The risk of neoliberal reforms is that the prospects for many people are likely to worsen unless there is a conscious commitment to address problems of absolute poverty so that "common folk" can become true "citizens." It is not just the troubles of the powerful, in other words, but the inattention to the troubles of the unempowered that has created a crisis of representation. Effective democratic governance demands that the voiceless be heard.

## Reforming State Institutions

In response to the crisis of representation, the legacies of authoritarian rule, and the inefficacy of government economic management in all countries in the early 1980s, government institutions came in for close scrutiny after the demise of authoritarian rule. The result was a widespread and intensive effort to reform the institutions of the state. This section describes the strategies pursued and analyzes their limited success.

We focus on three major areas of attempted institutional redesign. One is the effort to break the gridlock between, and improve the democratic responsiveness of, the executive and the legislature. The second is the effort to reform the administration of justice: to combat crime and corruption, to depoliticize the courts, and to improve access to the court system. The third is the attempt to bring about territorial decentralization and to devolve responsibilities to subnational governments while seeking to improve their capacity to handle their new duties.

### Reshaping Executive-Legislative Relations

With the return of constitutional government in Latin America, scholars and politicians advanced proposals for institutional reform designed to help solve the problems that they believed had contributed to the previous breakdown of democratic institutions. In many cases the nature of legislative-executive relations was blamed; in particular, fixed presidential terms and the stalemate between the legislature and the president in presidential systems were seen as crucial factors in democratic breakdown.

The most commonly heard prescription was parliamentarism. Its scholarly advocates believed that incentives for cooperation between the two branches would be increased by tying the legislators' tenure in office to the success of the executive.[18] Legislators who would face the prospect of losing their ballot positions in new elections called by a stymied prime minister would be more likely, the proponents of parliamentarism believed, to organize in disciplined parties and form effective government coalitions. Similarly, executives in parliamentary systems would face votes of no-confidence and thus would have more incentive to negotiate with legislators than would a president elected separately from the legislature and unaccountable to it. Despite these arguments, parliamentarism was not adopted in any Latin American country.

In the Anglophone Caribbean, the problems were different. In their existing parliamentary systems, the first-past-the-post electoral system and the small size of parliaments gravely weakened the capacity of the legislature to represent political minorities or to balance the executive. Elections produced large parliamentary majorities, denying even large minority parties adequate representation in parliament. Moreover, parliament was left with few means to check unbridled executive power. As Munroe reports, almost one-third of the region's members of parliament are also cabinet members. In effect, they are constitutionally debarred from independent and critical stances in relation to the executive because they are also in the executive. These problems remain unsolved for the most part.

Although politicians in Latin America and the Caribbean have been unwilling to undertake a wholesale change of state institutions (from presidentialism to parliamentarism, or vice versa), they did make a variety of institutional changes. Argentina (1994), Brazil (1988), Colombia (1991), and Peru (1978 and 1994) convened constituent assemblies to rewrite their basic charter. In Bolivia, Chile, Nicaragua, Paraguay, and Venezuela, legislators undertook constitutional reforms. In Ecuador a commission of experts drafted a new constitution based on widespread consultation and subsequent submission to a referendum.

There have been two waves of constitutional reforms. The first wave accompanied the transition to democracy and was aimed at solving the problems that were believed to have plagued previous experiences with democracy, especially gridlock and exclusionary practices such as the effective disenfranchisement of large numbers of citizens. Exclusionary practices also came in for sharp criticism in the long-established constitutional polities of Colombia, Venezuela, and the Anglophone Caribbean, where the most widely voiced demand was for an opening of the political system to greater participation (a cry heard also in Mexico). The second wave of constitutional reforms responded to long-standing problems of democratic governance that came to public attention as governments attempted to implement market reforms: corruption, excessive concentration of power in the presidency, and irresponsible behavior by legislators.

The goals for reform advanced by the two waves were broad and potentially contradictory: (1) to break the stalemate between the executive and the legislature; (2) to encourage the democratic responsiveness of the executive by checking its unbridled powers; and (3) to increase the democratic responsiveness of the legislature. This third point had two aspects: to encourage responsible, programmatic behavior by legislators and to increase the effective representation of voting minorities.

In order to break the stalemate between the executive and the legislature, several kinds of reforms were passed to strengthen the executive. The most widely adopted reform was the ballotage, that is, a "second round" in presidential elections in order to ensure that the president would be elected by a majority. Since the late 1970s, this has been introduced in Argentina and Nicaragua (where a candidate needs only 45 percent of the vote to avoid a second round), and also in Brazil, Chile, Colombia, the Dominican Republic, Ecuador, El Salvador, Guatemala, and Peru. A second reform was to give special powers to the executive to make macroeconomic policy. Such reforms first occurred in gridlocked democracies: Uruguay in 1967, Colombia in 1968, and Chile in 1970. They would be introduced in Peru in 1979 and 1993, Brazil in 1988, and passed by plebiscite in Ecuador in 1994.

A third change, introduced in Peru in 1993 and in Argentina in 1994, was to permit the president's immediate reelection, ostensibly to strengthen the incumbent's capacity to govern. The fact that incumbent presidents Fujimori and Menem benefited from the reform, however, led many to see this change as a resurgence of personalism in contexts where partisan, judicial, and legislative checks on the executive remain weak.

A different approach to breaking stalemates between the president and the legislature focused on the electoral law and the incentives it provides to legislators. The electoral law is often cited as an explanation for the stable governmental coalition in Congress in Chile and for unstable coalitions in Congress in Brazil. Brazilianists point to electoral law incentives that hinder cooperation, foster party indiscipline and disloyalty, and induce preferential attention to pork-barrel politics over policy issues. In contrast, Scully calls attention to Chile's quite different electoral law of the early 1990s, whose "almost inexorable bipolar logic" has provided strong incentives for interparty cooperation at the polls and in the legislature.

In order to check the president's powers, politicians in various countries have granted greater prerogatives to legislatures. In Colombia, the Congress was authorized to censure ministers. In Nicaragua in 1994, the Assembly acquired greater authority over tax policy. In Argentina the 1994 constitutional reform created a cabinet chief accountable to the legislature and curbed the president's power to rule by decree. Bans on presidential reelection, already in place in most countries, have been added to several constitutions. In 1994 Nicaragua and the Dominican Republic banned immediate reelection; in 1991 Colombia banned reelection at any time. This strengthening of congressional prerogatives is largely a reaction against the abuse of presidential power that occurred as chief executives attempted to stabilize and reform the economies of these countries. (This happened only to a limited degree in Brazil, where the 1988 Constitution increased a great many of the legislature's powers but at the same time made the president's decree powers, established in the prior authoritarian constitution, even more arbitrary.)

Meanwhile, some reformers tried to end exclusionary practices and foster the legislature's democratic responsiveness by increasing representational pluralism. In many countries, expansion of the suffrage was expected to provide a constituency for reformist parties of the Center and Left. The ballotage in Argentina and Colombia was designed to encourage the proliferation of presidential candidates, and consequently of parties as representative vehicles, by permitting "sincere" voting (in which voters support the candidate they truly prefer) in the first round. Colombia's use of national districts for the election of senators allows voting minorities not concentrated in a particular region to gain representation in this chamber. Venezuela's shift to voting in part for individual candidates, not just for party slates, seeks to promote greater pluralism and weaken control by party leaders as well.

The most striking characteristic of these reform processes as a whole, however, has been their failure to improve the quality of democratic governance. Constitutional reform has proceeded the least in the Anglophone Caribbean, but the Latin Americans, frankly, have relatively little to show for their efforts, either. The greatest disappointments are evident in Brazil, Colombia, Ecuador, and Honduras, where little seems to have changed, and in Chile, where the electoral laws and the standing and structure of Congress remain well below acceptable levels for democratic constitutionalism. There, executive powers are excessive, one-fifth of the Senate is unelected, and the electoral law overrepresents conservative rural districts and impedes the effective representation of voting minorities.

How can this failure be explained? Some of the problems are genuinely intractable. Even if "smart people" were omnipotent in implementing reforms, they would still find it extraordinarily hard to determine how to balance the trade-off between accountability and effectiveness. The somewhat contradictory goals present early in the reform process were just as evident at the end.

In some cases, the diagnoses and prescriptions advanced by reforming elites turned out to be faulty. Ecuadorian academics, Anita Isaacs reminds us, expected radical changes even though the modifications enacted in 1979 were for the most part limited to the extension of the suffrage, party registration, and ballotage, stopping well short of reforming the institutional relations between the executive and the legislature. Ecuadorian elites erroneously focused their attention on creating incentives for short-term *electoral* coalitions (such as the ballotage), failing to realize that these incentives did not facilitate longer-term *governing* coalitions. Similarly flawed was the exercise in Brazil. Brazilian constitutionalists in 1988 did not address the electoral law's incentives for politicians to focus on pork-barrel politics and its disincentives for party discipline. Lamounier argues that this neglect can be traced to the mistaken notion that fragmented ("pluralist") representation in the legislature and concentrated power in the executive are the best ways to reconcile democratic government and effectiveness. (Although Brazil has long suffered from representational imbalance and electoral fragmentation, the 1988 Constitution continued to over-represent the northeast while failing to establish a minimum vote threshold that parties must meet to win representation in Congress.) In both Ecuador and Brazil, constitutional reform did little to solve the problem of governmental gridlock; president and congress continued to confront each other, the former often resorting to rule by decree.

In many cases, necessary reforms were not passed because they threatened the interests of elites. Munroe shows that the first-past-the-post electoral laws common throughout the Anglophone Caribbean protect the interests of the dominant parties best because they exclude third parties from ever gaining significant parliamentary membership.

More generally in Latin America, Hagopian's study of traditional elites shows that the interests of such elites are best served by existing electoral arrangements that reinforce the clientelistic nature of parties. Clientelistic party systems are characterized by fragmentation, personalism, a patronage or rent-seeking approach to the state and public policy, and a lack of party loyalty on the part of legislators and voters. Party indiscipline is especially evident when politicians desert the parties on whose tickets they ran, as a majority of Brazilian members of Congress have done since the restoration of civilian government in 1985 and as a comparable proportion of Ecuadorian members of Congress have done since a similar transition in 1979; in each of these two countries, as many as a third of the members of the legislature change parties during one term of office.

In clientelistic party systems, parties fail to articulate the interests of their constituents at a programmatic level, which fuels voter apathy and, in some cases, social violence. Collective action is difficult when power is dispersed among many parties (as in Brazil and Ecuador, for example); even where parties are fewer (as in Colombia and Honduras), internal factionalization and lack of discipline within large parties frequently results in an equally paralyzing de facto multipartyism. Members of congress pursue pork-barrel objectives at the expense of legislation or administrative oversight, permitting the excessive concentration of powers in the presidency. Traditional elites can make such conditions work well for them.

In clientelistic systems, presidents can employ patronage to co-opt the opposition, weaken congressional supervision over executive policies, and lull legislators into permitting the use of presidential decree powers. For these reasons, presidents, too, often prefer the constitutional status quo, therefore. For example, as Kline notes, Colombian presidents since 1946 have routinely ruled under "state of siege" provisions authorized by the constitution, relying on decrees rather than laws for the governance of the economy.

In this book, Hagopian argues that traditional elites are less predisposed to respect democratic institutions and processes and more likely to abuse the state for ends that are both antidemocratic and antimarket. Lamounier, Kline, Isaacs, Edelberto Torres-Rivas, Rosario Espinal, and Rosenberg and Ruhl document the long-standing clientelistic features of party systems in Brazil, Colombia, Ecuador, Guatemala, the Dominican Republic, and Honduras, which have had the effects summarized above. As Rosenberg and Ruhl put it, the two principal parties in Honduras have offered little effective leadership because their interest is largely directed at meeting the needs of their respective clienteles. Power is rarely exercised to effect a larger vision of the common good. In all such cases, democratic representativeness suffers, and effective constitutional reform to improve governance becomes highly unlikely.

Nevertheless, there have been some modest improvements, especially in countries with little experience of congressional assertiveness or efficacy. Ironically these improvements have resulted less from constitutional changes than from a more even balance of power between executive and legislature. For the first time ever, the Congress of El Salvador plays a role of oversight and legislation in the 1990s, with all of the country's political forces represented in its midst. During these same years, the Mexican Congress began to question the executive more systematically. Also in the 1990s, albeit (as Spalding shows) after excruciating difficulties, Nicaragua's Assembly began to legislate to address some of the country's ills. After the 1993 national elections, as Diego Abente Brun points out, Paraguay found itself with a divided government for the first time in its history; at issue was the capacity of president and congress to deepen a still-incipient process of constitutionalizing the government while maintaining acceptable levels of governability.

History also shows the importance of political learning in improving democratic governance. Consider the problem of resolving executive-legislative gridlock. The cases of Costa Rica in the 1950s and El Salvador in the 1990s exemplify the capacity of politicians to learn to cooperate for the purpose of fostering civil peace and establishing constitutional government. In each of those cases, civil wars came to an end and constitutional governments were installed. Venezuela in the 1950s and Chile in the 1990s provide related examples: various parties were able to cooperate to end dictatorship, install constitutional government, and fashion effective relations between president and congress.

Bolivia in the mid-1980s is equally remarkable. As Gamarra shows, Bolivia had had a textbook example of a weak, fragmented party system that permitted the military and, later on, drug traffickers to influence the exercise of power. In 1985, Bolivian politicians responded with inventiveness and creativity to a runaway hyperinflation. They have been able to form three kinds of partisan coalitions: one to contest elections, another in Congress to identify the next president (in the past three elections, the winner of the plurality of votes became president only once), and a third also in Congress to fashion reliable congressional governing majorities. The very same parties that had brought the country near its grave made possible its resurrection.

Each of these five countries was in the midst of effecting an epochal transition from economic chaos (Bolivia), civil war (Costa Rica and El Salvador), or dictatorship (Chile and Venezuela). In each case, politicians successfully responded to the problems of their times. These examples suggest that institutional changes are most effective and lasting when they are backed by strong political coalitions and serve the interests of the dominant political forces at a critical juncture.

### Reforming the Court System

Judiciaries throughout Latin America are in dire need of reform, but little headway is being made. The problems with the court system occur at nearly every level, for four general reasons: (1) the corruption of judges; (2) the politicization of the courts; (3) the gutting of judicial independence by the president; and (4) the operational incapacities of the court system itself. In the 1980s and 1990s, reform efforts have attempted to expedite the administration of justice to combat crime and corruption, depoliticize the courts, and improve societal access to the court system. This section looks first at the four explanations for the malperformance of the court system and then turns to reform efforts.

In some countries, especially Bolivia and Colombia, the judiciary has been corrupted by drug traffickers. In Colombia, Kline recalls, drug leaders have been convicted infrequently because they have bribed, threatened, or killed judges. In response, the Colombian judicial system acknowledged its incapacity and came to rely more on plea bargaining: any person could receive a reduced sentence upon surrendering and confessing one crime. The problem of judicial corruption from drug trafficking has spread to other countries.

Meanwhile, the extent of politicization of judicial appointments by political parties is a threat to impartiality. In Ecuador in 1983 and again in 1993, Isaacs reports, congressional majorities deeply politicized the appointments to the Supreme Court, gutting its independence and threatening constitutional order.[19]

The threat to judicial independence comes not only from the legislature but, even more frequently, from an executive eager to reduce all obstacles to the implementation of presidential policies. In Argentina in the early 1990s, De Riz reminds us, President Menem increased the size of the Supreme Court to add his appointees and at the same time reduced the scope of Supreme Court jurisdiction over cases bearing on the "economic emergency." The Supreme Court's deference to the executive seriously compromised its legitimacy in the eyes of much of the public and the legal community. In other places—such as the Dominican Republic, as Espinal tells us—presidentialist personalism in the appointment of judges is routine and has greatly weakened the independence of the judiciary.

Presidents have also meddled with the courts to avert the politically costly prosecution of their allies. In February 1994 President Fujimori used his legislative majority to prevent the Peruvian Supreme Court from trying military officers accused of extrajudicial executions, the killings of nine students and a professor from La Cantuta national teachers' university.[20] In Argentina, President Menem replaced the independent judges who were slated to try some of his associates on corruption charges with more compliant court officers.

Finally, the operation of the courts is itself defective. In Bolivia, for example, Gamarra notes that the most serious problem facing the judicial system is the non-Spanish-speaking population's lack of access to the courts. By law, all proceedings must be conducted in Spanish, even though this is not the primary language of a substantial proportion of the population. As a result, many people look for justice outside the courts.

Operative deficiencies are also apparent in Colombia, according to Kline: in the early 1980s, only one in ten reported crimes ever led to a verdict, and in the early 1990s that figure had dropped to one of twenty. Similar statistics, regrettably, are common throughout the region. In many countries the court system is severely underfinanced, as Millett and Isaacs point out for the cases of Panama and Ecuador, respectively.

Despite these enduring and serious problems, there are glimmers of reform. In many cases, sustained efforts are under way to allocate greater resources to the courts, to improve the training of judges, and to professionalize the circumstances of their work. Colombia's 1991 Constitution created a National Prosecutor's Office (Fiscalía Nacional) with the authority to investigate and prosecute cases and to coordinate the activities of all military and civilian agencies gathering evidence on crimes. Thus the new constitution broke with the Napoleonic Code tradition in which some judges investigate crimes and others adjudicate them; the reforms freed the court system from investigative responsibilities. During the first two years, the judicial system processed 50 percent more cases than under the old system. This change holds promise for expediting the administration of justice.

Argentina's constitutional reform of 1994 also holds promise. In the so-called Olivos Pact between Alfonsín and Menem, a new council was created to nominate all judges prior to their appointment. The constitutional reform created a new General Accounting Office to audit the government's accounts and thus combat corruption. These agreements enhanced the independence and professionalism of the judiciary system, created more effective means to combat corruption, and attempted to depoliticize the judiciary. Parties in El Salvador, Nicaragua, and Paraguay have also been able to reach agreements and appoint balanced supreme courts. The willingness of political actors to compromise raises the hope that one of the root causes of judicial politicization, legislative-executive conflict, might be reduced.

Most ambitious has been Costa Rica's experiment with judicial activism to facilitate societal access to the court system, as described by Gudmundson. Since the 1980s the Fourth or Constitutional Chamber (Sala IV) of the Supreme Court has become involved in an ever-widening number of disputes. Nongovernmental organizations (NGOs) have gone to the Fourth Chamber to challenge the neoliberal economic policies implemented by Congress and the executive. The Chamber has also become involved in tourist, coastal, and national park development projects and in disputes about the rights of indigenous peoples, labor unions, and prisoners. Virtually all important economic interest groups have litigated to oppose the elimination of protection or subsidies. Plaintiffs often try to generate publicity and controversy to provoke the executive to modify its policies. Although effective at channeling discontent in the short run, this approach could lead to the atrophy of legitimate political channels for interest articulation and conflict resolution, and a heightened sense of popular cynicism regarding the judiciary.

### The Territorial Decentralization of State Powers

In the 1980s and 1990s most Latin American countries placed territorial decentralization on their national agendas.[21] Many see it as a way to unburden the national government by turning over some of its responsibilities to local entities that may understand local conditions better and, reformers hope, may be more effective; at times, it is but one way to cut the national budget.

For others, decentralization is widely regarded as a means to increase the participatory nature of regimes, especially in countries that have come to elect local officials only in the 1980s or 1990s, such as Colombia and Venezuela. For many groups in civil society which have had trouble articulating their interests at the national level because of a reluctance to form close ties with political parties, local government holds hope for meaningful participation in community affairs. Parties of the Left, as Angell notes, hope that territorial decentralization will allow their officeholders to prove their competence in government at the local level, paving the way for a claim to national office; Causa R in Venezuela's Bolívar State, the Frente Amplio in the city of Montevideo, and the PT in São Paulo exemplify this strategy. Finally, local governments can provide new participatory opportunities for the informally disenfranchised, including indigenous groups and the poor; their increased participation at the local level might have positive implications for democratization at the national level.

Government and opposition may have contradictory objectives with regard to decentralization, however. The example of Chiapas illustrates this tension. For the Mexican government, territorial decentralization in Chiapas is a means to pacify the region and co-opt some indigenous elites. For the Zapatistas who began an insurgency in January 1994, the objective is to establish bases from which to launch wider political challenges, as they did in 1994 and 1995.

Despite these high (and somewhat contradictory) hopes, the results are discouraging. In most countries, local governments possess neither the funds nor the technical expertise to assume the new responsibilities assigned to them. Under these circumstances, subnational governments can undermine the efforts of national executives to carry out economic reforms. In Argentina and Brazil, for example, fiscal powers and prerogatives were extended to states and municipalities without corresponding responsibilities; the resulting deficits and debt contracted by subnational governments have hampered the consolidation of economic reforms.

Decentralization can also undermine democratization by reinforcing the power of local elites, their practices of clientelism (to which Hagopian calls attention), and the power of their military or paramilitary allies, as in Brazil, Colombia, El Salvador, and Mexico. Especially in the rural areas, these countries suffer from the inability of the central state to enforce the law equitably throughout its national territory. Instead of increasing the accountability of local elites to civil society, decentralization would decrease even further their accountability to national authority, and it might permit the consolidation of petty tyrannies. Decentralization is also likely to remove certain issues from the national agenda, which has been more likely to be hospitable to initiatives from the political Left. Decentralization may some day empower ordinary citizens to take better charge of their government, and permit a wider range of innovation at the local level, but there is still a long way to go before these promises are realized.

## Economic Reforms, the Market, and Democratic Consolidation

Free markets and free politics are celebrated throughout much of the region, and thoughtful arguments are advanced about why they "go together" in Latin America and the Caribbean in the 1990s. Yet many scholars and political activists also argue that the rapid implementation of "neoliberal" market reforms has disrupted democratic representation, hurt the poor, and increased social conflict.[22]

Market reforms (especially deregulation, privatization, and the termination of business subsidies) can serve the goals of democratic politics. Statist economic arrangements often permit and foster close connections between economic and political elites, reducing the prospects for wider participation and fair contestation. Statist economics privilege business groups whose profits depend on political connections, not necessarily on efficiency or quality. Market reforms can break the ties between political and economic elites, reduce the opportunities for corruption and rent-seeking behavior, and create a level playing field for economic actors. Insertion into international markets provides external actors with the leverage needed to defend constitutional government in the region; such leverage helped to thwart Guatemalan president Jorge Serrano's attempt to overturn the constitution in 1993. In the 1990s, external actors have also used their economic leverage to prevent authoritarian reversals and to widen political openings in the Dominican Republic, Mexico, and Peru.

Some governments—most notably in Argentina, Chile, and Costa Rica—are establishing a "happy partnership" between market reforms and nationalism, replacing the historic alliance of populism and nationalism, as a means to consolidate both constitutional government and a market economy. In Chile, for example, defenders of constitutionalism and market openings appeal to nationalist sentiments suggesting that a proud nation would surely wish to meet these standards of "civilized" peoples; similar arguments are made for the integration of the poorest sectors into the national economy.

Democracy, in turn, can help to consolidate a market economy. In countries where levels of societal contestation and political instability have often been very high and organized opposition forces have been strong, democracy can reduce many transaction costs. There may be fewer disruptions from labor strikes or insurgencies if the would-be supporters of these strategies can find more cost-effective alternatives to advance their interests within democratic politics. In addition, democratic regimes can involve the political opposition in support of a market economy more effectively than can authoritarian regimes. In Argentina and Chile in the 1990s, for example, key decisions—Argentina's convertibility law governing monetary and exchange rate policies and Chile's tax laws—have resulted from negotiation between executive and Congress. By giving the opposition a voice and vote in the creation of fundamental long-term market-conforming policies, democratic regimes can set the foundations for credible and stable long-term rules. In these circumstances, rational investors can expect that today's rules will endure tomorrow even if the opposition wins the general elections. The procedures of democracy help to consolidate the market economy.

But the connection between democracy and the market is complex. Many of the devices designed to maintain fiscal discipline barely meet the test of democracy. For example, a closed and technocratic style of decision making reinforces the unresponsiveness of the state to societal demands and may well be authoritarian. At times presidents rule by decree, deliberately bypassing the legislature. These concerns were raised most often in Argentina and Bolivia in the 1990s. Even strong parties such as those in Chile, which have adapted well to the challenges of governance, must still prove their ability to articulate societal interests; there is so much "consensus" in Chile that dissenting interests and values may be neglected.

The turn toward a market opening has coincided with spectacular cases of corruption that led to the impeachments of presidents Collor in Brazil and Pérez in Venezuela. Concern about corruption also looms high in nearly all other countries. During the early stages of the privatization of state enterprises, for example, there are substantial opportunities for government officials to favor certain business groups. Mexico illustrates a related problem: because PRI politicians can no longer rely as much on state resources to pay for their campaigns, they resort to private funds in a political environment where rules governing campaign financing are weak and often unenforced.[23]

In the short run, moreover, the shift in economic models has contributed to the crisis of representation discussed earlier because parties must overhaul their economic programs and find new ways to gain support from their often surprised constituents. New parties and social movements have arisen to protest these policies, invigorating democratic contestation, to be sure, but also challenging the scope and durability of market reforms. Populist parties and corporatist forms of interest representation had in years past tied labor and other groups to the political system, but in the 1990s these forces have weakened precisely at the moment when public support must be found to help guarantee the stability of economic reforms and constitutional government, especially in Brazil, Mexico, and Venezuela. And, as noted earlier, Yashar traces the rise of indigenous mobilization throughout the hemisphere in part to grievances exacerbated by neoliberal reforms and left unarticulated by eroded representational networks.

The change in economic models has also altered the roles of the political Right, the political Left, and the traditional elites, shaping the quality of politics and the stability of constitutional government. The political Right has increased its participation in party politics in many countries, as Edward L. Gibson demonstrates. Parties of the Right, or parties with strong support from the Right, have proven far stronger than some eminent scholars had thought as recently as the early 1980s that they would be.[24] As the 1990s opened, for instance, elected parties or coalitions with strong support from the Right governed in every Central American country. This development portends well for the stability of constitutional rule, at least in the short term, because conservative interests (most often those of business) are well represented through the party system.

The marriage between democracy and the market also makes it possible for many economic actors to pledge their allegiance to constitutional government. Few incentives now exist for business to knock on the barracks door to alter national economic policy. The military is often judged to be too incompetent to manage the economy, given its generally poor record in government in the 1970s and early 1980s. Labor unions are weak, and macroeconomic policies benefit property owners. Business participates in politics, often supporting parties of the Right (though sometimes also other parties), mainly through the deployment of resources at election time (such as purchasing television time during campaigns), not through party building. The connection between business and parties may be close in El Salvador (with regard to ARENA) and in Mexico (with regard to the PRI), but it is tactical at best in most countries.

One obstacle to building parties of the Right has been the tendency of formerly populist parties in Argentina, Bolivia, Mexico, and Venezuela to usurp neoliberal platforms. One question for these parties is whether they can incorporate the Right as leaders and as constituents and still retain lower-class support. In the mid-1990s, perhaps surprisingly, the answer (except in Venezuela) seemed to be yes—a true feat of partisan skill.

The stability of constitutional government in the short term depends on the representation of the Right, but the long-run consolidation of democracy depends on the representation of nonelite interests, often by parties of the Left as Hagopian argues in her chapter. The development of a social democratic Left in Latin America, as Angell shows, has been encouraged by the same events that have weakened the Left in general: authoritarian repression, the collapse of communism, the decline of labor unions, and the narrowing of economic options. Widespread corruption and inattention to social needs have become key issues for these parties. The parties of the social democratic Left are very strong in Brazil, the Dominican Republic, Nicaragua, Panama, Uruguay, and Venezuela, and strong in Chile and El Salvador. For them, constitutional government holds the only route to national power in the 1990s. The Left's lack of governing experience in most countries and the absence of a clear economic alternative are liabilities, however.

Finally, as Hagopian notes, most traditional elites have opposed market reforms because such reforms threaten their control of resources and their access to government policymakers. To the extent that reforms succeed in shifting control over clientelistic resources from traditional elites to the executive, or reduce the salience of such resources by means of privatization and deregulation, the reforms are likely to advance the cause of both freer markets and freer politics. Traditional elites undermine democracy and markets by skewing electoral laws in order to block the emergence of political rivals who articulate mass interests, by placing limits on market and other policy reforms as a condition of their support for constitutional government, and by deforming the mechanisms of political representation with clientelism. These practices have pernicious effects on the extent and effectiveness of democratic governance. The alienation of citizens from the political system and the obstacles to market reforms are greatest where traditional elites are the strongest, as in Brazil, Ecuador, and Guatemala.

In sum, market reforms in many countries have strengthened the Right's allegiance to constitutional government[25] (especially evident in the export business sectors), while they have revivified the prospects for parties of the Left[26] that can channel some of the discontent aroused by such policies. Traditional elites, in contrast, are the enemies of both markets and democracy.

Empirically, in the mid-1990s voters signaled their preliminary approval of the shift toward a market economy. They abandoned the punitive electoral behavior noted at the beginning of this chapter. They began to reward officeholders who had managed the economy and other fundamental tasks well. Colombia's Liberal Party won three consecutive presidential elections in the 1980s and 1990s, in part in response to good economic management. Chile's Concertación Democrática coalition (including Christian Democratic, socialist, and other parties) won a second consecutive presidential election in 1993 thanks to its consolidation of a transition to a democratic regime and its excellent economic management. El Salvador's ARENA party, credited with securing internal peace and reactivating the economy, won a second consecutive presidential election in 1994. Ernesto Zedillo won the fairest-ever Mexican presidential election in 1994 in part because his party, the PRI, was perceived to have rescued Mexico from the economic depression of the 1980s. Fernando Henrique Cardoso was elected Brazil's president in 1994 mainly because of his successful control of inflation during his term as finance minister. Alberto Fujimori was reelected president of Peru in 1995 because he was credited with taming inflation, reactivating the economy, and controlling a virulent insurgency. And Carlos Menem, having presided over the termination of hyperinflation and the revival of economic growth, was reelected president of Argentina. In these and other instances, rational voters supported new market-oriented policies, thereby wedding the future of constitutional government to the success of the market economy.

For the "happy partnership" between democracy and markets to prosper, however, more needs to happen. Poverty must be reduced if citizens are to have the needed resources for effective participation; only with a widespread capacity to participate is democratic consolidation achieved. The reform of social services—their financing, organization, and effectiveness—awaits attention throughout the region. And the capacity of the state to raise revenues to rebuild infrastructure, and to improve the quality of health and education, requires ongoing effort. Special care must be taken to ensure that privatization decisions and implementation are transparent, not opportunities for corruption. Other issues include the balance between direct and indirect taxation, as well as the efforts of middle-class groups to resist reforms that hurt their interests (most notably in Uruguay, as Juan Rial points out, to protect and increase middle-class pensions through the use of a plebiscite). Successful defense of past rent-seeking achievements limits the resources available for other urgent needs.

The worry, best expressed by Castañeda, is that the political system will be unable to handle the pent-up demands that are bound to be expressed as the memories of authoritarian governments and hyperinflationary crises recede. Creating the understanding that democracy cannot solve everything is essential for a democratic culture, but it is not sufficient for stability; sooner or later constitutional government must provide some answers to the material problems of the poor. To justify his authoritarian methods, former Peruvian strongman Manuel Odría used to argue that people cannot eat democracy. For democracy to be consolidated and for the poor to resist the temptation of would-be authoritarians, democratic polities with market economies must make it possible for the poor to eat.

## The Armed Forces and the Consolidation of Democracy

Since the mid-1980s there have been three types of military assault on constitutional government; they are discussed here in increasing order of concern. One, evident in the early 1990s in Haiti, as Anthony P. Maingot notes, is for the high command of the armed forces to overthrow the civilian government. In the 1980s this was the principal means to rotate rulers under authoritarian regimes, as in the case of Panama throughout the Noriega years. As Abente Brun notes, it was also used to terminate General Alfredo Stroessner's regime in Paraguay. This practice had been common in much of South and Central America from the mid-1960s to the early 1980s, but no successful military coup led by the high command has occurred in other South or Central American countries since 1982, when one group of Guatemalan military officers overthrew another. In the 1980s and early 1990s, the less professional the military, the more likely that its high command would publicly lead an overthrow of the government—the opposite of the pattern that prevailed in the 1960s and 1970s.[27]

In several countries with professional armed forces, however, there have been military mutinies against constitutional governments in the late 1980s and early 1990s. These revolts were led by disgruntled middle-ranking officers in Argentina, Ecuador, Guatemala, Panama, and Venezuela;[28] each of these countries except Panama has seen at least two coup attempts in these years. The motivations for the coups varied. In Argentina and Panama, they were related to the downsizing of the security forces, and in Argentina to the prospect of trials for human rights violations. In Argentina, Ecuador, and Venezuela, ambitious and popular officers led the coup effort. In Guatemala, opposition from some business elites to tax and other economic policies played a role. A common aspect of these mutinies was that the military chain of command broke down; the mutinies were aimed at the high command as much as at the constitutional government. Consequently, the capacity to maintain civilian control was shaken because the generals could no longer ensure the loyalty of the lower ranks of the armed forces. Military deprofessionalization was associated with the increased likelihood of coup attempts. All of these attempts failed in the end because they were opposed by the military high command and because civilian politicians, for the most part, closed ranks in support of constitutional government. But will the high command and the civilians be able to retain control in the future?

Finally, a grave threat to constitutional government may come from a coup led by an elected civilian president supported by the high command of the armed forces against the congress, the courts, the political parties, and all vehicles that help civil society seek advocacy and representation for its interests. Pioneered in Uruguay in the early 1930s and repeated in Uruguay in the early 1970s, this pattern is associated in the 1990s with Peru's president Fujimori. Thus far only Guatemalan president Jorge Serrano has attempted to emulate him, without success. (Susan Stokes discusses Fujimori's case in detail.) In these cases, presidents have claimed that extensive corruption in congress generates gridlock as well as the pursuit of illicit objectives at the expense of the public interest. Presidents thus call on the military to establish a temporary civilian dictatorship. This pattern of coup-making is particularly worrisome, even if it has succeeded just in one country, because the problems of corruption and gridlock are real, and the disenchantment with the performance of constitutional government has been considerable in many countries.

The aftermath of Fujimori's coup in Peru has made his suspension of constitutional government especially appealing to antidemocrats. The economic reforms initiated in Peru in the early 1990s before the coup finally began to bear fruit, while good police work led to the capture of Abigael Guzmán, the founder and longtime leader of the Sendero Luminoso insurgency. Though both outcomes could have occurred without a coup, Fujimori claimed that his decisive anticonstitutional act brought them about. Right after the coup, the Organization of American States (with strong backing from the U.S. government) pressured Fujimori into calling internationally supervised elections for a constituent assembly (which would double as a parliament) and to agree not to prolong his presidential term without a free election. In April 1995 Fujimori was reelected president by a strong majority. Despite some irregularities, the election was fair enough.

This combination of circumstances recalls the potentially great appeal of a Caesar who proclaims the need for a temporary interruption of constitutional government to save the country and constitutionalism in the long run. The problem, of course, is that such interruptions often last for a longer time. Fujimori's economic and military policies, together with his acquiescence to international pressure in returning to the procedures of constitutional government, may have had the paradoxical effect of making a "Fujimorazo" much more appealing than either Fujimori or the international community ever imagined: he seemed to have fulfilled the promise of a short and effective dictatorship.

On balance, however, the barriers against *successful* military coups did rise in Latin America in the 1980s and 1990s and remain high in the Anglophone Caribbean. In general, the "demand" for coups has been constrained by the generally disastrous performance of military rulers in the late 1970s and early 1980s. The economies of Latin American countries collapsed when military presidents governed. The military lost the reputation for competence beyond its specific professional sphere, though the Pinochet government in Chile regained such a reputation during the second half of the 1980s. The demand for coups has also been reduced by the strength of parties of the Right, as noted above; many business elites no longer rely on military coups to advance their objectives because they are effective under civilian rule. The "supply" of coup-makers has also been limited because military officers recall their frustration, their unpreparedness, and the loss of their own military professionalism when they attempted to run the government. If the memories of military misgovernment fade and the performance of constitutional governments remains weak, however, the prospects for such coups might increase again.

Another reason for the decline in the frequency of coups is that in many cases the armed forces can have their demands met without resorting to such tactics. The military retains significant prerogatives in countries as different as Chile and Nicaragua, Cuba and Honduras, Brazil and Peru, Colombia and Guatemala. Military courts defy civilian jurisdiction over the criminal activities of some military personnel. The military continues to control police forces and intelligence agencies in a great many countries, without significant civilian oversight. Retired and, at times, active duty military officers continue to control important state enterprises directly or indirectly; in Chile a portion of earnings from copper exports is explicitly reserved for military use. In these ways, the armed forces in many countries retain an independent source of revenue to shield them from budget austerity. In some countries, military commanders also maintain significant subnational influence through their alliance with local power elites. In countries where civil violence is particularly high, the armed forces exercise even greater power; despite transitions to constitutional government and despite elections, much of Colombia, Guatemala, and Peru has remained under direct military rule. For the rural citizens of these countries, no "democratic transition" has taken place. Such military prerogatives remain important obstacles to the realization of democratic practice.[29]

There is considerable debate about the appropriate roles of the armed forces in contemporary Latin America. In Argentina and Uruguay, civilian governments have eagerly promoted military participation in international peacekeeping and peace-enforcing operations under the auspices of the United Nations in order to focus the armed forces on these new professional issues. The hope is that the military will be less likely to interfere in domestic politics if so occupied.

One persistent concern about any military operation, including military involvement in combating drug trafficking, is the need for effective means of civilian control. For the most part, such mechanisms remain insufficiently developed, and in some countries they have yet to exist because too many civilian "defense experts" have been specialists not in controlling the military but in aligning with them to make coups.

There is a related concern about military involvement in the development of infrastructure or the improvement of public health. Such normally praiseworthy activities may blur civilian and military lines of authority, reviving the notion (proven false during the economic crises of the late 1970s and early 1980s) that military officers can handle the routine affairs of government more effectively than civilians. In short, the task of establishing civilian supremacy over the military remains daunting, and the likelihood of coup attempts remains high. Nonetheless, the prospects for continued constitutional government are better than at any time since the great depression of the 1930s.

## The International Defense and Promotion of Democracy

Never before has there been such a strong international commitment to the defense and promotion of constitutional government in Latin America and the Caribbean. Such a new commitment is yet another barrier to successful coup attempts. Propelling the international activity on behalf of constitutional government is a change in the attitude of many Latin American governments toward intervention. This shift is best exemplified by Resolution 1080 of the Organization of American States, enacted in Santiago, Chile, in June 1991; it requires OAS member governments to address the interruption of constitutional government, should it occur.

There is also a marked change in the behavior of the U.S. government. Twice since the end of the cold war in Europe, the United States has deployed tens of thousands of troops to a near neighbor, motivated at least in part by the need to establish or restore viable constitutional government. In Panama in 1989 and in Haiti in 1994, U.S. troops deposed a military ruler and installed a civilian president. In Panama, international observers found that Guillermo Endara had won the 1989 presidential elections but was prevented from taking office because the military government stopped counting the ballots when it became evident that its candidate would lose. In Haiti, Jean-Bertrand Aristide was duly elected and took office, but was subsequently overthrown.[30] While the renewed commitment to constitutional government is encouraging, the lowering of barriers to the use of force across international boundaries is a source of concern.

The U.S. and other governments in Latin America, the Caribbean, Canada, and Western Europe, as well as the United Nations and the OAS, have also played valuable roles in ending wars in Nicaragua, El Salvador, and Suriname, making possible a transition toward more open politics. Through election observation, moreover, foreign governments and transnational NGOs have fostered a climate for freer elections in the Dominican Republic, Guyana, Paraguay, Peru, and Mexico. These international actors have supported trends away from electoral abuse and fraud, assisted with the logistics that permit freer and fairer elections, and denounced violations of the electoral process where they occurred. In Guatemala the international community played a decisive role in foiling President Jorge Serrano's attempted coup against constitutional government. And in the early to mid-1990s, the international community, including the Clinton administration, helped advance peace and constitutionalism in Guatemala, El Salvador, and Nicaragua, as well as defending constitutional government in Venezuela.

The defense of constitutional government has had some noteworthy limitations. Transition to civilian rule in Haiti was not accomplished without military force. And Peruvian president Fujimori's coup against constitutional government was not reversed; its thrust was mitigated through international pressure and negotiation in ways that, inadvertently, may have increased its appeal. On balance, however, the international community has had a good record defending constitutional government in the 1990s.

There is also the hope that the increased international engagement of certain countries will promote constitutional government within them. Mexico's participation in the North American Free Trade Agreement (NAFTA) may help consolidate the economic reforms enacted in the late 1980s and early 1990s, assist the country's recovery from the late 1994 and early 1995 currency devaluation shock, and foster a more open political climate. As Dresser's chapter shows, the administrations of presidents Carlos Salinas and Ernesto Zedillo were required to change many undemocratic political practices in order to safeguard Mexico's participation in NAFTA. Under international scrutiny, Mexico created mechanisms to protect human rights, reduce the likelihood of election fraud, and recognize opposition victories for subnational offices. Similarly, Paraguay's engagement in international trade and other economic relations through MERCOSUR (with Argentina, Brazil, and Uruguay) may help to open the political system further, years after the end of Alfredo Stroessner's dictatorship. Freer markets in the global economy, as in domestic economies, may contribute to the consolidation of freer politics in the long run.

By the same token, however, international factors may also create pressures that destabilize domestic politics. NAFTA, for example, is making it very difficult for Mexican maize producers to compete with imports from the United States, fueling discontent in already volatile rural areas and giving credence to the enemies of NAFTA (and of the government) within Mexico.

These perspectives offer a window into the future of Cuba, which Marifeli Pérez-Stable reviews in this collection. Will the future of Cuba be like the past in Panama in the 1980s and Haiti in the early 1990s, where massive U.S. military intervention occurred after unarticulated civil societies and weak and fragmented opposition movements within and outside the country were unable to launch a successful process of democratization? Will it be like Nicaragua and El Salvador in the 1980s, where extensive civil war with external participation lingered for years? Or will the future of Cuba be like the 1980s and 1990s in much of Central America, Mexico, and Paraguay, where an engaged international community aided a peaceful transition toward more open politics? The third scenario would require, of course, that Cuban leaders be more willing than they have been in the past to negotiate new rules of governance with the domestic opposition. From the perspective of democratization, the prospects are not good; the current political regime seems likely to endure, though it has already become much friendlier to international market forces. For the reasons Pérez-Stable reviews, however, we believe that the third scenario has the better chance of achieving Cuba's successful transition to democracy because it would impose the lowest costs on its people and its neighbors.

## Conclusion

"Like all men in Babylon," Jorge Luis Borges wrote, "I have been a proconsul; like all, a slave. I have also known omnipotence, opprobrium, imprisonment."[31] In many ways, this characterizes the experience of many prominent Latin American politicians in the 1990s. Some, like Argentine president Carlos Saúl Menem, spent years in prison under military government. Others, like President Fernando Henrique Cardoso of Brazil, spent years under official opprobrium and exile during his country's period of military rule. As Latin America and the Caribbean approach a new millennium, the task is to banish forever slavery, opprobrium, and imprisonment without succumbing to the temptations of the omnipotent proconsul. The power of presidents and ministers to govern is at times vast and injurious to democratic practice, for it presumes falsely that the executive alone has been elected by the people.

In this work we call attention to the importance of institutions and procedures that remain fundamental for democratic practice. In particular, we have focused on parties and their key role as bridges between state and society. And we have pondered the issues and concerns that arise within governments regarding executive, legislative, judiciary, and military institutions. These institutions and relationships are at the heart of the future of constitutional government in the Americas.

With regard to the prospects for military intervention in politics, we have echoed the alarm of others and have noted the extent to which the military may remain involved in politics short of staging a coup. Nonetheless, we are heartened by the decreased frequency of successful overthrows of constitutional government.

Thus the task at hand is to improve effective democratic governance. We are especially encouraged by the capacity of many to organize peacefully to participate in political life, but we are discouraged by continuing evidence that the design and redesign of the institutions of constitutional government have fallen well short of the needs of these countries. Between these two trends lies the future of democracy in the region.

# Notes

This is not a freestanding chapter. Instead, it calls attention to, and to some degree summarizes, themes that emerge in the chapters in this collection and in other work that has been part of the Inter-American Dialogue project on democratic governance. Because the introductory chapter by Jorge Domínguez and Abraham F. Lowenthal highlights certain policy issues, this chapter concentrates on more scholarly questions. This chapter relies occasionally on textual references to other chapters, but our debt to the authors in this collection is much greater than these citations suggest. The views expressed here are ours alone. The Inter-American Dialogue and the authors are at liberty to claim that all the errors in this chapter are ours and all the insights are theirs. We are also grateful for comments on an earlier version from Alan Angell, Michael Coppedge, Rosario Espinal, Peter Hakim, Harvey F. Kline, Abraham F. Lowenthal, Marifeli Pérez-Stable, Rose J. Spalding, Michael Shifter, and Deborah J. Yashar. An earlier version was presented at meetings of the Harvard University comparative politics faculty group and of the University's Sawyer Seminar, sponsored by the Mellon Foundation; we are also grateful for the comments from the participants, Eva Bellin, Daniel Goldhagen, Torben Iversen, Stanley Hoffmann, Stephen Krasner, Anthony Pereira, Theda Skocpol, and Deborah J. Yashar. We thank Linda Lowenthal for very fine editing. All mistakes are ours alone.

1. Jorge Amado, *Gabriela: Clove and Cinnamon*, trans. James L. Taylor and William L. Grossman (New York: Crest Books, 1964), 75, 80.

2. Reelections had occurred uninterruptedly only where there had been no competition (Cuba), or where doubts have existed about the fairness of electoral procedures (Antigua, the Dominican Republic, Mexico, and Paraguay). Only in Colombia (except in 1982) and elsewhere in the eastern Caribbean have fair elections resulting in repeated incumbent party victories been the norm.

3. United Nations, Economic Commission for Latin America and the Caribbean, *Preliminary Overview of the Economy of Latin America and the Caribbean, 1994*, LC/G.1846 (December 20, 1994), 39.

4. On this linkage function of social movements, see Kay Lawson and Peter Merkl, eds., *When Parties Fail* (Princeton: Princeton University Press, 1988).

5. The Mexican case is complex for two other reasons. Civilians have ruled in Mexico, and, despite important irregularities in Mexican elections, the evidence from public opinion polls shows that a plurality of voters have preferred to vote for the Institutional Revolutionary Party (PRI) than for any of the opposition parties. See Jorge I. Domínguez and James A. McCann, "Shaping Mexico's Electoral Arena: The Construction of Partisan Cleavages in the 1988 and 1991 National Elections," *American Political Science Review* 89, no. 1 (1995): 34–48.

6. See also Karen Remmer, "The Political Economy of Elections in Latin America, 1980–1991," *American Political Science Review* 87, no. 2 (1993): 393–407.

7. This and the next two paragraphs draw on Jorge I. Domínguez, "Transiciones democráticas en Centro América y Panamá," in Jorge I. Domínguez and Marc Lindenberg, eds., *Transiciones democráticas en Centro América* (San José, Costa Rica: Editorial Instituto Centroamericano de Administración de Empresas, 1994), 19–62.

8. For a discussion of bargains that may lead to democratic outcomes, see also Adam Przeworski, *Democracy and the Market: Political and Economic Reforms in Eastern Europe and Latin America* (Cambridge: Cambridge University Press, 1991), chaps. 1–2.

9. Robert A. Dahl, *Polyarchy: Participation and Opposition* (New Haven: Yale University Press, 1971), 15.

10. For a more elaborate discussion of the costs and benefits facing guerrillas and governments, see Matthew Soberg Shugart, "Guerrillas and Elections: An Institutionalist Perspective on the Costs of Conflict and Competition," *International Studies Quarterly* 36, no. 2 (1992): 121–51.

11. For the general concepts, see Albert Hirschman, *Exit, Voice, and Loyalty* (New Haven: Yale University Press, 1970).

12. Barriers to entry by new parties in the electoral law are, however, often low; in some cases, they have been lowered in recent years. This is why dissident politicians can form new parties instead of seeking to overthrow the government by force.

13. For a discussion of the historic role of Argentina's provincial parties, see Edward Gibson, *Conservative Parties and Democratic Politics: Argentina in Comparative Perspective* (Baltimore: Johns Hopkins University Press, 1996).

14. See Domínguez and McCann, "Shaping Mexico's Electoral Arena."

15. For a classic discussion of the utility of "reliability" and "responsibility" in parties, see Anthony Downs, *An Economic Theory of Democracy* (New York: Harper & Row, 1957), 96–113.

16. We recognize an anomaly. If this argument were right in every instance, a major third party should have emerged in Jamaica in the early 1990s in response to the People's National Party's turn from statism toward promarket policies and the continued resistance of the two dominant parties to changing the electoral law to lower the threshold for third-party membership in parliament. Our argument with regard to the Latin American cases requires, therefore, permissive electoral laws—proportional representation. This is exactly what the Anglophone Caribbean does not have.

17. For further discussion, see Jane S. Jaquette, "Rewriting the Scripts: Gender in the Comparative Study of Latin American Politics," in Peter H. Smith, ed., *Latin America in Comparative Perspective: New Approaches to Methods and Analysis* (Boulder, Colo.: Westview Press, 1995), 111–33.

18. See Juan J. Linz and Arturo Valenzuela, eds., *The Failure of Presidential Democracy* (Baltimore: Johns Hopkins University Press, 1994); Juan J. Linz, Arend Lijphart, and Arturo Valenzuela, eds., *Hacia una democracia moderna: La opción parlamentaria* (Santiago: Ediciones Universidad Católica de Chile, 1990).

19. For an overview of supreme courts, see Joel G. Verner, "The Independence of Supreme Courts in Latin America: A Review of the Literature," *Journal of Latin American Studies* 16, no. 2 (1984): 463–506.

20. For a general discussion of human rights issues during democratic transitions, see Manuel Antonio Garretón, "Human Rights in Processes of Democratization," *Journal of Latin American Studies* 26, no. 1 (1994): 221–34.

21. For a general discussion, see R. Andrew Nickson, *Local Government in Latin America* (Boulder, Colo.: Lynne Rienner, 1995); Jonathan Fox, "Latin America's Emerging Local Politics," *Journal of Democracy* 5, no. 2 (1994): 105–16.

22. For a theoretical argument about the economic advantages of democracy over autocracy, see Mancur Olson, "Dictatorship, Democracy and Development," *American Political Science Review* 87, no. 3 (1993): 567–76. See also the special issues on "Economic Liberalization and Democratization: Explorations of the Linkages" in *World Development* 21, no. 8 (1993), and on "Economic Reform and Democracy" in *Journal of Democracy* 5, no. 4 (1994).

23. For a related argument, see Barbara Geddes and Artur Ribeiro, "Institutional Sources of Corruption in Brazil," *Third World Quarterly* 13 (1992): 641–61.

24. See, for example, Guillermo O'Donnell and Philippe Schmitter, *Tentative Conclusions about Uncertain Democracies: Transitions from Authoritarian Rule* (Baltimore: Johns Hopkins University Press, 1986), 62–63.

25. The greater allegiance of the Right to democracy can be found to varying degrees (listing from south to north) in Argentina, Chile, Colombia, Panama, Costa Rica, Nicaragua, El Salvador, and Mexico.

26. Opposition to some of the negative consequences of market reforms has strengthened the long-term prospects for parties of the Left to varying degrees. Listing from south to north, this is evident in Argentina, Uruguay, Brazil, Panama, Nicaragua, El Salvador, and Mexico.

27. For discussion of the earlier pattern, see Alfred Stepan, "The New Professionalism of Internal Warfare and Military Role Expansion," in Abraham F. Lowenthal and J. Samuel Fitch, eds., *Armies and Politics in Latin America,* (New York: Holmes and Meier, 1986), 134–47.

28. This pattern has been common elsewhere as well. See Samuel P. Huntington, *The Third Wave: Democratization in the Late Twentieth Century* (Norman: University of Oklahoma Press, 1991), 234.

29. A number of scholars stress the prerogatives retained by the military after the transition to constitutional government and the threat that this poses to democracy. See Alfred Stepan, *Rethinking Military Politics* (Princeton: Princeton University Press, 1988), 68–127. See also Brian Loveman, "'Protected Democracies' and Military Guardianship: Political Transition in Latin America, 1978–1993," *Journal of Interamerican Studies and World Affairs* 36, no. 2 (1994): 105–89; and Felipe Agüero, "The Military and the Limits to Democratization in South America," in Scott Mainwaring, Guillermo O'Donnell, and J. Samuel Valenzuela, eds., *Issues in Democratic Consolidation: The New South American Democracies in Comparative Perspective* (Notre Dame: University of Notre Dame Press, 1992). In contrast, Wendy Hunter shows how democracy has helped to limit military prerogatives in Brazil. See her "Politicians against Soldiers: Contesting the Military in Postauthoritarian Brazil," *Comparative Politics* 27, no. 4 (1995): 425–43.

30. To be sure, the main U.S. motivation for intervention has not always been the promotion of democracy. In Panama the main motivation was to curtail drug trafficking and financial laundering, while in Haiti it was to make it easier to stop the flow of immigration and to return undocumented immigrants. Another important difference between the two interventions is that in Haiti the United States had sought and obtained prior authorization from the United Nations Security Council and a commitment that other countries would eventually join a peacekeeping effort; in Panama the United States acted unilaterally.

31. Jorge Luis Borges, "The Lottery in Babylon," in his *Labyrinths: Selected Stories and Other Writings,* ed. Donald A. Yates and James E. Irby (New York: New Directions Books, 1964), 30.